# I AM WHO I AM

## 25 YEARS OF WORKING WITH THE POOREST IN CAMBODIA

## JANNE RITSKES

**author**HOUSE®

AuthorHouse™
1663 Liberty Drive
Bloomington, IN 47403
www.authorhouse.com
Phone: 833-262-8899

Published by AuthorHouse   08/24/2021

ISBN: 978-1-6655-3156-6 (sc)
ISBN: 978-1-6655-3154-2 (hc)
ISBN: 978-1-6655-3155-9 (e)

Library of Congress Control Number: 2021914070

This book is dedicated to:

The people of Cambodia whom I love

To Tabitha Cambodia Staff, Workers and Families

To My Nokor Tep Foundation co-founders:
Ing Kantha Phavi and Trac Thai Sieng

To my beloved Daughter: Miriam Rose Ritskes

"Nothing is Impossible with God."
(Luke 1:37 NIV)

# CONTENTS

# PROLOGUE

This memoir is about my 25-year journey working as God's hands in Cambodia.

My passion for the people of Cambodia started many years ago when the bombing and genocide were taking place in this country. I knew then, as I know today, that this is the country I must serve. I am a woman of extraordinary passion that makes me different from many others. My passion is rooted in the pain I see in others, pain that I know I can impact and not turn away from.

Like all people, I am terribly ignorant of all the types of pain people suffer. I have discovered, over the past 35 years, that helping to ease pain is something which is learned not from books but from life itself. Over the years I have learned the pitfalls of community development. I have also learned that there are better ways to do it, not because some book told me or some professor taught it, but because I could see and feel whether or not what I did actually alleviated the pain.

I learned during all these years that the cost to myself in some ways was enormous but in so many other ways, was nothing. As long as I persevered and was faithful doing what I knew was right, not for me, but for the people I served, then there was no other option. The learning had not always been easy. Starting Tabitha Cambodia, I had only one other person who believed in me, not in what I was going to do, but in me. My brother John said to me, "Sis, I will help you but understand me, no matter how many will stand with you, you are alone. It is your vision, your faith that will make this happen. We can only stand with you."

Tabitha is my vision and drive, and every aspect of Tabitha came about through personal knowledge of the pain and suffering of others. Savings is the only way to help those who stand and live in fear. Their choices are made with no threats. I knew Cottage Industry was the only way forward for women who had their dignity stolen from them through sexual violence and abuse. Being handed an orphanage full of children filled with pain gave me no choice but to find them a home. My gorgeous daughter who was a defiled child, a throw away child, gave me no other choice but to call her my own. House building, I learned from people who had no home and from people who needed to serve. Water programs came from the death of one of my staff who on his death bed said, "They need water Janne, give them water". Schools came from people who needed to serve, and from children surrounding me because there was no school, or space, or money. Nokor Tep Women's Hospital came because I suffered and it was my own suffering that made me so aware of the suffering of women here.

In all these instances there was one clear marker for me. I could do something about the pain! Once I knew that, I never had any other choice but to do so. Doing less would have taken away who I am; it would have made me empty. I am who I am. The visions I have, and the work I must do. I can only accept that this is something I must do.

I know that for many people, my visions at times seem to be far-fetched, yet I must be who I am. I know I can make a difference in the lives of millions of women through the women's hospital. It is not an easy task, nor a quick one, but it is one I must do. I have no other choice.

And yes, people will stand with me in this vision, people we know and people we have yet to come to know. Each person will add and be a part of that vision. For some, in ways they never imagined nor could I have imagined. And that is good, for that is what life is all about.

My inner strength and conviction comes from my God who has been and always will be with me. In that sense my brother was wrong. I have never been alone. I am grateful to each and every person who joined me on my journey and shared my vision for the people of Cambodia.

In many cases I have changed the names of characters and locations of events to protect the privacy of the families we worked with, the staff, and volunteers who participated in our work. In addition, some characters represent composites of more than one person in order to protect identity.

# THE BEGINNING

This is the story of Tabitha Cambodia for it is my story, it is the story of our staff, it's the story of our volunteers, and it's the story of each person who has stood with us in so many ways.

Tabitha Cambodia is about my personal faith, my walk with God, our relationship, my beliefs that derive from this relationship. It's about learning this in my youth from parents who had gone through two world wars, a depression, immigration and their personal walk with their God; values and beliefs shared with their children. I learned first-hand the strength they had as they went through their varied and difficult life.

The values that are the core of my being are as follows:

- That all people are created by God and created in His image, whether or not they acknowledge that is not an issue for me (Genesis 1:27, NIV);
- That my role is to search for God's image in each person I meet, to seek out the good;
- That each person is of equal value in God's eyes and there is no discrimination (Ephesians 1:4 NIV);

- That each person is accountable for each and every decision that we make (Romans 14:12 NIV);
- That there is a consequence to those decisions that we make (Jeremiah 17 5-10);
- That every individual has been given talents and that each of us are accountable for those talents, whether that talent is physical, material or spiritual (Matthew 25:14-30 NIV);
- That each of us is in total control of the direction our lives take, in both bad and good times. (Romans 14:12 NIV); and
- That each of us must live out our given talents/gifts that God has given each of us, those gifts that make us unique and that fulfill His plans for us (Romans 14:12 NIV)

These are a few of my very core beliefs, ones that help me to determine the decisions I made and how to implement those decisions.

## Why Cambodia?

I grew up in a small town on the St Lawrence River in Canada on the border with the USA. I was a teenager when the Vietnam conflict erupted, a conflict that captured my full attention. It was also a time when color television came into being, with color being a bit skewed, showing scenes that were gory and uncensored. It was a time when my American friends were under threat of being drafted; young lads, too young and too inexperienced to fully understand the enormity of the war, young lads who gave their lives, others who returned broken by what they had done and seen.

I learned that war is about denying that people are images of God, and that wars are won and lost by ideologies that totally ignore the humanity of people. I learned that humanity is erased by renaming human beings through nonsensical terms such as "Gooks" during the Vietnam War. This renaming gave the war mongers the right to eliminate masses of people with impunity. The war reporters changed the war by reporting vivid scenes of not Gooks being killed, but of people being blown to pieces. I met several of these reporters, men broken by what they had seen and reported.

I watched with horror as the secret war began in Cambodia, a nation severely punished because they would not allow the allies to use their country as their base to fight Vietnam. I watched village after village bombed into oblivion, the reporters standing in the Mekong River pointing out the carnage that was left behind.

I watched as the United States withdrew its troops from Vietnam, Cambodia and Laos, not because they wanted to but because so many courageous people at home began protesting against a body count of young Americans who had lost their lives. The protesters brought back a sense of humanity; they made humans valuable again which finally ended the Vietnam War.

But the mayhem had left behind other personalities within these countries who had learned that ignoring the value of humanity is the one and only way to impose their will upon their people. In Cambodia, Pol Pot came into being, a man who wanted to show the ultimate implementation of an ideology called communism. For Pol Pot, the people were simply dispensable things to be used, abused and thrown away to fulfill his vision.

I took note of the stories coming from Cambodia, of Pol Pot's vision to completely destroy Cambodia and its people and then rebuild

Cambodia from the ashes. The stories were grotesque, the pictures horrifying. How can this be? Why is the world not protesting, how could we support such inhumanity? The one time I thought I should do something was while I was in college in the United States. I thought we should protest the loss of humanity but I was told gently but firmly that my protest would end up in jail time and I would be an unwelcome person. I was a coward and so I did nothing, but I knew then with certainty that one day I would go to Cambodia. I was guilty of ignoring their humanity. I was guilty of being cowardly.

The intervening years between college and Cambodia were years spent in the Philippines and in Kenya. It was a time where I learned that my values required systems that respected the dignity of each human being, systems that allowed people to make their own choices, systems that required time for people to explore these choices and decide what choice was best for themselves. It required evaluation of my approaches, changing what was not beneficial to what was beneficial. It required patience and a firm belief that each person was accountable for his or her own choices. It required a system that allowed time for failures and a time to pick oneself up afterwards. It required a system that rejoiced at each step forward taken by a family; systems that required encouragement when it did not go well. It required a system that allowed me not to become too rigid in what we could do but also to be always open to new and better ways of doing things.

I learned that hurt is universal. I learned that being able to empathize with another is crucial to hearing their voices, that being able to cry would allow others not to cry. I learned to be able to reflect their strengths and weakness by doing the same myself. I learned to walk a mile in the shoes of another.

## Arriving in Cambodia

In 1992 when my sojourn in Kenya was finishing, I was invited by an international relief organization to take up a position as training manager for their organization in Cambodia. I was loath to join them but I wanted to be in Cambodia. So, I went.

The country was in serious flux as various groups and individuals vied for power. Amongst these groups were the Khmer Rouge and Pol Pot, a group and leader supported by the international community. The country was rife with insecurity. Life could be taken for less than fifty cents and guns and immorality were widespread throughout the nation. The internally displaced population was close to 80% and the capital city of Phnom Penh was a city of refugees, living by the millions in absolute poverty. The countryside had been reduced to ashes with everything destroyed: homes, schools, hospitals, banking, commerce, infrastructure and yet, like most poverty, in strangely astonishingly beautiful surroundings, a factor that has always struck me as odd; so much misery in such beautiful surroundings.

My work with this organization was problematic from the moment I arrived. My task was to encourage the foreign staff to train nationals to take over their jobs. The foreigners were unwilling to deal with this issue and the Cambodians were equally unwilling to cause any issues because they were cowered and traumatized by the past 30 years of absolute terror.

The training began by asking them to tell me three bad things and three good things about this troubled country. All of them insisted that there was nothing good about Cambodia, it was all bad. I insisted that there was good, so what was it? It went from bad to worse as I asked each of them to write down and tell me what their goal was, what they would hope to accomplish in the next three years because this would be the basis of designing a training program for nationals. Their anger at this request resulted in my being called before the Director and told not to ask so much of the foreigners. I changed tactic and asked them all to define poverty for our definitions would determine the kind of programs to be instituted. The answers all started with the word NO: no food, no clothes, no money, no home, etcetera. My response was simple, could they show me a Cambodian who had no clothes, no food, no home because if it was all no, then our answer was simple, give them food, clothes, homes. Simple, right?

The anger that met my question was increasing in volume for no one had seen any of this. The answer was not "No". So, then what was the answer? They don't have enough; they have some but not sufficient. Then the next question was then what was sufficient? Again, the decibels rose but people were now beginning to think a bit more.

I became very disillusioned by all that was happening in my work. I knew I wouldn't be able to sleep for months if I continued to train. For me personally, it was untenable.

# 1994

I returned to Canada determined to start my own NGO in Cambodia. I was totally disillusioned by the development community. I felt like they wanted me to sell my soul. I also felt that rather than criticize others it was time to put my money where my mouth was. I talked with my brother John who told me to go ahead. He would set up a foundation but reminded me that I would be doing this all alone. I was never alone for my God was always with me. With John's blessing, I took out my savings and cashed in my pension, a move that all around me felt was very foolish at my ripe old age of 44. But my walk with God was paramount! He promised He would provide for me if I did His will (Joshua 23:14 NIV). I believed God and so I returned to Cambodia with my funds. The money was enough to rent a rather decrepit home for six months, to start up a program or two, and to pay staff salaries for two months. It was a small start. Thankfully I had developed some amazing friendships to fall back on: Jannette Fawcett made sure I was never hungry and Nerida Nettlebeck made sure I had moral and some financial support.

My first task was to find a building for Tabitha Cambodia. I was staying with Nerida, a colleague from my former organization. Poor Nerida was quite distraught with the whole concept of starting an

NGO with so little money. We talked about my needs for a building with at least ten rooms and where I could live for under US$1000 per month. She said it was impossible because the United Nations and newly opened embassies had driven up the cost of rentals. Later that same day, several Cambodian staff from my former NGO came to welcome me back. They also said it was impossible.

The next morning, I asked Nerida to drop me off at a realtor's office on the way to work. She stayed for a bit as the Cambodians gathered around to hear what I wanted. They brought out a photo-album with pictures of buildings and their rents. For what I was looking, none came under US$1500 a month. Nerida gave me a smile of I told you so and went off to work. I told the people that this was not acceptable. I could go no higher than US$1000 a month. I was talking to six gentlemen at the time. Behind me stood a woman. She listened then asked me what I wanted to do. So, I shared my vision about Tabitha. She took out a little black book and said she might have two possibilities. Would I have the time to look with her? You bet I did. She took me to this house. As soon as I saw it, I knew it was the place. It was a two-story building with enough rooms to be able to do everything I had envisioned. And all of this for US$800 a month, which I had negotiated down from US$1000, payable every three months. This was a rare thing as a six-month deposit was normally required. The building was rustic and well-used and came complete with a security guard, a much-needed thing at the time. It also came with a generator which was an important asset as electricity was not always a given. Nerida was stunned by it all.

The house also came complete with its own selection of natural inhabitants. This was traumatic for me as I had recurring nightmares before I started work overseas. My nightmare was that I would be met with a man-sized cockroach the minute I stepped off the plane. It was the one thing that almost prevented me from working overseas. The ants and cockroaches in the building were unmerciful for they were everywhere, including my bed. I committed my own version of warfare against these beasts. My second warfare was with the bats. I entertained a whole neighborhood with my evening ritual of avoiding, catching and releasing bats but what really did me in were the snakes. Every other day, another snake would slither out of the woodwork and Peap, the security guard, along with my maid Sunbat, would be frantic in their efforts to catch the thing. I would be hysterical as Peap had an unnerving habit of catching the snakes by the tail, whirling them around his head and flinging them away from him, often in my direction. It is a miracle that he lived after each episode. I was beside myself with fear, disbelief and anger.

My second task was to hire staff, which was an upsetting task for one and all. The common denominator all the staff shared was their deep trauma. Each and every one of them had visible physical symptoms such as trembling, shaky voices, and the inability to breathe at the slightest sign of trouble. Each one was terrified to leave the safety of the building. How they made it to work each morning was a puzzle to us all. Every night was filled with sounds of gunfire and exploding grenades throughout the city. The first hour of the workday was always about calming down and so I began to have devotions each morning. A time of quiet reflection, sharing of fears and anxieties and ending with a time of quiet prayer.

As we began to settle into a team, two mothers came to the office. What a horrible couple of hours this was as both mothers asked if I knew what I was doing by hiring their daughters! The girls were not worthy of being hired. The vitriolic haranguing by the mothers continued for half an hour. By the time they caught their breath, one of the girls was rolled into a ball at my feet, sobbing and trembling. When the mothers had finished their tirades, my response was simple. I told them I didn't know what they had gone through in the past 30 years for it was beyond anything I could understand but, I said, I believe you are trying to keep your girls safe. Please could I talk with their daughters?

I asked the girls to look at me. Neither girl could lift their eyes. I asked them quietly, what do you want? There was no answer for several minutes and so I asked again. Through her heaving sobs, the one whispered, I want a job. I said, I can't hear you, stand up and look at me, and tell me what you want. It took five minutes for her to stand up; I want a job she said with downcast eyes. I said, look at me and tell me what you want. It took some time before she could face me. I want a job she said. The job is yours. This woman has been with Tabitha ever since, an amazing woman. I turned to the other girl; the anger in her eyes was frightening. I want the job she muttered. It's yours I said.

One of the mothers ended up adopting three children to replace the children she lost during Pol Pot's regime. The other mother has never forgiven her one remaining child for surviving and is still as vitriolic with her. Her saving grace was all of us at Tabitha. What war and a genocidal regime does to people is quite frightening.

## Cottage Industry

I decided to start with Cottage Industry which involved producing saleable products from Cambodian materials. All the staff were too traumatized to do much more than this. We talked about development but it was too soon for staff to leave the building and go out on their own. Instead, we all became involved in searching for local resources. One fine morning all of us trooped off to Olympic Market, a large wholesale market in town. Our chat was negative as usual for the staff were convinced there was nothing of value that Cambodians made, surely nothing that anybody would want!

As we walked through the endless market aisles, I saw silks of every color and hue, silks with beautiful patterns. I asked how much it was. The staff were quick to tell me that the price and the story behind the silk for each piece was made for a specific reason. The silks were made in skirt lengths and the pattern and colors represented various occasions such as weddings, single, or married, holidays, etcetera. If you wore a silk outfit then people knew what occasion you were celebrating, whether you were single or married, whether you had children or not, the stories seemed endless.

Fascinated as I was with the history of each piece of silk, I saw the material with a very different eye. This particular pattern would be good to make Christmas stockings, I said. There was an immediate and stunned silence, Christmas? What is Christmas, they asked. Oh boy, I shuddered, you don't know Christmas? They reaffirmed their ignorance of Christmas. How can that be? The past forty years of isolation, war and genocide had left them ignorant of the outside world.

So, I said, okay, buy me three skirts of red and green checked silk, and the rebellion began. You can't buy those I was told; those are for the ploughing ceremony! Yes, that's true I agreed but they are also material, a Cambodian resource we can use to make Christmas products. No, no they argued, you can't do that, they are for ploughing

11

ceremony only. I asserted my authority; buy them, I ordered. They did so reluctantly. Then we purchased cotton, many meters of cotton in red and green. Wrung out from the emotions and efforts involved, we returned to the office.

On our return trip to the office, one staff, Chanthou lamented that we don't have any skills, we can't even cut. I looked at her rather dumbfounded and said nothing. Once we arrived back at the office, I took a sheet of paper and drew the outline of a Christmas stocking. I asked the girls to place this pattern on the green and red material, material folded over a dozen times. With chalk, they outlined the pattern on the material and then I asked them to cut out the pattern. The girls didn't blink an eye as they cut with confidence. Once done, I looked at Chanthou and said, see, that's the skill of cutting. Her face lit up with surprise and then pleasure, we do know something, she said.

I then took the checkered silk and drew out pieces to accent the stockings. The girls were less than thrilled to cut the ploughing ceremony silk but cut they did. Mari was our Cottage Industry manager at that time so I showed her how I wanted the pieces sewn together. Call me when it's done, said I. Do a red one first.

After thirty minutes I was called but no one looked very happy. I was delighted because they were beautiful. What are these for, you are not going to wear them are you, they muttered? I began to laugh but stopped as rebellion was brewing. I tried to explain Christmas and its decorations but no one was willing to listen. I ordered them to sew a green one and again call me when it was done. Dark mutterings greeted this news.

I returned in due time to admire their handiwork. Mari, the delegated spokesperson, muttered that you are going to embarrass us if you wear these stockings. Cambodians will laugh at you! They will laugh even more when they see one red stocking and one green stocking! Soklieng, not to be outdone by such boldness, spoke her mind, we are embarrassed that you don't have a 4x4 car, live in the office, and hardly have anything! You are not like all the other NGOs that have everything! (This was during the time of UN intervention bringing with them all the trappings to make sure their staff never did without any of the basic necessities of life).

As I was admiring their handiwork and listening to their words, Janette arrived. She took one look at the stockings and said, you can't sell these Janne! The staff were delighted with her statement, big self-satisfied smiles creased their faces. No, said Janette, you can't sell these for I want to buy them, in fact I would like 20 stockings in all! They are beautiful! Thus, began our 25 years of making cottage industry goods.

Cottage Industry was designed to be self-sufficient from the onset of the program. The concept was that all the costs had to be covered, materials and labor and a small percentage per item towards costs of office rents, electricity, etcetera. Cottage industry had to be based on quantity as women had to earn enough to feed their families and pay expenses year-round not just part of the year. This meant developing a product line that was diverse enough to provide work year-round but priced in a way that people wanted to buy more, not just one item.

The women working in Cottage Industry were deeply traumatized. These women had been sold into the sex trade by their families, families that had lived through war, genocide and insecurity which left them broken and destroyed. As a result, this left its mark on product development. A number of the women working in Cottage Industry could not use a sewing machine but they could crochet and knit. There was a fad at that time called beanie babies. The first batches we made were crocheted dolls about 8 inches long with gangly arms and legs. Since we had started just before Christmas I thought this would be a great product. We had the pattern and a prototype was done by Phally.

When the doll was done I was ecstatic for the doll was simple and cute, or so I thought. The workers were not so happy! We can't make these, said Phally, they remind us of the bad years, years when people lost their hair, their eyes were huge and staring like this doll and then they starved to death or were executed. It is a bad thing to make. Phally stood before me, tears streaming down her face. Yes, said I, these are a bad thing to make.

We built a showroom from leftover pieces of wood and dismantling a wall. There was a remarkable side benefit to having a showroom to show our products. One day the mother of one of the staff came to see what we were all about. Well, she got so excited; she just kept hugging me and kissing me. Both of us were in tears. She said God was really in this work. She just couldn't believe it. She also knew how little money we had. She then asked: what kind of car would I like to drive? I thought it a rather strange question. She asked me again and I said that I didn't know what she meant. She asked me if I would be willing to drive a small car. I said yes, I would. She then said: you will have my car. It is a Toyota Cressida, an older one. She never used it and she thought I should. I couldn't take it but she kept saying we were the same, working for God. God had given her the car to use but she preferred a motorbike and she would feel like I was saying no to

God. I was totally speechless. The car arrived several days later, after some much-needed repairs.

Word got around about our showroom and people started arriving to buy our products. Nerida's parents arrived from Australia for a visit. Her mother taught us how to make moveable teddy bears, a product that sold in the thousands over the years. What was most memorable about that visit was our trip to the markets to buy materials to make the teddies. Nerida's father had lost his leg and was wearing a prosthetic leg. Begging was rampant in Phnom Penh at the time. There were so many people who had also lost their legs through the ongoing and continuous civil war. A number of these people were beggars at the market we went to. I had become rather immune to the clutching arms grasping our arms and legs but her parents were not. One persistent fellow, a double leg amputee, was on a homemade skateboard contraption which he pushed along with his arms. His constant badgering finally got to me. I turned around and pulled up the pant leg of Nerida's dad, showing his prosthetic leg. His reaction was immediate and actually made me laugh for the beggar's eyes were huge with disbelief. He turned on his skateboard and left. To say everyone was stunned by my behaviour was an understatement.

I returned to shopping as if nothing had happened. Ten minutes had passed while we shopped unmolested. Then the pulling of my leg started again. I turned and there was the amputee with a number of fellow beggars in tow. He held up his hand to Nerida's dad with a hand full of money that he insisted we take. My eyes filled with tears; the beggars had understood the pain of another amputee and they reached out in grace to help Nerida's dad overcome that pain. It was an invaluable lesson I learned that morning. I learned that Cambodian people are compassionate beyond understanding to others in pain. It is a trait that would be repeated again and again in my years of work. It is one of the reasons that I love them so!

The changes in the lives of our workers were amazing. The workers had a variety of ugly stories to tell. One woman was in process of selling her three-year-old boy for ninety dollars when Vutha, a development staff, found her. She started crocheting and she kept her boy. Another girl of 14 was an orphan with 3 younger siblings. Their mother died giving birth to the last one two years previously. People in the area felt pity for the kids and gave them leftover scraps of food and clothes. With crocheting, the young lady was able to feed herself and her siblings. I visited the group after three weeks. I couldn't believe my eyes. The two families had rebuilt their cardboard and plastic shacks into sturdy homes of wood with tin roofs. The biggest change was in their health. When I met them the first time, they were all very ill looking and very dirty. They were now eating fish and vegetables with their rice and they were eating regularly. They looked much healthier with cleaner skin and clearer eyes. They wanted to know about this Jesus person who tells our staff to work every day with them and who work so hard. Of course, the staff were very excited about what they were doing and it showed in their talk and manners. That was very catching.

Those first two months we made Christmas decorations, from misshapen balls to garlands, from leftover materials. We made crocheted finger and pencil puppets and sewed toys like centipedes and teddy bears. Our customers were few but we continued to produce. Cottage Industry was eating up capital, what were we to do?

I had several gifted staff in a variety of areas. Mari was an expert cook; several other staff spoke English well. Many of the expat women complained about the lack of cooking skills of their cooks and all complained about the poor English of their Cambodian staff. So, we designed several classes, one for cooking and one for teaching English. The classes were filled very quickly. I was delighted not just for the income, but now my meals were much tastier. Cambodia stir fry had lost its glamour after eating it three times a day. I also had developed abhorrence for rice which was the Cambodian staple, so the change was very welcome. The money earned from these classes covered our expenses for two months.

## Community Development and Savings

It was time to start our development work. The values underlying our development work required that we work with people in a way that would bring out their best without fear of reprisals. It required that people truly could make their own decisions, choose what they would like to save for. It required accountability for their decisions. It required trust.

Cambodia was just emerging from the horrific past of forty years of war, genocide and isolation. Everyone was deeply traumatized, deeply hurt. There was very little security yet; the nights were filled with shootings and grenades and no one felt safe. The staff were no exception. They were terrified to leave the safety of the office, terrified of people they would have to meet.

The litany of excuses began of why we could not do development, couldn't do savings. The people were too poor, they did not have money. My response was: show me a person with no money. The people are bad and they will steal from us, kill us, not trust us, they are lazy. My response: who told you that? Show me a lazy Cambodian!

The arguments continued for several weeks. I finally said, we, you and I, are the barriers to development because we don't let the people speak, instead we speak for them. We will never be able to help anyone with our preconceptions! We need to develop a baseline questionnaire asking people about their life's realities and then we will decide our best approach to helping people.

Their resistance continued until I finally said, you have a choice, keep your job and go to the poorest and talk with them or you can quit right now. Vutha was the first to take up the challenge. She left the office to go to Kilometer 6, frightened and at the same time angrier than I had ever seen her. She returned several hours later, her face lit up with unbelievable joy.

Vutha told her story. She had driven her motorbike to Kilometer 6, determined but terrified. Kilometer 6 was one long road of unbelievable poverty at that time. She had stood at the top of the road and started to sob, she was so terrified. She couldn't stop crying until a woman stopped and asked her what the problem was. Vutha poured out her heart to this woman. She told her how she had to interview poor people but she knew they would hurt her and laugh at her. The woman gently asked her to come with her.

In the depths of the village, the woman invited her to sit down on a mat in front of a very small thatched hut. Seven children appeared from all directions. The woman's husband appeared, dressed in a krama and nothing else. The children were severely malnourished, dirty and dressed in rags.

The woman apologized that they had no food to offer her but instead asked one of her children to get the last remaining coconut out of the house. She told Vutha to go ahead and ask her questions for she was poor. Very quickly, neighboring families joined in and family after family answered her questions. Vutha visited each small shack, she was welcomed wherever she went, and she saw and felt the poverty around her. What changed Vutha that morning was that each family offered her whatever food was left in the home, a piece of fruit or a scrap of rice, and she was welcomed wherever she went. She had returned to the office to pick up more surveys and couldn't wait to return to the village. This was the start of our development work.

A few days later, Vutha and Soklieng and I went to Kilometre 6 together. The poverty was so very stark and painful. I taught them what a target population was. In order to find the poorest of the poor, we had to set a baseline. This baseline turned out to be anyone who made an income of 0 to 1000 riels a day, roughly 15 cents a day or less. Both ladies had worked with poor people before or so they thought. Soklieng became very disturbed. They had found the poorest people but it was much different than what they had believed. Soklieng, who always said she was poor, said that she would never say that again. That made my day.

We found eight very poor families in very short order. It turned out that two of the women were able to sew. We decided that both should come to the office and be trained to make our products. Tabitha would buy them both a sewing machine, which they would repay out of their earnings. Chanthou had changed dramatically from being a suicidal cleaning lady into a transformed woman. She became a teacher of others. She would teach these ladies how to sew our products. What an unbelievable change that was! It made all my efforts with her worthwhile.

Another family we talked with consisted of a woman with nine children, the youngest a month old. Their shack was a meter square. Half of her children had to sleep outside as there was no room within. She made piggy banks out of mud from a nearby stream. She was also in debt to a moneylender. The moneylender would pay her one cent for each piggy bank which normally sold for five cents apiece. He owned the lady because she was too poor to refuse the penny per bank. I challenged both Vutha and Soklieng, as to what should we do to make her life better. Their answer was quick. Let's buy all she can make for five cents and sell them at the office. Then they would find a local market for her. We took the ten banks she had and would come back the next day for another ten. The lady was thrilled. During the night it rained, and all her banks were destroyed by the rain. The girls were heartbroken, but she made more banks and we sold them at the office.

Two other families made Cambodian designs out of beaten tin. Again, they were very poor and had little market for their product. The girls said we had to find a market for their work. One of the things we did was sew a few of them on the stockings, making them really Cambodian. Another fellow was severely handicapped because of stepping on a land mine. He made money for his family by begging. There was no end to the poverty. Everyone looked much older than they were; they looked so very tired and beaten. We decided to start community development in earnest. We chose Kilometre 6 as our first village where 3000 families lived in absolute poverty.

It was the week of Christmas and I decided to throw a Christmas party for the staff and workers. It was very poignant. Many of the workers had only one set of clothes so they came early to wash their one set of clothes in the back of the building. They did each other's hair up. We had decorated the place with lots of color and lights. Their kids were fascinated. The party was magical. The staff did their version of the nativity, a shocking portrayal of how the Khmer Rouge would have conducted the census of the people, and then their version of Santa. It was hilarious. We played several games and then gave everyone a small gift. Then there was lots of food and drink. The people thought it was great! A tradition begun and continued for many years.

In the midst of the celebrations a woman arrived from the French Embassy. She needed decorations and toys. We all gaped in disbelief as she emptied shelf after shelf, not a decoration was left, no matter how misshapen or ill-conceived it was, then shelf after shelf of toys. We were left with one misshapen centipede and two finger puppets. Then the miracle happened for she paid in cash! Cottage Industry was solvent again. The Christmas miracle!!

On Christmas Day I held my first Christmas party, the one party I threw that continued throughout all the years I was in Cambodia. The people that were invited were friends and families that I knew along with several families and people who were in Cambodia for the first time and were homesick. On average there were roughly fifty people who came each year. It was always a pot luck dinner with everyone having to bring food and drink, and everyone had to bring a White Elephant gift, beautifully wrapped, which was something they owned that they didn't like and wanted to get rid of. The White Elephant broke the ice as people chose a number with which they could choose a gift from the table or take a gift from someone who had already chosen one. There was so much laughter!

After the game we had a proper sit-down dinner. We always opened with a prayer of thanksgiving and remembering our loved ones so far away. After dinner was carol singing and then the Christmas pudding! This was always done with trepidation as lighting the pudding put everyone in danger. We then played games like charades. The evening ended with quiet conversations amongst ourselves. A day well spent with friends and loved ones. It was a good way to end the year.

# 1995

The year started out with money being depleted and not much coming in. I had written two proposals to embassy slush funds, one of which was the Australian Embassy. I had also signed a contract with another NGO to do some training. Despite these efforts, the money was not forthcoming at the speed that I needed it. What to do?

The next day being salary day, the staff knew I had no money. I spoke to God. I told Him this was too hard. He told me not to worry. I went to bed at eight, no longer worried but wondering how this would all work out. A little after nine there was a banging at the gate. I was not too keen on opening the gate as the normal night time lullaby of shooting and grenades going off was in full swing. But the knocking continued. I slowly opened the gate and there was Margret Cormack, the wife of the Anglican pastor, Don Cormack. Several weeks before Christmas, Margret had packed several hockey bags full of our products to sell to her church in Singapore. Her husband was not too keen on this when he saw the packed bags. He looked me in the eye and asked what I had packed? Was it marijuana? I started to laugh but he was serious so I said no, it was all products that we had made. Don had a point as several of the local markets sold nothing other than marijuana, rows after rows of the stuff.

Margret was white with fear as I let her in. She told me her story. Like many of us, she went to bed early and had fallen into a sound sleep. Thirty minutes later she awoke and heard Gods' voice. He told her that she had to come and pay me the money for the sales, enough money to pay salaries the next day. She argued with God, it was too dangerous to be out in the streets but God would not let her alone. I told her my story of no funds. We both laughed and she headed home amidst a volley of shots just down the street.

In the meantime, our community development program was beginning to take off but not without some serious issues to deal with. I was and still am a very strong advocate for savings with the very poorest. Savings was and is a simple concept. Perhaps because it's so simple, it's hard to understand how anything simple can work? The tendency is always to make a simple concept, difficult! It seems to be a part of human nature. Tabitha staff were no exception to the rule. Right from the beginning they insisted on making what was simple, difficult! In training staff, I already knew that without learning first-hand the hard lessons, we would never have a successful program. So, the training program began in earnest.

A system that tends to be indigenous in all developing countries was the concept of savings within a group. There would be a group of an average size of ten families where each family would save the same amount. Then the families would draw numbers and each family in turn would receive the entire amount. The system came with inherent problems. Those whose turn was to be within the first five weeks of the cycle loved it because they received money to buy their dreams immediately. Those in the last five turns often did not receive the funds, since the families who had received the entire savings earlier tended not to put in their savings after their needs were met.

A second problem that always emerged was allowing members to bid on receiving the funds first. If a member bid by adding ten percent to the total as a fee for getting the money first, and no member bid higher, then that family got all the funds first. The bids would increase to an alarming percentage, often over one hundred percent! It took away the purpose of the savings group. A second impact was that only a few strong members ever got the cash as weaker members were unable to pay the exorbitant fee.

I insisted that we start with the group savings program, a program indigenous within Cambodian society but I made rules that would address the challenges in the system. The families would receive funds in turn but there would be no bidding wars. Each family would get their turn. On the second go round of the system, those who came last in the first cycle would be first in the second cycle. We called it the merry-go-round system. It worked well but was slow and subject to pressures from the people to always be first to receive funds.

The staff were happy about the merry-go-round but insisted that it was not a fast enough system. They insisted that loans were necessary so that all families could move forward on their dreams at the same time. Over my years in the Philippines and Kenya, I knew that loans were very dangerous to the poor, people who had an uncertain income, people who worked extraordinarily long hours for a mere pittance. They never earned enough to feed their hungry families. Any emergency such as an illness threw them at the mercy of loan sharks with very little to offer as collateral. If they did not own their land or small house then it was often a child that became the collateral.

Loans were an ideal way for land hungry people to obtain even more land; for those whose business dealt in the trading of human flesh, loans were a sure-fire way to always have a fresh child for sale. There was no discrimination, male or female, children were good bargains.

It was also true that the vast majority of the poor were illiterate. They could not read the loan contracts, nor were they aware that the conditions of loans such as collateral would be followed through on. They had no legal recourse because they had put their mark on the loan contract. The safest loans were from family members, often people as poor as they were, but it was never quite enough.

The attraction of loans was the instant money, a release from the immediate stresses that the poor live with. It was a temptation they often could not resist and it would become a source of pain and regret with no other options immediately to offset the consequences. So many children lost, homes and land forfeited. Their rationale to these occurrences was simply to say, it is because I am bad and the gods are punishing me for there could be no other rationale for living lives of deep misery.

The staff were adamant that we give loans and I was just as adamant that we did not, so we started with savings. All of us went to Kilometer 6 and we talked with families. We talked about their needs, simple things like towels or dishes, things that were very cheap and readily available. I always asked the question but why don't you have these things? The answer was always the same, we have no money. I would gently point out that they had some money for they had store bought clothes, mats to sit on. The people would stop and stare at me for a moment and then came the answer, we don't have enough money. Why don't you save, I asked? We cannot for we earn very little and our families are big. There is always a claim on any money we have. There is no safe place to keep money because our homes are very flimsy and small and someone will come and steal our money if we left it in the house. As one woman said it: I am like a mother pig, the kids come and suck me dry.

I asked: if they could save a little each week, enough to buy a towel or a dish, would they be willing to save? Of course, they would but how could that be? What if we came each week, same day, same time and we kept your money safe for you? After ten weeks, we would return the money and you would buy that thing you were saving for. You would keep a small book where we would record each week's savings and you would make your mark when we returned the funds. We would also like to take pictures of what you have bought.

People were wary of this concept for how could they trust us when their world was filled with evil and distrust. I said, we will pay you ten per cent on your savings, and here is my address and phone number and you can come and tell me when it is not working.

The staff were dumfounded. This is not the way we should do it! I said this is the way we should do it. Well, let's make groups the staff said. I said no, if you make groups, the strongest in the groups will get all the savings for they will bully the weaker ones and they will never get their savings. Our arguments continued until I finally said, you can have your groups but only for the collection of savings and the people must choose their own leader. When we return the funds, it must be given directly into the hands of each person with no intermediary and each savings passbook must be signed by you and the family member of the savings.

For the next few weeks, I went with them as they talked to families and people began to save. As the staff became confident, they started to argue again, we must give loans so that people can buy bigger things like chickens and pigs. No, I said, loans will cause problems. But Vutha, Soklieng, Tharry, Srie were adamant about loans.

I capitulated but made very tough rules. There would be no loan bigger than US$20 and no interest but instead each person had to save the same amount each week as the loan repayment. Each staff person would be a guarantor for the money, no repayment, the staff would pay. And, most important of all, they had one year to prove their point.

So, the new system began. Oh, the people were so happy to have the cash! Some bought what they said they would while others changed their minds and bought something else like a case of beer or used it for gambling. When the pressure became too much, Srie came with her head down followed by Vutha and Tharry. Srie was trembling and could hardly speak, she said, the people are running away from us because they can't repay their loan. Some are good but many are not. What can I do? You must repay out of your salary I said, or you chase the people down. You all told me that loans were the only way to help people. I said no, loans were bad and now you must live the consequences because you are responsible for the funds. The staff were disheartened! This was too hard but they persevered.

The one thing I did do at the beginning of the year was to force each staff and worker to save. I forced them to open a bank account which was a very traumatic experience for all of them. Soklieng came back from the bank in sobs because the people at the bank had laughed at her, telling her she was stupid for trying to save $10 a week. I told her, don't listen to them. In time you will be the one laughing; a prophecy that turned out to be true in the years ahead. Each person had to give me their bank book which I kept under lock and key. On paydays they got their books and deposited their money. It was a habit we kept up for the first ten years by which time they were mature enough to do it on their own. I believed that they could not teach savings without doing savings themselves.

In the meantime, the answer for my proposal from the Australian Embassy came back. The answer was no. I was truly angry and went to the Embassy to ask why. The young man responsible for this decision met me and simply said, none of you NGOs do what you say. I said come and see for yourself! To his credit, he came and he saw. He saw the products and talked with the workers. He came to the communities and talked with the loan recipients and savers. He checked all our accounts which showed him the receipts for everything and our monthly financial statements. He liked what he saw and heard us. The no became yes and we received a grant of US$35,000. Part of the proposal was for vehicles: US$1000 for a car for my use and US$500 for three motorcycles for community development staff. This changed everything for us, for now staff would be able to work in three different communities instead of all in the same one.

In addition to the sales from the Cottage Industry and the grant, I supplemented our income by providing training to another NGO. The focus of the training was to see the resources within the communities and families and how to take those resources and multiply them. It followed the principles of the biblical story of the talents. I was doing training with this NGO, a government run seed and vegetable station, some of whom were staff I had trained with the organization I had worked with before. It was so wonderful. There was genuine joy in meeting again and genuine joy in their sharing how very much they had accomplished. My heart lifted to God in pure thankfulness and a hunger to visit with them again. They all talked at once, trying to tell me about the ponds and the fish and the pigs and the gardens. It was so good.

Work was going well. Every week we had new groups and did new things. One woman earned enough from donated candy from a friend to get a new roof on her house. Actually, there was no roof. She was so poor and had five kids, all of whom were the same size because of malnutrition. She praised God endlessly and put me to shame. I really enjoyed going to the communities to see what our impact was on the people.

The changes in the lives of some of our Cottage Industry workers were amazing. Seng Somali lived with her husband and five children in the slums of Kilometre 6. Her husband worked for one of the government ministries and his monthly take home pay was $20. For the past five years, they had lived in a thatch house that did not keep out the rain. They were unable to send their children to school. They were always hungry, with the diet consisting of only rice. Malnutrition had taken its toll on the parents and the children.

Last November Seng Somali began crocheting for Tabitha and joined the crocheting savings group which was mandatory. The differences in the family's life were dramatic. They all ate good food every day. The children attended school for the first time. From the savings they bought pigs to raise and sell and from the proceeds were able to buy squatters rights on a piece of land and built a sturdy, comfortable home. She bought a sewing machine and did tailoring at night to bring in extra income. Seng Somali smiled a lot. She walked with her head high. She said "With Cottage Industry we have gone from nothing to much. One day, I would like to see my children graduate from school and get good jobs. Little by little we will be able to buy furniture and maybe even a radio and TV. I praise God for what He has done."

Mauchan was 14 years old and an orphan. Nobody wanted her, nobody cared except for Sokoom. Sokoom was a sewer in Cottage Industry. She used to live in a thatch house, had trouble feeding her five children and herself and her husband was jobless. Sokoom joined the sewing savings group and very quickly was able to buy a moto-taxi for her husband to work. On their next turn, Sokoom and her husband rebuilt their shack into wood and tin. Sokoom saw Mauchan and took pity on her. She took her into her house as her daughter and asked us to teach her how to crochet. Mauchan now earned her own living and was saving money so that maybe one day she could return to school.

I asked Sokoom why she had adopted this young lady whom nobody wanted. She answered slowly and thoughtfully. "You see, Janne, Tabitha had pity on me and my family. I am now able to have pity on another. It once happened to me. I was an orphan that nobody wanted. Now, maybe I can help one other person not to go through what I did."

Cultural clashes were inevitable. One of my friends brought in a Valentine's Day cake, big enough for all the staff and workers to have a piece. What was this Valentine's Day anyway? Once again, something celebrated in the West was unknown in this country of sorrows, but the cake sure was good. Over the years this Valentine's

Day was imported on a national basis. Coming from a background of unbelievable horror and girls being seen as chattel, a bouquet of flowers became the prize on Valentine's Day to capture a girl's heart.

The ignorance of sex for girls was immense. I received a phone call from one of our villages because the girls were all pregnant and the turmoil amongst the villagers was immense. When I arrived, I asked what had happened. There had been a national holiday, Khmer New Year, a traditional event that brought everyone home to the countryside. It was customary for girls and boys to dance traditional dances and an opportunity to check each other out but traditional dances forbade the touching of the opposite gender. These celebrations lasted late into the night. The old people had taught the girls that they had to beware of the males in their community. If a boy held their hand or stepped over them, then they were pregnant and therefore spoiled and unmarriageable. It so happened that a number of the girls had held hands with boys and believed that they were now pregnant and unmarriageable which was an unthinkable scenario. In their ignorance, they had panicked and become inconsolable. I spoke with the elders and together we sat the girls down and taught them about the real process of getting pregnant. Not an easy afternoon.

## Moving Office

Our first office left a lot to be desired. My living space was a bedroom and a toilet, and much of the upstairs space had no outside walls. Electricity was an erratic and schizophrenic visitor. 1995 was one of those very rainy years and boy, did it rain. The first big rain came after months of very hot, dry weather when rained and rained buckets. It started at two o'clock in the morning and when I got up at five o'clock, we had a foot of water throughout the building and in the yard. And still it rained. I think I know how Noah must have felt.

The staff showed up at work and we all gathered on the porch upstairs. Not much damage was done because the maid and security staff had lifted up everything important at two o'clock in the morning. Nevertheless, we all walked in water up to our knees. Slowly all the toilets, twelve of them in this building, backed up and added to the mess. I was in shock. I asked the staff pick a happy song for devotions. They picked, How Great Thou Art, which set me giggling. Then I said, let's read Isaiah 61 -NIV so I can remember why I am here. This also set them giggling.

Then, horror of horrors, a customer came and insisted on wading through the muck to shop. I warned her to come back on a better day but she insisted. She slipped, got really wet but bought a lot. I said: we need a new place. The staff really liked that idea. They, too, were tired of living in rusticity.

Mari and Soklieng took compassion and comforted me. At 5:00 pm the work day was finished, at 6:00 the two ladies were back to show me five new places. We settled on one. It was a modern home, for Cambodia. It had enough space to do what we needed to do; it had a better showroom, and a terrace that could handle up to 30 sewers at a time. There was enough office space and a small living space which thrilled me. It didn't flood with the rain, was on a better street and it had ELECTRICITY! The house came with a huge generator, enough that we could still iron, have fans and lights on and use the air conditioners when the electricity failed.

The move to our new building proved to be quite a day. We actually moved all our stuff within two hours in four trips with three trucks. Our former security guard decided that he wouldn't let us leave the old place without him. He waited until we had the trucks in the yard then he closed the gate and put the biggest padlock on that I have ever seen. It took us fifteen minutes to cut the thing off and then he started taking stuff off the trucks as the others were loading. He came very close to meeting his maker before his time. I had him by the throat before Mari convinced me to let him go. So, we loaded double time and moved in one big hurry. By six at night most everything was in its place. The staff were thrilled with the new building and worked like slaves. We celebrated with champagne. The staff were tickled because most of them had never had champagne before and they felt that they were just like expats when I treated them to wine. We laughed a lot.

Nature was rampant in this new building as well. We had hornets that attacked customers and staff alike. The problem was that the hornets' nest was firmly imbedded around electrical wires and in our bougainvillaea tree. In desperation, several young lads from the community came to save the day. They were well prepared with rubber boots, raincoats, rubber gloves, plastic bags over their heads, crowned with motorbike helmets. I was rather dubious that the plastic bags would be helpful and my message was understood as one of the young men slowly turned blue while gasping for air. They had come in the early evening while it was raining. They assured me that the hornets have an aversion to rain and that they would be asleep. I just hoped that the hornets had read the same book. The entire neighborhood came to watch the show, rain or no rain. The young men began to break apart the nest while spraying it with chemicals. An angry hornet got under the helmet of one of the young men.

The other promptly started beating him on his helmet with a stick. God was merciful and the hornets left for a better location and we were safe from attack. I am thankful to say that the two young lads survived into manhood.

## The Orphanage

June Cunningham, whose husband worked in Cambodia, was a good friend of mine. She came and talked to me about an orphanage. It was set up by a woman who was subsequently expelled from Cambodia and had left 24 orphaned children behind, children all under four years of age. The expelled woman promised to send funds but clearly forgot to do so. The orphanage reeked from a block away and I was very reluctant to get involved and did not want to see it. June and Audrey Harte, whose husband also worked in Cambodia, talked me into it and so began another journey in Cambodia which was to have a huge impact on Tabitha. It was just one of the many ways that God worked in my life for the betterment of many.

The orphanage was so very sad, the children were so little, and it smelled so bad. The kids were desperate to be held or touched and stood there with stretched arms begging to be noticed. I didn't want an orphanage so I made it clear I would only get involved if we placed the children up for adoption. I also made it clear that I wouldn't get involved unless I headed the board. I didn't want to deal with the endless chatter and little effort which was so typical of boards. We agreed.

We organized the board for Cambodia House. As Chairman I managed to get things moving in the right direction. We had ten board members representing seven countries. We had mothers, grandmothers and singles, a perfect group, and at least 15 volunteers to work on various committees. It was a big task. We started with nothing more than an empty house with 24 children. We were offered 32 additional children but wouldn't take any more until we had a clear picture of what we wanted to do and how we were going to do it. Audrey and June sighed with relief. I didn't mind being boss; it meant I got to delegate everything.

Our next exposure to the Cambodian community was the International Red Cross Day event. The Red Cross was headed by HM Queen Monineath at the time. They invited NGOs involved in making crafts to display and sell our wares at the venue marking this auspicious day. As usual, there were rules, with the biggest rule that only two people from Tabitha were allowed to man the stall. This caused a stir amongst the staff, all of whom wanted to be there to meet the King and the Queen. What to do and who to choose?

The problem was solved. First, we were given eight meters to display our wares as there were not enough NGOs or products yet available to make a good display area. The area was outside near Sisowath Quay, a big road with lots of space near the Royal Palace. All the staff came to help set up the display. Security was high and so problems with numbers of people helping drew the attention of the security guards.

This was to my benefit as the guards were North Korean and spoke very little English and I spoke no Korean. They kept gesturing at me with two fingers. I knew perfectly well what they were saying but pretended not to understand. What I did was put two Tabitha staff every meter and told them to get on their knees. The guards were beside themselves as I would nod with a big smile and say yes, two people, two people every meter. We were at an impasse when the Royal entourage arrived. The guards were now busy making sure no one got near the Royal couple or near the two Prime Ministers, and their wives.

After the official ceremony, the King and Queen followed by the two Prime Ministers made their way to the display area. My staff knew protocol much better than I. All of them were on their knees with their heads bowed and their hands placed together in front of their faces (they call it *satu* which was a sign of deep respect). The King came first and praised our products. He spoke English which was good for me. Then came the Queen. My, what an extraordinary person she was. She took the time to take the hands of each of my staff, lifted them to their feet and had a kind word for each. I was in tears for my staff who had suffered so much, who were so very poor and stressed, being treated with the outmost dignity and respect by this wonderful woman. It was a moment none of us will ever forget.

The Royal couple were then followed by the two Prime Ministers and their wives. Each spoke glowingly of our products; each was respectful and kind. Prince Ranariddh greeted us quickly and moved on while Princess Marie took the time to look at each item and praise our women for their excellent work; another woman of amazing grace and kindness. Prime Minister Hun Sen stopped and picked up several of our Christmas decorations. Buy these, he instructed his staff. Unknowingly his wife Bun Rany had entered the stall and was standing behind me. I stepped back to get a bag for the purchases and inadvertently tripped over her. I shuddered in horror. I will be expelled from the country. My staff faces said it all, but Bun Rany started to laugh as I was apologizing profusely. It can happen to anyone she said, it's alright. A third woman of grace and humour. I knew then, that despite all the negative reports about Cambodia and its leadership, I knew there was also a measure of grace and kindness with the women that stood behind their men, women who would influence and encourage kindness and grace for the people.

My staff experienced a gift of respect and dignity that day, something which had been denied them for forty years. It was a moment that changed them all from being somewhat ashamed of this small, insignificant NGO to taking pride in who we were and what we stood for. For many years we would take part in the Red Cross Day and each time we would meet the people who ran the country and each time the women would take a moment and let us know how much we had improved and how proud they were of our work. Each time I was thanked for what Tabitha was doing and for the wonderful staff we had. Something that would bring many benefits over the years to come.

Several weeks later the staff almost lost this newly discovered sense of respect for being a Tabitha staff member. Cottage Industry continued to grow. A lot of the expats working within Cambodia came and shopped for everyone wanted something from Cambodia to give as gifts. There were very few others making Cambodian products. Then came Cambodia's Independence Day and there was to be a parade, the first in forty years. There was an NGO working in Cambodia at the time. They were involved in supplying condoms free to anyone who wanted them. They came and asked if we could make a 12-foot condom to be used in the parade. Of course, we could, I said. That condom required a lot of creative thinking and construction after I explained to everyone what a condom was. The explanation and the laugher involved was worth every minute of frustration. We worked as a team. Trying to make this thing stand took a bit of patience. The day of the parade all of us went out to watch. Our condom took the glory for it was big and beautiful! Staff didn't know whether to be proud or embarrassed by what we had created. I loved it! It wasn't much of a parade by Western standards but it marked the changing times in Cambodia. It also marked Tabitha as the place to go to for the weird and wonderful, but staff still didn't know whether to be proud or embarrassed by what we had created.

This year was a year of saying goodbye to good friends, something that was a normal part of life overseas. It was not always easy making friends and then having to say goodbye. I said farewell to Tony and Lorraine Culnane, friends who stood with me in the starting of Tabitha. Charles Twining, the US Ambassador, was leaving and we just kissed and hugged good-bye in front of everyone. He was in tears because he had been a good man in Cambodia and had earned our respect. I wished him God's blessings and just held him for a moment. He was sad that he was going and wished that he could stay, like me. I said he could work for Tabitha. The salary was lousy but the work was great. That got him laughing.

The Australian Ambassador was very impressed with the royal stamp of approval we had received from the Queen. He felt very proud that the Australian Embassy had helped us out with funding. I said the feeling was mutual. Gordon Longmuir, our Canadian Ambassador, just gave me a hug. I was on the Canada Fund committee and met with him once a month over various projects that Canada supported here. He called me his diamond in the rough. I was never quite sure how to take that comment.

I was always amazed at people thinking they actually knew more than me about what I should and should not be doing. Audrey was appointed the administrator at Cambodia House. She complained to me about visitors and people coming to the orphanage: "Does everyone come in and tell you how to do your business?" Colin, her husband, had come in the day before. He was opening a new store. He said "I understand about everyone thinking you're not too bright. Each and every person that comes in tells me how to do the work. How do you put up with it?" My answer was that I ignore most of what people say, I only listen to the odd piece of wisdom that comes out of their mouths.

Politically things were not good. A big power struggle was going on with the King's brother put under arrest and tanks and guns on the street. The King and Queen left the country in protest which did not bode well for us. I prayed that nothing more would happen but nerves were on edge and it bothered me that they left. The King was a buffer zone and did carry clout so it was unnerving when the safety net walked away. Threats, arrests, guns, and tanks became a daily part of our lives. We were all praying that cooler and wiser heads would prevail but when power is an issue, wisdom is at a premium. I lived in the middle of the conflicting parties so that did not make me feel any better.

The Christmas parties that year seemed endless. The British Embassy had generously donated enough money for us to be able to buy new clothes, shoes and a toy for all the children at the orphanage.

The Tabitha staff party numbered 150 staff and workers, an amazing growth during the year. My annual Christmas party became a part of June's family party. The best white elephant present was a pair of underwear wrapped up by a friend who weighed a little over 300 pounds. It was chosen by a young teenage lad. The look on his face was a sight I will never forget nor the laughter that accompanied it.

Tabitha was always on the verge of financial troubles but that was far outweighed by the number of families helped in the savings and loans program, far outweighed by the 80 plus workers in Cottage Industry and the changes in the lives of the families involved. It was very good.

# 1996

1996 started with a breather of sorts with a slowdown in visitors. It was good way to start the year. That lasted about a week before we picked up $4000 worth of orders and opened several new communities in community development. I was visited by a fair number of people who were trying to help the poor. All of them were looking for my help in resolving some of the issues they had created and had not quite worked out the way they believed they should have happened. The most remarkable was a woman who wanted me to work with a group of twelve women who had sold their daughters into the sex trade. The women had all bought televisions with the money they received for their girls. Their lives hadn't changed; could I teach them how to save? My suggestion was that the women sell their televisions and buy their daughters back. This suggestion was met with disbelief. I can't do that, she said, you must help them instead. The answer was a very firm NO for she had created an untenable situation.

I was struck by how many people passed through Cambodia, people who were stunned by the poverty and suffering of the Cambodians they had met, people who thought they had short term, quick-fix answers to the problems of poverty. People who were disenchanted by the failure of their short-term solutions, people who decided that my job in Cambodia was to serve their needs rather than the needs of the Cambodians. Could I help this family or that child, could I give money to this family or child? No, I could not. People constantly came to me for advice but what they really wanted was my approval for what they were doing. My standard response then was, and is now, the same. You know whether what you are doing is good or not, you know whether you have helped or not. You are the only one who can decide what is right or wrong, whether or not you can sleep at night. You don't need my approval. The approval must come from you. It was not the answer people were looking for. It made them stop and think and for some, it was good; but for many it was not.

We made committees for the orphanage. One of the most exciting was the committee to approve potential parents. The buying and selling of Cambodian children was rampant at the time. One fellow had been caught in Italy selling 60 Cambodian children for body parts. We decided that prospective parents had to have a complete file of information before we would consider them. We required home studies, psychological studies, medicals and criminal clearances not just from their home countries but from Interpol as well. None of us wanted to be accused in the future of placing a child in an abusive home.

The placement committee met when we had a number of files on hand. The rules for these meetings were quite simple. Each person received the file three days before every meeting. They were required to write down their issues with a set of parents. At the meeting for decisions on prospective parents, each person would state what their concerns and strengths of the applicants were. The rest of us were allowed to ask questions for clarification on a presentation but none of us were allowed to say I agree or disagree. Every point made was considered to be a valid point. The end result blew me away: nine different people with nine different views. At our first meeting, one of the committee members decided that she could not approve the parents because of health issues. The issue was that the woman was overweight, which she felt was a potential health issue. I was stunned, really? I never thought about that aspect. By the time meetings were over, we had a thorough knowledge about potential parents. The consensus was always easy: a unified yes, no, or we need more information based on nine very different views of a file.

In conjunction with this was the need of approval from the Ministry of Social and Veterans Affairs. As a board we had written up our vision, goals and how to achieve these goals. Included was our list of how we would vet potential applicants. I met with the Minister and submitted our forms. His assistant was a man named Menrouen. Menrouen and I became very close friends over time. The Ministry accepted our plans except for the criteria of vetting parents. The minister asked me point blank if we were telling the Ministry what to do. I said no, but none of us wanted to be accused later of placing a child in an abusive home. The minister smiled and said: that's what I thought you would say. May the Ministry use these criteria as well for vetting parents? Of course! If I had known then what I knew later, we would also have developed criteria for vetting orphanages that were placing children.

Over the next few months, we became aware that the placing of children was a business, and our orphanage had been one of these. Several couples would show up at our gates asking to be given this or that child. They claimed that they had paid for these children and wanted them. All were rejected out of hand and told they could reapply if they wished. None ever did. To cap it off, one of those foreigners who would buy and sell children under the auspices of an orphanage came to me one day and offered us $500 for each of our children. Clearly, we were philosophically miles apart and the answer was no. She eventually was arrested, charged and sent to prison in another country for her abuse of children. I felt vindicated but she was not the only one. Eventually this practise brought all adoptions to a halt. I believe that was a tragedy as so many legitimate orphans did need a home.

Our awareness led us to notice that several of the staff we inherited were abusive to our children. These staff were fired and a direct result was Audrey becoming the administrator and Violy, June's maid, became an employee. Things at the orphanage improved considerably.

We were in a rented building where the rent hadn't been paid for a number of months. The owner of the house had no sympathy and kicked us out overnight. To my surprise and shock, the house the orphanage ended up moving to was the first Tabitha office. What a nightmare!

We had no money and worry about paying the bills was tantamount in our minds. June had lived in Singapore before she moved with her family to Cambodia. A friend of hers, Amy Ferguson, was a teacher at the Singapore American School. Amy had raised some funds with her class and heard of our financial woes, so she sent a donation. June said: we must send a thank you letter and some pictures, which we did. This changed everything. Amy's class had donated several times to international aid agencies but had never received a thank you. Our thank you made Amy a strong supporter of the orphanage and of Tabitha Cambodia.

We approved four sets of potential parents. One particular set of parents was Andy and Mary Payne. The process of child selection was quite simple. We had a playroom which was a room without walls but had mosquito netting. The children had playtime each day for two hours in the morning and again in the afternoon; times when we allowed outsiders to visit. Prospective parents were asked to sit in with the children and just watch and if a child struck their fancy, then they would be asked to spend one on one time with that child by taking them out on several excursions.

We had knowledge of the prospective parents because of the vetting process and we knew the children. Each of us had side bets on which child would match with which parent. It was magical as it wasn't just the parents who chose but the child also chose the parent. There was an unseen connection, a deliberate choice process taken by the child as well as the parent. Many of the prospective parents had expressed a strong desire for a newborn baby but we made it clear that such a child was not possible. We would encourage them to come and meet the children before they made a decision. And come they did.

Andy and Mary came and went to their first play session. We met afterward for lunch and they were downcast for they had not seen a child they thought would fit their family. I was a bit taken back. Did you not see Chan, one of our youngest girls? Chan was shy and would hold back on her emotions and feelings. She would stand in the corner and watch. I encouraged them to go back in the afternoon and look for her. June and I both believed that they would make a good match.

They returned later in the afternoon to Tabitha, so very excited. They had found their child and Chan was to be their daughter! So now what was next? Next was the approval process of the Cambodian government, something that was to be a very trying process, but a process that allowed parents and child to get to know each other and to bond.

Mary and Andy wanted to know about Tabitha. We talked for several hours. The next day I showed them the communities we worked in, showed them Cottage Industry with the workers and the products and we talked about my vision and dreams. Mary looked me in the eye and said, our students, (both were teachers at United World College in Singapore), need to come and experience what poverty is. What could they do? It would be several months before we came up with the answer: House Building. In the meantime, both Mary and Andy thought they should carry some of our products back to Singapore and help us to sell these products. What a gift, as Marg and Don Cormack had left and we had no one who wanted to do this.

We packed several bags of products that the Payne's carried back with them and sold to friends and fellow teachers. They also met with Amy Ferguson who in turn also started to sell our products to friends and fellow teachers. The beginnings of Tabitha Singapore and the amazing growth of Cottage Industry had started.

I met a couple of reporters from the Canadian Broadcasting Company, Wivina Belmonte and Edith Champagne. They had been working on some stories in Vietnam and needed to renew their visas so they had come to Phnom Penh for a visit. We met at the Foreign

Correspondents Club where mutual friends introduced us. The ladies asked if they could do a short piece on our work and I was happy to show them around. This short piece on Tabitha Cambodia eventually resulted in a half hour episode on a CBC series called Man Alive, filmed later in the year.

The staff and I met and talked about all that we had accomplished and what our future plans looked like. Heng and Vutha were adding 40 new families apiece in Phnom Penh. We had reached a milestone and were working with more than 500 families in community development. Each family had their own story of courage and perseverance. In the past two months, seven of the women gave birth to babies. Each child was born healthy, with normal weight and healthy lungs. All the families had saved money and made preparations for the new arrivals. Gone was the past of struggling to find help and money for the births. On Fridays, the new babies were brought to me for show and tell. The babies got passed from arm to arm and we spent a few minutes oohing and awing over each child. We also spent part of the time talking about child rearing practices.

The past thirty years saw the destruction of the basic family unit. Children were taught very early not to cry or express themselves in any way. The communist regime often asked children to spy on their parents. When they reached school age, many of the children were removed from the home to work in children's camps. They knew little love and learned to hide all emotion. Now there was freedom, freedom to love their children. But they had little experience with this so I talked to the babies, making them gurgle. I held them in different ways, giving support to their heads. We talked about breastfeeding and sore nipples. We talked of weaning when the teeth come in and cause pain. We talked of family planning. They began to talk of their childhood. It was always in a monotone, with little or no emotion. They taught me about suffering and pain in a way that left me torn and sorrowful. They reminded me of the blessings and grace in my own life. They reminded me that I am a privileged person, allowed to be a part of lives that have known great meanness and yet show such promise. They reminded me of God and His passion for His people.

On a visit to our communities just outside Phnom Penh, we met Oun Dina and his family. Oun Dina used to be a soldier. He lost his leg in 1990 when he stepped on a landmine whilst fighting the Khmer Rouge. He met his wife, Somme, in 1994. She lost her leg in 1973 when there was civil war and she was hit by a rocket. They lived in a small house in Chamkamorn, an area the Government gave to injured soldiers. They had met and married whilst they were both training at Wat Than.

Life was very hard for them. Dina told us that it was like living in the border camps: very little food and water, beatings every day. He thought that he would die. Dina spent much of his time drinking away his misery.

In January 1995 Soklieng found Dina and talked with him. Soklieng had thought that he was different from the other handicapped beggars. Soklieng asked him to work with us because he was very poor and his wife was pregnant. He was a good worker and he worked hard. Then one day, just before Khmer New Year, we lent him some money. He drank that money away. Soklieng was very angry with him. I was very angry and wanted to let him go, but I wanted to give him one more chance. Soklieng told him he must change all his bad ways, if not for himself, for his wife and baby daughter. He said he would change, but Soklieng didn't believe him.

She was wrong. He did change. He had bought, and was still paying for, a half hectare of land an hour outside Phnom Penh. He had built a house with his own hands. He had planted 140 banana, papaya and jackfruit trees. Even though he had one leg and his wife told him the work was too hard, he had done all the work by himself. Soklieng thought this family had a good opportunity. They now had land, a house, and fruit trees. It made Soklieng very happy to see. She told me that when we see people do wrong, then we must tell them again and again to try and change. Eventually they will listen and they will do good.

Dina has asked for and received a loan to dig a well. This would ensure that there was enough water for all his dreams. I asked him what was next. He told me to come with him. We drove through the dusty countryside until we came to a beautiful home. See that house, that is what I will build when we sell all our fruit. My children will live in a good home. He gave us a big smile and pedaled off to work his land.

The staff felt that we should expand our programs to Pursat and Siem Reap. This came about because I was offered a plane ride by Vincent, a good friend, to visit Krakor a small town in Pursat province. We flew in a small plane, a tin can really, with six big people. Krakor was in the middle of nowhere. We landed in a cow patch and were met by heavily armed soldiers. It was all a bit unnerving. The town was on the Tonle Sap Lake which was a large inland lake. We drove to town on motorbikes, very fast over very rough roads leaving my butt sore for a week. We then took a boat through several large floating fishing villages. It was quite a sight and experience, for poverty was everywhere. Poverty looks romantic but romance wears thin pretty quick. I shared my impressions with the staff.

The staff suggested that we start our new area in Siem Reap instead, the area of the famed Angkor Temples. I had not yet gone for I was jaded. You see one temple, you've seen them all, I said. This did not impress the staff. I capitulated and decided that the staff should do a baseline survey of the area. We would make our final decision based on that survey.

I had a problem employee at that time, a man who had all the answers but no questions, a man who knew all about poverty but had not touched it. I firmly believed in the Peter Principle: promote people to a position they can no longer handle and they will resign on their own. He was assigned as the manager in Siem Reap, with Ani as assistant manager and Soklieng to oversee both their work. For weeks after he was assigned to Siem Reap he would phone every day complaining about how bored and lonely he was. I just told him you were bored and lonely at work in Phnom Penh as well, you are simply not a happy person

My problem employee finally resigned a few months later. Ani became the manager and I sent Apo, a former sewer, to work with her. Ani and Apo did a wonderful job and enjoyed it; my old employee had done the work but complained the whole time. He knew I had sent him to Siem Reap to either bite the bullet or resign. It was quite a relief.

# House Building

Andy and Mary and I had talked about providing an experience for young people through Tabitha. I had met a group of teachers from another international school in Singapore, a school that took in young foreign students who had been expelled from other international schools. I talked with the staff and we agreed that these young people should build a home for an old grandmother who was raising six grandchildren. They all lived under a blue tarp with many holes. The staff believed that we should build this grandma a home made of thatch and wood materials, the common materials available at that time.

Nine young people were on that first team representing eight nationalities. Several had serious behavioural problems. I started with orientation, explaining the background of and recent history of the people we would be working with. I explained some of the rules about our behaviour. James, the most troubled teen, made some smart remarks. I turned to him and told him that he was the leader and I expected great things from him. None of the young people had ever held a hammer or a saw. The work was brutal. The wood posts for the foundation weighed a ton but they managed to place them properly. Hammering the thatch walls together was a nightmare and the heat was unrelenting. One young lad, Sunil had shaking arms from being unused to work. They taught me how to say expletives in eight languages. Sunil got very frustrated and had me rolling on the ground as he let loose with a ten-minute version of "angst and frustration." Tabitha staff had a blast sawing and nailing with them.

While the students were busy hammering, I had my arms picked raw and my nose picked red from the local women determined to see if my body was all real. They thought I was beautiful. I had a very red face which made my eyes turn very blue. This brought about considerable concern as the Cambodians thought I was going blind. Cataracts were endemic in Cambodia and turned their brown eyes blue.

The house was finally finished after three days of hard labour. We presented the home to grandma and she was in tears. She was overwhelmed by it all and couldn't understand why we did this. I couldn't understand it either except it is called grace, receiving without deserving. I gave the kids a "thank you and proud of you" speech at the end. For the troublemakers, especially James, it brought tears. Then he started to laugh and asked if I could send this little speech to his parents. He said "This means I finally did something good."

A few months later I received an unexpected visit from James's parents. He was sent on the house build as a last resort after being expelled from three schools. House Building really turned him around. His parents said that he was now very positive and, on his return, he was reinstated at his old school without his parents' knowledge. He wrote entrance exams and passed, wrote apologies, and accepted supervision cheerfully. His parents didn't know until the principal telephoned and told his parents he was reinstated. At first the parents said "No", but the principal talked them into letting him return to a normal school. They came to thank us for our part in this turnaround. That brought me close to tears and made it all worthwhile.

Shortly after housebuilding I went to Singapore on my first work visit, which became a semi-annual event. Singapore was an experience in reverse culture shock. It started the night before I left when the staff took me out for a surprise dinner for my birthday and Khmer New Year. The staff paid for it all which really surprised me. Next morning at the airport, the women were in tears and the men gave me the biggest bunch of flowers you have ever seen. Soklieng kept saying "my mom is leaving." Ye gods," I thought. June thought it all quite touching but very funny. First, I tried to leave the flowers with June but she refused to take them. Then I tried to leave the flowers in the waiting room but some man chased after me and gave them back. Then I gave them to one of the crew as a gift which they returned at the baggage counter in Singapore. I then gave them to Barbara who picked me up but she returned them the next day saying they were meant for me.

I had appointments from 8 o'clock in the morning till 11 or 12 at night. Of course, Catherine, a friend of mine, kept me sane with lots of laughs, meals and a few drinks. Going to a bookstore was heaven. Mary Payne managed to get us lost going from one appointment to another. She kept asking if I recognized any of the buildings. She had to be kidding? We arrived an hour and a half later than expected for one appointment. The hostess was not pleased but I thought it all quite funny. The hostess told me I had to wear my poor dress so she wasn't high on my most favoured people's list anyway. Singapore Rotary members were all the highbrows in the country. I got them laughing when I said I wouldn't eat anything I couldn't pronounce. There certainly was wealth in Singapore and I was treated royally but I couldn't wait to get back to Cambodia.

While in Singapore I met with an adoption support group as a representative of our orphanage. It was a strange meeting. Several parents had adopted through agencies or individuals who are in the business of buying and selling babies. (The going price was

US$40-45,000). These people were antagonistic to our requests for home studies and police clearance. They were also the ones that could not get papers for their adoptive children. Others in the group had gone through the correct process and the children were legally theirs. The "illegal" parents thought we were critical of what they had done but the others were grateful for the clear message of how to go about things. It was quite a night but we ended up with six applications going out, plus we were asked for applications for another three couples who wanted to adopt.

The orphanage was going well. We took four of the older boys on the river to celebrate my birthday. This was Janette's idea because she thought that I should adopt. (That would not happen!). The boys were enthralled with the outing. Everything was new and exciting. We had to look at every passing boat, bird and piece of sewage floating by. They loved the water and ate as if they had never eaten. It was a special afternoon.

The orphanage was always on the verge of financial disaster so we decided to do a fundraiser. We organized a Quiz Night with Conor Harte being the MC. We had space for 120 people and we were sold out within days. The evening was lovely and we raised enough money to keep the orphanage afloat for several more months. The only problem we encountered was that we had rented dishes and glasses for food and drink. One glass was broken and so the rental group thought we should pay $75 for that one glass. I was not pleased but in the end they settled for $5. Over the years, it has become clear that I am not a trivia person. Every time we had quiz night, my team always came in last but we had the most fun.

Our products were going to Singapore in increasing amounts. We had made black hockey bags so that people could carry bigger loads back. There were some concerns about customs and duties but I said, no worries, just say they are gifts. Andy and Mary Payne and Amy Ferguson opened their homes to hold sales and as word got out, more and more people wanted to shop as well as take some of the products to sell to their friends. It was a work of trust. As God said, see the good in people and they will be good.

Money from sales was hand carried back. This became an issue when the money was in the thousands of US dollars. The banking system in Cambodia was developing but it took time as the financial institutions were all destroyed in the forty years of war, genocide, isolation and insecurity. People were very nervous to carry so much money but I never worried for this was God's work and He would protect, something that proved to be true time and again. No one was ever stopped in either direction. I think God made customs on both sides blind to what we were doing.

The exchange not only included goods and funds but it also involved new ideas for more products. We started adding cushion covers and handbags to our product lines. Initially, most of the Cambodian silk was produced for ceremonies and so it always involved a traditional design. This was suitable for a number of products but we needed plain silk colors for our growing product line and customers. We made the decision to go directly to silk weavers rather than go through middle-men selling silk in the local markets.

We did our research of which provinces produced silk. It was not an easy thing to do as security throughout the country continued to be an issue. The Khmer Rouge were still very active in many areas so it was not always safe to travel. Another issue was the presence of landmines throughout the country. Eventually we decided to work with the weavers in Takeo province.

We went to do a survey of the weavers and to learn about how silk was made. What a long and onerous process it was to make silk. The people who still remembered the skill were bringing it back to life for the silk industry which, like so many things in Cambodia, had been destroyed by the Khmer Rouge. The weavers were in their 60s and 70s, bowed by the past forty years of hardship and misery, women who had lost so very much, including husbands and children, to the ravages of the war and genocide. All were single, raising grandchildren whose parents had died as a result of war, landmines or the scourge of the emerging AIDS epidemic that was devastating the country.

There were no locally grown silk threads left in Cambodia. The mulberry trees needed to feed the silk worms were destroyed by the Khmer Rouge so the women bought the silk worms from neighboring countries such as Thailand, Vietnam, and Laos. They would boil the worms until the silk threads were loosened and then they would start the carding of the silk, tying the fine threads together in a process called carding. This resulted in bundles of raw silk thread. The women would then boil the thread in local dyes such as red from beets. This process would result in over 150 silk colors as the boiling process needed to be watched at all times. But the women were just like us; busy with household chores, busy with children and spouses, busy with farm animals and growing food, busy dealing with physical ailments and so the silk would be boiled in dye for a variety of times. Sometimes the color would be a very dark red, next time a wine red, the following time a brilliant red. All beautiful to see, but frustrating when we needed consistency in color.

The women then spun the silk into fine threads, sometimes a single thread, sometimes two threads and sometimes three. Tabitha decided that the two threads was the one we wanted to work with; strong and pliable enough to do what we needed to do. The women would set the loom, a process that could take as long as a month, sometimes two if the pattern was very intricate. We wanted primarily single color thread; something the weavers very quickly adopted for the work involved in setting the loom for patterned silk was drastically cut. They would then work the looms producing four to eight meters per day. The looms were handmade wooden looms just big enough to be handled by one woman. The materials would be as long as 30 to 35 meters in a bundle, more than that the looms could not handle. The width of the material was also severely restricted to anything between 90 and 100 cm. For pieces required for scarves, it was anywhere from 45 to 55 cm. The fact that every process was hand done was a source of continued frustration as customers wanted exactly the same silk color and length each time, which was something that we could not guarantee, even today. This was especially important when we received large orders but variations in shades of colors always caused concern.

Our first major order came from a chain store in France. It required a great deal of attention to quality and color. I acquired a few white hairs throughout the production of that order. It was a large quantity, which not only caused us grief in terms of having the same color all the time but it seemed we were forever one or two pieces short of an item that we had counted numerous times. Another major issue was payment. It cost us money to purchase the raw materials and money to pay for labor. The company was unwilling to pay any more than the bare minimum of the total value of the order at the onset. I finally solved the problem by refusing to ship the order until final payment had been remitted.

During the six-month production of that order, Tabitha was constantly under financial constraint. I had approached a number of organizations such as Singapore and New Zealand Rotary Clubs, church groups and slush funds of embassies in Cambodia. Those small grants came in timely increments and the work continued.

The number of our workers continued to grow. The impact on the lives of these women was phenomenal. Siew Mouw was 33 years old and lived with her husband and one child in Chamkamorn. Mouw became a worker in Tabitha Cottage Industry a year and a half ago. Mouw's husband was a soldier who contracted malaria several years ago. His malaria returned regularly, which caused him to lose his job in the army. When Mouw began to work, she had no home, not even a plastic sheet, no food and no clothes other than what she wore. Over the past year and a half, her life, and that of her family, had changed dramatically. She learned to sew and earned enough money to pay for her sewing machine. She had no home to put it in, so for eight months she stayed working at the office. First, she bought a cyclo for her husband, so that on the days when he was well, he could earn a living giving rides to people. Together they pooled their resources and with the dream cycle bought a home and land. The house was large but rundown. A new floor and roof had been built and the new walls would come soon. They now had pots and pans, beds and dishes, clothing and food. Pedaling a cyclo was hard for her husband, so they planned how to use their next dream-cycle money to buy a motodop. He now earned an income from being a taxi motorbike driver.

Mouw told me that if it were not for Tabitha helping the poor like her, the poor would still be poor. She would have no hope. Now she could save money, because she learned how. Mouw was no longer afraid when her husband or her child was sick. She now had money to take them to the hospital for medicine. Mouw felt like she had no problems anymore. She wished all of us good health and a long life with happiness like we gave to others.

Politically, things in Cambodia were not going well and seemed to be moving towards a major showdown. The situation was very tense at the higher levels and it caused much fear amongst the lower levels. There was a unique form of anarchy among government circles. At the time, a reporter was gunned down shortly after a third party opened a new office. The people were confused, frightened and afraid that another time of Pol Pot would happen again. I'd been through this unrest a couple of times and believed that there would be a major blow-up affecting higher levels. During any time of political unrest and for a few months after, things would be unclear, but then settle down again. It did mean keeping our wits about us and keeping our heads down. That was easier said than done. Keeping staff and workers in a state of calmness took a lot of effort.

The hardest part of life for me was saying goodbye to good friends. It was time for Nerida and Janette to leave Cambodia and June was preparing to leave for the summer break. (Ninety percent of expats working in Cambodia left the country each May, as soon as children were finished school.) Janette, Nerida, June and I went to the beach for our own farewell. Janette's and Nerida's leaving left me feeling sad. They were both super support people for me. We had a great time at the beach, despite the rain. I inherited all their mechanical gadgets: a wonderful music, tv and video system and a computer complete with e-mail. Nerida was convinced that if all of us had e-mail, we would keep in constant contact. All this technology had an effect on me that was not necessarily good, a problem that persists until today. I am definitely not an IT person.

## Siem Reap

In the meantime, Ani had completed the survey work on poverty in Siem Reap province. The poverty there was striking and, as a whole staff, we decided to open an office there. Choosing the office was an experience in itself. Siem Reap was still insecure, just two hotels and surrounded by the Khmer Rouge. Our nights were disturbed by gunfire and grenades, never a dull moment. Angkor Wat was overgrown and eerily quiet. Being the only foreigner left me feeling very vulnerable. All of us felt like we were constantly being watched.

We found a building that would allow us to have an office, living space for staff and a display and work space for our products. I didn't like the place and refused to stay in the building at night. There was a strange eerie feeling in that building. Ani was fine with it. Several months later I sent Soklieng to Siem Reap to assess the work being done. She came back to Phnom Penh rather shaken. The first night she slept upstairs in the office. She was woken around midnight by a woman cleaning the room. Terrified, she went downstairs and woke Ani. Ani, being Ani, volunteered to change rooms. She was woken at 2:30 am by the same woman cleaning the rooms. Our morning devotions had had an impact on her for she asked Jesus to keep her safe and then spoke to the woman, do a good job she told her, and went back to sleep. The next morning all was spic and span. Seeing ghosts by nationals and foreigners was the norm throughout the country for the past forty years had left souls searching for peace.

The people were so very poor and there were no roads. I had an audience with the Governor who told us we could start the work but that we needed to be formally registered as an NGO by the government. I told him that the government had given us permission to start but because of the constant ongoing turmoil with the differing parties, no one was willing to do this. The Governor wrote a wonderful plea to the Ministry of Foreign Affairs in support of our registration approval. On my return to Phnom Penh, I went to the Ministry and our approval and registration with the government was completed in record time.

A representative from the Ministry of Foreign Affairs came and told us that we had to attend a formal signing of the agreement with the Government. It was a tremendous moment when it was signed. They had a big ceremony, complete with all three television stations, champagne, and a very formal signing ceremony. Then the Minister gave us a congratulatory speech and I broke into tears, which drew the cameras even closer and made the Canadian and Australian Embassy representatives emotional as well. Tabitha staff members stood proud and were so excited. It was a true recognition of their work.

It really was another miracle. Organizations had waited for three years to be registered and we achieved it in five weeks with the help of the Governor. The staff were flying high and we had more champagne when we got back to Tabitha. Several other NGOs celebrated with us; bemused at how we could do it but not them. Politically, things were not so good and there were fears that all registrations would cease until after the elections. We were extremely thankful that we were legal and under the protection of the Government. How good that was!

I needed a place of my own for my little living space at the office was being overrun by the products and showroom. It had been a long year-and-a-half working and living with Tabitha for seven days a week. It was obviously the right move in everyone's mind because I received many gifts of furniture and dishes from a number of expatriate friends. I thought my apartment looked wonderful but Bev and Glynnis who helped me move, didn't think so. They came and saw and left, and then came back with carpets, a dining table and chairs, huge porcelain vases and stools, and then the place looked terrific. They were thrilled with the move, a move many of them had been praying for, for months. Their generosity and joy at the move truly surprised me. The staff sewed curtains and cushion covers and the place looked great! The neighborhood was totally Khmer and I was their pet cause. The army had a pétanque court across the street, so I had them all watching over me. The landlord lived downstairs and he was very nice even though the electricity was very iffy every evening from six until ten o'clock.

Four adoption applications were at the Ministry of Social Affairs where a large number of people had a say and a stamp in the process. For several months I would go to the Ministry twice a day and ask about the progress of the papers. It was getting quite comical as

Ministry staff knew the files and would tell me this file was at this place and that file at another place. Menrouen became their front man in our twice daily meetings. Finally, one day, I said to him in front of all the Ministry staff, I think it's time you and I got married for we see each other in the morning and at the close of day. I giggled and walked away. The whole room broke into laughter and it was the moment everything changed. Menrouen and I became very good friends and the files began to move through the system. In August our first four files were completed at the Ministry and moved to the offices of the Prime Ministers. Menrouen made sure these adoption papers were cleared and our first four children started a new life with their adoptive parents. It was so very good.

1996 was a year of flooding, severe flooding. Cambodia has floods each year, floods which are not too high and which replenish the rice fields with new soil. Every so often though, these floods are quite severe. This was one of those years. Vutha and I got caught in a downpour while we were looking at her new area. About 150 of our families were in the middle of the rising river and had to move to higher ground. This past summer about 30 of the families built their houses on sturdy cement piles above the water and so were able to stay in their homes. What blew me away was that their animals, chickens and pigs, were moved into these houses as well, an average living space of about three square meters. These animals were their source of income so they took priority over people. Poverty was a harsh task master.

We spent most of the day visiting our families by boat as they were living under very stressful conditions with water, water everywhere. Visiting the people by punt boat leaves a bit to be desired and with my physical expertise, or lack of it, I had managed to lighten the lives of a number of people by falling in. One of our business people offered us lunch. She was on a platform of plastic bottles with a tarp. The stools were underwater and I missed the stool. In many places the water was 20 to 30 feet deep. I promptly tripped over the edge of the stool and fell into some pretty yucky stuff. I thought my body was going to grow some cells that didn't belong there.

Once off the boat we moved on to drier land where they put me on a bicycle with a little box on it. My butt fit in the box, but little else. We drew quite a crowd, who were thrilled with the spectacle. The staff were concerned with my propensity to fall into holes and were determined that I not miss this wonderful opportunity to lose whatever pride I had left. We finally got to drier land and onto a motodop. My legs were shaky from all this travel and I managed to tip us all over in a hurry. Nobody was hurt but I was a bit bewildered. What amazed me was that my mind was completely numb through it all. It was when the staff took over my life that this always happened. There were fears that the river would overflow its banks in the next few days and then the whole city would be underwater. What a nightmare that was!

But it was not all doom and gloom in Community Development, in fact quite the opposite. Nie Seng was a 48-year-old woman who lived with her husband and six children in a village called Doeum Sleng. When Vutha began to work with her a year and a half ago, none of the children were in school; she had no business with which to earn money to buy food; her home was just a bare shelter. She received a loan to start a small business and wrote down her dreams for improving her life. She was part of a group of 10 families, all with similar stories. Nie Seng said "that the interest free loans enabled her to change her life. I was in debt to the moneylenders and could not repay because of the high interest and because I have to repay the total loan amount back in one time. I thought I was in debt for the rest of my life." Nie Seng repaid the moneylender and was free to regain her dignity.

She said "the savings and dream cycle is a good system for poor people because they can help themselves not to be poor anymore." The savings-dream cycle involved each person to set aside a part of the income they earned to do the small steps to improve their lives. Each of the ten members in the group received the full amount of the savings once in every ten weeks, allowing them to do big things. Nie Seng's dreams were to buy a motorbike for her husband so that he could earn an income from being a taxi service. Her dream was to put all her children in school: all six were now getting an education. She had a dream to buy land and build a house: her new house was built on sturdy cement pilings, made of wood with a tin roof. She had a dream to buy pots and pans and dishes, to buy beds and mosquito nets, to buy a small cupboard to put it all into. She now had those things. She had a dream to buy a small dugout boat so that the boat could be used to ferry people. The boat was sturdy; I know because I rode in it. Nie Seng was no longer poor. She and her husband and children continued to dream and hope. Flooding was no longer a problem.

In Heng's area he introduced me to So Malia. So Malia had a hard life. She lost her husband several years ago as he fought in the war. She had three children to raise and when we began to work with her, she had no place to call home, had no food, no money and was deep in debt. She once had a home but the house and the land it stood on fell into the river with the floods two years ago. Then she was in a motodop accident and lost three toes off her foot. The medical costs put her deep into debt.

She received her first loan a little over a year ago. With it she began a business selling Khmer noodles. Each day she hoisted her baskets on her shoulders and walked the pathways of her community. She could sell all her wares three times in one day bringing in a daily income of more than 10,000 riels. (US$3) Her dreams were to pay off the debts that she had incurred with her accident. Her children were all in school. Her new house stood on sturdy pillars and she was slowly furnishing it with beds, pots and pans, dishes. She asked us to come and see the expansion to her house. She had just built a new kitchen, not one like ours, but one that served her needs. She said "I could not think of how to do this before. I lost my hope and I was losing my mind. I now like to get up each morning; there is so much I can do, so much I would like to do."

The year was coming to a close. I went for a second time to Singapore to speak at a Global Concerns Conference sponsored by United World College (UWCSEA). UWC was a school that had become a steadfast partner with us in our work at Tabitha, a school that would eventually have me come twice a year, a school that sold our products faithfully each year, a school that brought housebuilding teams, up to seven teams a year to build houses, a school that has built five schools over the years, a school that is synonymous with Tabitha Cambodia. This was all thanks to Andy and Mary Payne believing in us.

The year ended with our community development programs growing from strength to strength, our Cottage Industry program doubling in size, changing the lives of our women. It ended with the CBC team making a documentary of our work on a Canadian television series called Man Alive. It ended with twelve of our children at the orphanage finding new homes with their families, a bright future ahead of them. It ended with our annual Christmas celebrations. It ended with a growing turmoil in the political scene, anarchy threatened, life was dangerous with guns and violence a norm. It was a wonderfully busy but an amazing year.

# 1997

The year started out with a wedding as Mari, our Cottage Industry manager, got married. Now weddings in Cambodia do not even come close to western weddings. Most of it has to do with taking pictures and more pictures. The custom in Cambodia is that the bride and groom change their wedding outfits up to twelve times in the space of two days. Mari changed eight times. There were about 250 guests and we were served a ten-course Chinese meal. There was a live band. For the first hour it was the normal eating and visiting and then the majority of guests left, leaving about 80 of us behind. Mari's brother was a high-ranking person in the military and regular police, so all the head honchos were there, complete with guns, but without their wives. The dancing started and it was a real eye opener. These guys got up and started dancing with each other, started singing serenades, presented each other with flowers, and, in general, had a great time. We, of course, also had to dance.

I decided then that peace would come to Cambodia as soon as we could set up karaoke for all the military. Give them all a beer and music and let them be free. I was quite deaf and bemused at the end. Mari looked great in her dresses but she had that lost look in her eyes. Mari was marrying a Frenchman and moving to France. I would really miss her. I made Chanthou the new manager of Cottage Industry, a move that changed her into a mature and caring woman, fully aware of her responsibilities to the women working in Cottage Industry.

⸻

I went back to Canada for a much-needed break, for a time of renewal. I returned to Cambodia on what people call the flight from hell. What should have been a 26-hour flight turned into a 48-hour nightmare with cancelled flights and lost luggage.

The staff had managed well in my absence. They had problems, but were able to resolve those problems. The good news was that they were all still friends, but what was even better was that they were supporting each other in the work. It was good to be back.

It was a time of increasing tension in Cambodia. The political parties were vying for power and in that process, threats and counter-threats of violence were the norm to bring about individual and corporate wills. This tension had increased to a level that negatively affected the lives of the people. All of the staff and our recipients developed symptoms of post-traumatic stress syndrome. A malaise of helplessness and fear marked their everyday lives. We talked about the situation, comforted each other and encouraged each other. We spoke of our fallibility as humans, our tendency to hurt and disappoint each other and how this tendency was a common trait in the leadership of this country. We spoke of how this was not just true for Cambodia but for all nations and peoples. We spoke of choices, choosing to put ourselves first and foremost, no matter the cost to others or of choosing to put others first, costing us personal effort and pain but in the end, benefitting us all.

We spoke of our value as people, as individuals, each one of us being special and unique in the eyes of God. We spoke of how saddened God was that we chose to besmirch the beauty and preciousness of ourselves and others by choices that we made or allowed others to make for us. We spoke of His Graciousness that He had not made us mere puppets but people who can choose to do what is good or bad and the responsibility that comes with those choices that we make. We spoke of God's love that never changes, no matter what we do or what we say. We spoke of His power when we ask for it, the miracle of rains happening at the very times and days when violence is promised by the authorities, which dampened the ardour behind the promises. We spoke of the miracles that continue to happen despite our inertia and fear, cottage industry orders that make us busy and needs of others that challenge us to reach out. It was good to be His child, to live fully although not so easily.

Our morning devotions were a time of sharing everyone's fears, of calming the symptoms of that fear. Devotions always ended with a stern command from me to go out and do their work well. They needed to know where I was each day, whom I was talking to and what was clearly expected of them. It was the structure that gave the staff the ability to function despite the growing tensions within Cambodia. Everyone had guns and grenades, disputes on the streets were quickly resolved with the shooting of one or the other of the complainants. Night times were the worst when shooting, grenades, and screams were all part of the night-time lullaby. Rumours of impending doom and gloom darkened our spirits. Menrouen, my friend from the government, phoned each day to make sure that none of us went out at night or if we did, what part of town to avoid.

Despite the increasing tensions, our work continued. Each of us spent most of our days comforting and strengthening those we met. It affected the board members of the orphanage for we were in a panic to place our remaining children. We had papers in process for four of the children but we had six more children to place. The sense of urgency to place the children in secure and safe homes was enormous.

With the ongoing threat of the dissolving of the government, I spent hours at the Ministry finishing off our adoption decrees. One afternoon I sat in the Minister's office with Menrouen. The Minister and his staff needed a person to vent to and I needed the adoption decrees so we struck a deal. I would type up the four decrees and they would talk about their fears to me at the same time. Upon completion, they decided I should work in the Ministry as I typed slowly but typed well.

Several weeks later, the adoption process was changed, restricted to only children under six that could be adopted. This suddenly left our three oldest children unadoptable. I spent so much time with the Ministry, begging and cajoling to let our children be processed. We had found parents for all the remaining children surely this couldn't be happening! Two weeks later, the government decided that all adoptions would cease. June and I were in an absolute panic and so my hours at the Ministry increased tenfold and my knees developed arthritis from the begging and pleading. My typing skills improved to an amazing level. My ability to find the lost official stamps became a daily task, a task that served us all well.

Comforting and assuring our adoptive parents was a task June excelled at. I just supported everything she said. We practised evacuation with the remaining children in our care, evacuation from the orphanage for the day the country would explode. The children learned how to carry their backpacks, how to move quickly without panic when the barrage of gunfire and explosions was too loud to ignore. Even today, all of them still dislike the sounds of fireworks and backpacks, and even so many years later are still packed just in case. The tension was so great and the needs were so many that when two of our oldest boys left to go to their forever home with new parents, I cried.

All these years I never cried, but it was sign of the turmoil present during this time, that I cried over every child after that. It was my way to relieve the tension. To handle my feelings, I wrote a children's book about adoption called "Sunbat Looks for a Papa". Sunbat was the boy who understood the placement of our children. With every child adopted he would look at me and ask: where is my Papa? I always answered him by taking him out for an ice-cream sundae where we would drown our respective sorrows in that ice-cream. Sunbat was our last child to find a Papa.

Thankfully, Cottage Industry continued to grow through increasing orders and sales. This gave structure and comfort to all our workers. Community Development continued, enrolling more new families each week. One of the side effects of the tensions was the number of Cambodians fleeing the country to safety, selling their homes and land. I advised the staff that this was their time to buy. Thankfully a number of them actually listened. Prices were at an all-time low and several staff bought small homes and land. They had saved so they had funds. What they were short of in funds, I extended to them as small loans. Soklieng, Srie, Chanthou, Ani, and Mari all bought which gave them a sense of security, a sense of a future, despite the doom and gloom surrounding them. Heng was the fearful one and he could not do it. The tensions were too similar of the beginnings of another Pol Pot era.

In the midst of all of this was a surprising and lovely event. One of our female staff asked me to come and see her church. She had wanted me to come a year ago and help her build her church. She had an extraordinary faith, one of a direct relationship with God which was very similar to mine. My answer to that relationship was to build Tabitha; her answer was to build a church.

She and her husband were very poor when she started working with us in November of 1994. Her skills lay in her ability to crochet and sew and her extraordinary faith. I didn't need more staff the day she came to ask for a job. We had just started Tabitha and there was very little money and even less in terms of a program. Her eyes had that intense pleading look of someone who needs work. I resisted, but then she sat and made samples for me, and while I looked over the samples she slipped into the corner and fell to her knees. She prayed on bended knee, her lips moved and she stayed prone for many moments. I could not say no.

During the first year she spent much of her energy working her way out of debt, buying land and beginning a simple home. During that year she attended a local Khmer church and she tithed faithfully. She was also one of our leaders in daily morning devotions at Tabitha. In her second year she started asking me to come to her "church" in her home. I resisted because I know that, once a foreigner comes, the foreigner becomes the church. She would talk about the first five people, then ten people, then twenty people. I was proud of her. Her husband had also changed; he no longer beat her and he became a serious partner with her in the work. Each day he would be there to take her home, always with a smile.

Then last year she spoke about some foreigners who came to her church, but she was hurt because they had only been a couple of times. Her husband became a pastor and their little flock grew. From me she learned how to laugh with God, to sometimes rejoice in just being alive, and she lost some of the sternness and harshness that so quickly becomes a part of our faith. Last December she had asked me to come to dedicate the new church. It was a hectic time and I was too busy. That was not true either; I thought that, if I went to her church, I would have to go to Vutha's church and Sunbat's church and Chanthou's church, and I was selfish about my time, so I did not go. The hurt in her eyes then still haunts me.

One day, I said to her, "I will take you home." At first her face showed disbelief and then an indescribable joy crossed her face. We drove through the city and then turned down the road to the Killing Fields. I asked her if she really lived out here. Finally, we turned down a dirt road. I parked the car in the midst of a dung pile and we walked to her home. It was simple but spacious. "This is where we had our church," she said. "Oh, Janne, it was full of people." She proudly showed me the pictures of her people and our people at Tabitha. She showed me the bed and cupboard they bought with their savings. Downstairs she showed me the well and the latrine they had built. She could not show me enough. I was so ashamed of myself: how could I have denied her such obvious joy at my visit? How could I have been so selfish to wait so long?

Then she said, "Please, please come and see the church." Now my face was full of disbelief: "What church?" I thought her home was it. "It will only take a few minutes." So, we went and crossed a field to a group of houses. Tucked in the middle was a church, an honest-to-goodness church: it was 10 feet by 20 feet; it had a simple cross for a steeple; it was made of cement and had a tiled floor. Gathered around us were 30 of the 50 members, so very proud of what they had done, so very proud I had come. "No foreigners worship here," they said. "Won't you please come and worship with us, maybe this Sunday?"

Her face was filled with such a desperate look. "Please, just come once. You see, Janne, you helped me build this church. With my work at Tabitha, we could build a life and I could thank God by building a church just like you built Tabitha to thank God. Can we thank Him here together?" Yes, we can.

---

I travelled to Singapore for a week of meetings in the midst of the turmoil. The staff were beside themselves with worry. I had done the unthinkable and left them in their moment of need. Before I left, I made sure that a boat had been arranged to take them all to safety in Vietnam should it all go terribly wrong. While in Singapore, I phoned each day and talked with most of the staff. This kept their panic under control. My time in Singapore was necessary for we had Cottage Industry sales and orders. I talked on Singapore Am TV. Afterwards I went to the Singapore American School (SAS). Students were hiding behind pillars just to be close to me. They asked if they could touch my arm. Tongue in cheek, I said it would cost them 25 cents. Amy Ferguson was and still is a teacher there, and had arranged for a number of talks, which would become an annual event. UWSEA and the Paynes arranged for sales. We took in over $12,000 in sales and adoptive parents made sure I was fed properly. It was all very good.

On my return to Phnom Penh the staff greeted me with worrying news. They were convinced that civil war was about to happen. We talked for several hours and I calmed them down. All was well for a few days when there was a terrific boom heard throughout the city. That explosion resulted in absolute panic. People, including staff and workers, streamed into the streets, screaming and crying; cars and motorbikes went out of control, hitting and running over the people on the streets. I grabbed the staff and workers and forced them back inside the building and then I locked the gate. I would let no one leave until we found out what was going on. It turned out that an ordnance of landmines collected by demining agencies had blown up out by the airport, causing the reverberation heard throughout the city. It was hours before a sense of peace was restored, hours of talking and hugging before I dared to open the gates.

Ani phoned from Siem Reap with the bad news that soldiers with tanks and guns had entered Siem Reap. They were all very nervous. I promised to come up soon for a day. There were so many needs. June and I decided to take our remaining orphans for a swim at one of the hotels. On our way there, we were stopped by soldiers. I talked my way through the blockades and we arrived to an empty hotel. A couple of the boys in my car were very car sick. I empathized with this and started to throw up as well. June was disgusted and had to clean-up after us. I asked her why she hadn't told me to go home at the blockade. She just smiled and said, you were doing so well with the chatter, I knew we were getting through.

In the midst of all this, Ani decided to get married. Dara was a good man for he showed Ani a lot of respect. Ani married Dara against her family's wishes. The tradition in Cambodia was that families decided whom a daughter would marry and when. Ani left home a number of years before she joined Tabitha as a sewer and then became staff in Siem Reap. Now she was a manager and soon to be married to Dara, already a Tabitha staff member. With all the tensions and worries and the upcoming wedding it was time for me to go for a visit.

I sat on the airplane trying to comprehend all that had happened, was happening and was going to happen. I was tired and the staff knew that I was tired but I was also suffused with wonder and they knew that too. A trip to Siem Reap started very early at 4:30 in the morning to be able to leave for a 5:30 ride to the airport and a 6:15 flight to Siem Reap. Ani was late arriving at Siem Reap airport leaving me alone to fight off the hordes of taxi drivers. They all shook their heads in astonishment as I climbed on the back of Ani's motorbike and we zoomed off with luggage and legs sticking out in various directions. By 7:30 we were at the office and the work began.

The first half hour was talk of how each of us was doing. Apo was excited for she has just bought her first piece of land and could hardly wait to show me. Ani and Dara, now a young married couple, sat impatiently, so I knew they had something they wanted to share but in private. Sarouen, well Sarouen was a bit subdued. It was hard for her to sit in on our conversation when everyone around her was suffering the pangs of suppressed excitement and she had no excitement. I hugged her gently.

We discussed the latest government directive, the payment of income tax. Excitement was replaced by consternation. I explained it all in terms of democracy which was an over-worked, little understood word. Income tax meant that we become bosses because none of us liked to throw our hard-earned money away. Income tax was money to be used by the government to improve our country and if they didn't then, we must complain. If it still doesn't improve then we must act through an election process to change the government. Democracy costs us not only money but also costs us our time and our voice. This definition of democracy caused some deep thought; new concepts always did. I mentioned that we could also cheat and lie and not pay our taxes for that would not be hard to do. Dara, like Srie said in Phnom Penh, "Cheating would make us just like what we say the government is, corrupt. If we are like them then we cannot speak of what they do wrong." There was a unanimous shaking of heads in agreement and so we all agreed to pay our taxes. They made me so proud.

Our next item of discussion was the loans they gave to 118 families over the past two weeks. Eighty-nine families were repeating a loan and savings cycle, the rest were new families. I got to see pictures of 89 "dreams" of the improvements in their lives. It ranged from simple dreams such as pots and pans, school uniforms and mosquito nets, pigs and ducks, to more complex dreams like motorbikes and bicycles, land and house building materials, new wells and toilets. There was so much to see and to comprehend. To do so much with so little always surprised me. I told them about the students in Singapore and Canada who had raised money for some of these loans, money raised by people in another land so that people in this land could dream. They were amazed that others cared for them.

The meeting finished and Ani and I were off to the market. We had a new stall to sell Cottage Industry in a better location. Sophea was our 17-year-old staff person. She was delighted to see us. Four customers this morning she says. She practiced her English endlessly and enjoyed her work. No customer passed by without receiving her attention.

Ani and I left for a private meeting together. We began with expansion plans and both of us agreed that Apo had matured to a level where she could do development work. Ani had found a new area which would mean we were radiating from Siem Reap town in four different directions. Would I like to see it, she asked? Of course, I would. Before we left, Ani spoke of her and Dara's dream. They had found a new piece of land, 30 meters by 40 meters. The problem was that they had some money but not enough, could they borrow? We talked it through and I said, I must see and think. "After lunch, okay?"

Then we were off to the new area about 20 kilometers outside of town. The countryside brings a soothing mellowness to my soul for the colors are vibrant and the wind cools my hot body. The poverty was very visible with house after house of thatch and meanness, of hard work and lined faces. They were all farmers and had lived here for 18 to 20 years. They had so little to show for their labor. Ani said, "We think it's the right area." I agreed.

We talked with Apo about her promotion. She seemed to expand and her eyes took on a special light, for yes, she wants to try. Dara and Sarouen talked of how they will help her learn and surround her with support. It was good. We began lunch but they were finished before I even started to eat, they are so anxious to show me their new land. First, we stopped at Apo's land. It was in a good location in a poverty-stricken area. It was across from a new market being built by the governor. She showed me her dreams, where the well would go and the latrine. Then she pointed to a new house in the distance and said, "That is what my house will look like." We drive over and indeed it was a beautiful house. We talk of how she will do it given that she was a single young lady. It was unusual for singles to dream like this. All five of us help her to dream and to plan because we are her family, her friends. Her eyes could not get any brighter.

We climbed back on the motorbikes but by now my backside was beginning to ache as we drove through the community where Dara worked to Ani and Dara's dream land. Dara was loath to waste an opportunity to show me all this morning's pictures in real life so the trip was long as we stopped and went to see each family's success. It became an affirmation of life itself because it was not only joy in their own hopes and dreams but pride and joy in the hopes and dreams of others.

Finally, we arrived at their land. It was very large and empty. We walked through the dreamed of garden and measured the house out (my room will face the east). We could see the fruit trees and hear the laughter of hoped for children. It was a magical hour, reinforced with clear steps and plans to achieve.

As we finished and were leaving the field, I once again tripped and fell into a ditch. Sarouen helped me up with tears in her eyes: "What about me, what about my dream?" I was touched at this older lady, who had suffered so much and given so much to others. She never asked for anything. "What about your dream?" I asked softly. She had land but had not yet started to buy materials. We talked about how she could start to buy materials and to draw her house on paper. On the way back to the office, we stopped and bought her first load of wood. It would take another year before she had it all, but she had started.

The next morning at 7:30, Ani, Sarouen and I were off to see Sarouen's area. There was so much to see: corn fields and houses, toilets and land, bicycles and motorbikes, fishing nets and numerous growing businesses. We went to see the "new group", who will start soon and who have so many dreams. At 11 o'clock, we stopped at Chorn Huns house for a much-needed breather. She stopped her work and sat beside me in the shade. I lit a cigarette as she popped betelnuts into her mouth. And we talked about the 208 ducks from her last loan cycle and she explained how it all worked. She spent 25,000 riels a day on rice for her ducks but she sold between 30 and 35,000 riels a day in eggs. I also learned that ducks can drown because they not very bright birds. She was in her mid-forties, and had seven children who were finally all in school. She placed her hand on my arm, a sign that I am to pay attention, for she had something important to say. "Your program is good! We don't have to pay interest on our loan but we have to save our money instead. Then in 10 weeks we finish our loans and we get a new loan and our savings." She thinks she is teaching me. The hand on my arm began to squeeze and she became intense, "You know, I think that in two years with this program, there will be no more poor people in Cambodia, Yes! That is what I think." Ani and Sarouen were deeply touched by the sentiment. I was slightly bemused, because so many like her had done great things with so little, that I no longer was surprised. I was content. (Cambodia was much bigger than her area but I believed that what she said would be true for her neighborhood, something that proved to be true.)

Sarouen insisted on a few more house visits before I had to leave for the airport. Another new house, a small piece of land for another family and then we stopped in front of a very tiny shack. The mother was a widow with three children. The house was built from leftover thatch with holes in the wall, floor and ceiling. "This family, Janne, is very, very poor but the woman is very good. She needs a better house. Can the volunteer house builders come here next and build her a home?" (Every few months a group of volunteers come from Singapore to build a house). I thought this might be possible.

We returned to the office and we finalized plans for our expansion area and Apo's training. We talked about several new products they had developed and I approve several of them. The trip to Siem Reap was almost over and we were all tired, the time had been intense. We were all hopeful, for there were new dreams, new visions to explore. We spent a few quiet minutes in prayer and thanksgiving. It was time for the farewell hugs and the last trip on the motorbike. At the airport, we gave each other a final hug, had a final laugh and a final squeeze. It was all very good, a typical project visit.

Tensions increased tenfold in the country. The Canadian Ambassador went off to Paris to a meeting about giving Aid to Cambodia. I told him not to go, that things were not well. He left anyway.

Menrouen phoned me and warned me about the upcoming troubles. Life here was moving into higher and higher levels of tension. We had fireworks, but of the wrong kind. Things had turned ugly and the city was almost a ghost town. I was getting disturbing messages from both sides of the troubles. There were lines being crossed that bode ill and left little room for retreat. When the higher ups were nervous, then I got nervous. A convoy from one side was stopped and disarmed by the other which was a definite no-no. Both sides were now wondering what to do. I had answers but I did not think they would fit into either side's agenda. It made me nervous when they asked for advice. I felt for the underlings because the guys with the guns loved the hullabaloo for it made them feel like big boys for a while. The hunger for power was frightening.

The tension made me tired. Our ongoing adoption files kept moving but, my, what a job. Two files were finally finished but the process made us feel as if we had fought a battle, leaving us all weary beyond words, but triumphant. It was hard to get people to sign papers when their minds were on death and destruction. Adoptive parents were on their way to collect their children, for the message was: "Get here now, while you still can." I never thought I could worry so much about others as the kids have really gotten under my skin. With so few of them left, my relationship with the remaining children kept getting deeper and deeper. I loved them so!

The staff and workers were all jittery and nervous, but, as long as I stayed calm, they did fine. Word from above had just come in that another firefight was being planned. Terrific! I hoped it would rain buckets, the combatants hated getting wet.

I had a telephone call from Menrouen, (it was helpful to have connections) that a firefight would happen. Apparently, it would be a small firefight, with small guns, and far from town, so not to worry. Menrouen said he would send troops to pick me up from my home if it got worse, so, "Please, don't worry", he said. I told him that, as long as it's small guns with small bullets, I would only have small worries. He didn't think that was funny.

The staff were in a dither so I needed to settle everyone down again. We were to celebrate the 4th of July with the US Embassy staff on the riverfront in the midst of all this turmoil.

## July 1997 – A month not to be forgotten

It started on Saturday morning, July 4th when Soklieng said, "I think there is trouble at Pochentong Airport". I said that I would check it out and so I drove to the airport. I didn't see any problems until I reached the outskirts of the airport. Traffic appeared normal until the cars ahead of me suddenly started going off in all directions. I did a U-turn and the next thing a B-40 rocket landed 100 metres from my car. I must confess that my heart skipped a beat. I beat it back to the city, got the staff packed and sent home, locked the office, went to June's and arranged everything for the kids; then Andrew and I went to see if things were really going for broke or not.

We went to the airport and it was obvious that all hell was breaking loose. I lived a bit too close to the action so I spent a very long night on edge. On Sunday morning I went to check on everyone, dodging soldiers and whatnot. They were all safe so I went home. I was scared, but the staff were worse. The fighting continued for two days. Each day June and I would go and see what had happened. Tabitha had an armed bodyguard in front of the office put there by the government complete with a bazooka. As we were driving down Norodom Avenue we just squeezed through as soldiers were placing machine guns in the middle of the road. I drove June home and then went to my home. As I was driving up to my home there was an armed personnel carrier in front of my gate. The soldiers were waving at me to come closer. I didn't want to but the Cambodians came of out of their homes telling me I had to go because the soldiers were waiting for me. I was scared but went. The soldiers asked my name and then said, finally you are here. Menrouen had wanted to make sure I was safe from harm.

Monday was calm but extremely tense, with looting at an all-time high. The staff arrived at the office by six o'clock for they needed to see and feel me and make sure that I was not leaving them.

On Tuesday Ani phoned from Siem Reap saying there was trouble there and asking if I could come up. We talked and she settled down. The Filipinos, whose embassy was across the street from us, fled the country, so the staff were beside themselves now thinking that I'll be forced to leave. They are so traumatized that I could not leave even if I wanted to. On the phone that morning Ani begged me not to leave. Again, I promised not to leave. The pain of the staff was so terribly real and so horrible. Each day the workers needed to be touched and be reassured and the staff's job was to help me to provide comfort and assurance which made them strong again for that day.

It was also a time of miracles. The Australian Military attaché and his wife came by the office. There was leftover money in the Embassy Slush fund which they thought would help Tabitha through this difficult time. It most certainly did. Many other foreigners stopped by with gifts of money for they were leaving the country. All of them wanted my approval for their departure saying that the Cambodians understood. It's true Cambodians did understand: foreigners are good time people but people who leave when things get tough. The foreigners would tell me how much they loved the Cambodians but it was always conditional love.

The orphanage kids handled it well; they slept at June's house for three nights but then it was time to return to normal. We received the three passports needed for the children so they were all ready to go. All the parents were on standby to come and pick up the kids and then get out as soon as possible.

Menrouen asked me if I too, was leaving; I said "No." He then said, "What can we do for you?" I said I was concerned for my staff in Siem Reap and I wanted the kids out. I received a telephone call ten minutes later telling me that everyone in Siem Reap was safe from the ongoing fighting. He guaranteed me that all the final papers for all the remaining children would be completed by the end of the week, a promise made and kept. I received a telephone call each day from Menrouen to tell me exactly what was going on from their side and that gave us the knowledge to plan what to do next.

The Council of Ministers met and issued a statement. Politically things had changed for the better. Hun Sen had said: it is enough, no more killing! Then he made himself Prime Minister. Prince Ranariddh, the Prime Minster, who had instigated the trouble, had fled the country before it started. So typical of politicians. I was so very angry at all of them, to cause such pain yet again.

June and I went out each day to check the war sites as by 3 o'clock in the afternoon both of us were stressed to the max emotionally and needed to see and know what was going on in the city. We got around to all the places where shooting had occurred. We saw bodies and were saddened by the futility of it all. In the midst of all the turmoil, adoptive parents who were already in Cambodia along with their adopted children left Cambodia through airlifts organized by the home countries of the parents. June and I waved goodbye, relieved that the children were safe, but worried about the last of our adoptive kids who were ready to go as soon as their adoptive parents could make it into Cambodia. The airport had been bombed and flights in and out of Cambodia were sporadic.

I travelled to Siem Reap. The staff in Siem Reap were emotionally wrung out, shaking and tearful. Some workers were not able to do much, despite having orders to fill. That really tore me apart. So much comfort and strength needed to be spread around.

The town of Siem Reap was completely abandoned, everything was locked up tight and there were soldiers everywhere. We went to Angkor Wat later that day to give the staff a breather, but it was deserted and terribly creepy and we were followed everywhere by the military. I was the only person in my hotel and there were a few big shells lobbed during the night. I must confess I was scared but I kept repeating Psalm 91- NIV about keeping me safe from the terror by night. The Siem Reap staff were very emotional when I left the next morning but buoyed by the concrete plans we made. The staff back in Phnom Penh were so pleased to see me, they cried. Life was very difficult for so many. I wish that politicians all over the world could just see what havoc they wreak and what misery they spread.

One night, my neighborhood was under fire. It was a personal grudge that started with single gunshots at 1:00 am, then hand grenades at five which gave my neighbor a fatal heart attack. It all ended at noon the following day with CMAC blowing up a booby trap of five grenades sitting in a gallon of gasoline on my neighbor's gate! I must confess it was a horrible night. The explosion was phenomenal, with flames 50 feet in the air and a hole ten feet deep. They covered it with a ton of sand before they blew it. I really didn't need this, as we were running around trying to finish the paperwork.

Many people wanted to know why I stayed during this time when nearly all the foreigners left. For quite a while I did not want to answer that question for it was a very personal thing for me. It was not an easy question to answer, nor was the answer an easy one to share. I was afraid that my answer would be misunderstood, that it would make me to be something that I am not. I am not heroic, nor brave, nor exceptional, nor any of those things. I am just me, a believer in a God who is all-knowing, all powerful and all merciful. (Romans 11:33-34 NIV). He is more real to me than anything else in life. It is to Him that I respond.

The decision to come to Cambodia three years ago was one made in faith. I believed in His promises and relied on His strength and He has never failed me. I learned to see the Cambodian people through His eyes; the eyes of the Creator. And what He created was very good. (Genesis 1:27) These people are in His image, just as you and I are. Like us, they can choose to bring out that beauty or choose not to. They can choose to acknowledge that goodness or choose not to. I learned to love these people. Love is a big word, it encompasses a great deal. Love doesn't stop when times are bad, in fact, the opposite happens, it grows and develops for that is the time when we review just what it is we see in another and is it worth it. Love holds us accountable.

Being shot at or being near shelling is a terrifying thing. There is no glamour and no romance. It makes a person sick with fear; it changes everything in a flash. It makes one stop and think. And that was true for me as it was for everyone involved, those doing the shooting and those being around the shooting. I talked with my God. I made no promises if He would keep me safe, I just wanted to know what He thought. And He gave me his answer, one that has been there all along but just re-confirmed. It is found in the Bible in Isaiah 61 the first 3 verses, NIV. It brought me peace and assurance. I cannot leave.

Tabitha staff and the recipients of our programs were traumatized. So many were on an emotional edge which bordered on total despair and were at the point of giving up. During those days they and I travelled through the city to see and touch each other. It was a humbling experience. They just needed to see and touch, to ensure that there was still a chance the next holocaust was not beginning. Each day for thirty days, they asked me if I was staying. Finally, I shared my answer with them. I didn't want to because it was my reason, my answer, it was too personal. An amazing thing happened. As they read my answer, the tears started, for some those tears lasted for days. And with the tears came relief and a renewal of their own strength.

Tabitha was back to work but the work had changed. The staff saw the people with new eyes; they worked with a compassion that was stunning. They fought for the people, not with guns but with words and with patience. They encouraged and hugged; they cajoled and laughed. There was hope and renewed vigour.

Our last five Cambodia House children left with their new parents. It was an unbelievable weekend, first with meeting the parents on the tarmac at the airport, as most of the airport had been destroyed. We had one night together, with parents who had become very good friends leaving with children that we had bonded with and loved. It was good to see them all board the plane but it left June and I with holes in our hearts. It had been so much work; we loved the children so. It was as it was meant to be.

We gave away our orphanage furniture, most of which went to the Missionaries of Charity (Mother Theresa's organization) which started a new relationship, helping them to eventually register properly with the Ministry of Social Affairs. The relationship included my help in finding and vetting parents for their orphaned children. The leftover money was donated to Tabitha on behalf of the children and their adoptive parents, a gift that meant so very much to me personally. The children were leaving behind a helping hand.

Work slowly returned to normal. In community development we made the changes necessary towards a savings only program. We no longer granted individual loans, instead we had groups of ten families talking with each other about loans and savings and dreams. They would save as a group, using that savings as a loan to a family with a dream. That family needed to continue to save while repaying the loan to the group. This changed everything for now we could help many more families as money for loans came from the families themselves. I still was not happy because I knew what would happen. The strongest members of the group would always have access to the savings, while weaker members would not. But I agreed, since I knew this would change quickly when the weaker families started complaining.

The power of savings was beginning to be understood. I went with Vutha to visit one of the groups she was changing over to the new system of loans and savings, that is, teaching families how to use their savings as personal loans and making that money grow. The group had agreed and we got in the car; then Vutha turned and said to me, "Do you know what we are doing? We are giving the people power. Power to choose their own lives and power to solve their own problems." It was like a light bulb went on. After two years, she finally understood.

The staff in Siem Reap understood almost immediately and were changing all their groups at a rapid pace. Dara was a relatively new staff member. He'd been with us as a development person in Siem Reap for the last year and a half. Dara was a serious man, a man full of integrity and passionate in his work. His community was called Kok Chork, a community of 5000 families who have come from all areas in Siem Reap province. They had come because they were displaced by war and land mines. They were the unsung victims in a society where so very many are the victims. They were destitute, with little money, food, clothes, and no hope.

Dara was dismayed when I chose him to work in this community. "They are so poor" he said. I said, "It is your job to help them out of their poverty." In the past year and a half, Dara had transformed the lives of more than 250 families and each month he added another 15 families. He was untiring in his efforts. Every month I came and every month he showed me more. I met the woman with three children who had nothing and lost all hope. She told me how Dara forced her to get off the ground and begin a business. He had done that with many and they had built a bustling market. They had bought land and had built simple homes. They had given birth to healthy children and their children went to school.

In my visit this past June, Dara waited until the end of our busy day and asked me to see a family with him. My heart was torn with what I saw. There was a family of nine children, the youngest nothing but skin and bones. She was beyond the strength to even whimper. The other children were gathered in a huddle, too numb to respond. The father was working the land around his house, he had planted rice but the rains hadn't come. The mother was totally spent, her body bent in desperation.

I asked Dara what he had done to help this family. He had given a loan for the father to buy a cart and bicycle so that each day he could work on the fishing docks carrying loads. The father proudly held up that day's earnings for me to see. Two kilos of rice were all he earned but it was enough to feed the family one small meal that day. He hadn't been able to feed them for many months. In his hand he clutched the 1000 riels he needed to pay back the loan each day and 500 riels was for his savings. He broke my heart.

I could not speak and walked away. Dara knew it would touch my soul. We stood under a nearby tree and I asked him if he knew what was wrong with the child. He would not answer me. "She is starving, you see, and she will die." We cannot let this be." I said. He nodded his head and we stood in misery. "We must buy food and do it now." I took all the money I had in my pockets. It was enough to buy three months of rice. Dara never flinched but searched his pockets and he had enough to buy fish and eggs for one week. Ani, Apo and Sarouen all searched their pockets and we had enough to buy oil and medicine. We brought the food to the family. The mother's face shone with relief, the children gasped at the riches before them. "We must feed the little one," I said. She ate a banana and asked for more. I was fearful it was too much but she was so very hungry.

We went back to the office and I asked Dara why he needed to help these people. And he told me his story. In 1975 when Pol Pot came to Phnom Penh they shot his mother in front of him. He cried for days. They took his father away and left him with two young sisters to care for. They slowly starved to death despite all he could do. "Oh, Janne, how very terrible it was to watch them die like that. For many years after, I pretended not to remember but I carried a big ball within my chest. Sometimes I thought that ball would choke me to death. And then you asked me to work with these people. Each day I see my sisters and my family over and over again in these families. Each night I dream of what happened. Many times, each day, my head feels very light with what I see and I want to faint."

I am stunned by his words and said gently to him, "But you don't have to do this." Dara's eyes welled with tears and he said to me, "But I must. You see, I could not help my sisters but I can help these people. I can stand with them and work with them and plead with them, and we can have hope together. The ball in my chest is getting smaller each time I work with another family. That little girl today is my sister. Do you remember Janne, when we had the war last July and we were all so very frightened that you would leave. Do you remember what you said to us that day? You said God had called you here to help the poor, to comfort all who mourn, to bring gladness and to bestow on them a crown of beauty. (Isaiah 61 the first 3 verses NIV). Do you remember how I cried that day? It is the same answer for me; God has called me to help these people. One day they will suffer no more and the ball in my chest will be gone."

The little girl died three days later. We mourned for her. Her family was doing better. Her brothers and sisters were active in their play and work. The rains came and the rice was growing. The father continued to carry his loads. They finished their loan and got a new one. They saved enough to pay for school fees for three of the children. They walk with hope. One by one, Dara's nightmare is turning to dreams of joy.

—

Cottage Industry was growing steadily. During the troubles sales dropped dramatically which we made up for by sending shipments off to Singapore in record quantities and which Singapore sold just as quickly. Singapore was our lifeline in so very many ways during this tough year and excelled at selling and promoting Cottage Industry.

We had a very memorable housebuilding team come from Singapore to build a house for one of our workers. Things were still unsettled in the city and the nights could still be loud with gunfire and grenades. This team was a UWCSEA team of teachers led by Andy Payne. The house was to be built in Chamkarmon, a squatter area which was overcrowded and filled with poverty. When the team arrived in the area, the residents looked at us with fear and wary eyes as we walked through the narrow pathways to the site. The house to be built was four meters by six meters made of stone pillars, wood frame, tin roof and thatch walls.

The build started out well enough. Nine holes were dug into which the stone pillars would be placed. The holes were not much problem; it was the pillars that did the team in. Each one weighed about a ton and the team members struggled not just to lift the pillars but to carry and place them in the holes. Then we had to construct the frame and thankfully a number of local contractors helped with that. Since we at Tabitha didn't know enough yet about house building, we let the team decide what to do. The team decided that we should build the walls on the ground and then put them into place. It was very hot, and everyone was quite tired. Andy mentioned to me that the foundation was not very sturdy; in fact, it shook quite a bit with anyone walking on it. Several other team members joined in the conversation. What should we do? They decided to continue. As the newly built wall was being raised, the foundation collapsed. Andy broke a rib, Jonathan almost lost an ear and several of my staff had gashes that needed to be stitched. I went with the injured staff to get stitches, and Andy took the injured foreigners to an expatriate clinic for treatment.

Staff that were left behind to pick up the pieces and get things ready for the next day decided that House Building would not happen. I asked the staff why they did this. Their answer shocked me. "You know foreigners. When there is a problem, they run away." I told them that this group of foreigners wouldn't run away, they would be there in the morning. The next morning, as we walked through the community to the work site, people came out of their homes and started to clap. It was a truly humbling moment. The staff learned a lesson that day, that not every foreigner leaves when there is trouble. I learned a lesson that day, that House Building needed local contractors to do the foundations and frames with volunteers finishing the houses with flooring and walls. This system would allow for many, literally thousands, of volunteers to come and build in a relatively safe and very organized manner. I also decided that this was not a democratic exercise but would be well regimented and clear. No house has collapsed since.

We had had another miracle this year. All ten of our remaining children at the orphanage were kept safe during the troubles. Within three weeks, all of them were safe with their new families. Their early lives stayed with them for a long time, though. The orphanage was closed; all our kids were safe, and I was content.

# 1998

The year started out well. I had found a new place to live, closer to Tabitha offices complete with electricity. It needed to be renovated but was an apartment that was bright and airy and affordable. No more living in a shooting gallery!

I had also written a proposal for the British Embassy which would provide funding for three years. The British Embassy was following through on selecting Tabitha as their main in-country showcase, which meant $25,000 for the first year, $35,000 for the second year and $25,000 in the third year. What it meant was a larger building for the Tabitha office. We had grown and needed more space for expansion. It was an excellent way to start the New Year.

I was still training organizations and individuals on how to conduct development. Not an easy thing as people and organizations had their own philosophy on how things should be done yet they insisted I provide training. Brian was one of the people I was training at the time. Like everyone, he had all the answers to helping the poor. Getting Brian to actually stop talking and listen and learn was an onerous task. Our meetings would inevitably end up with me telling him to be quiet and listen and then I would explain the concept and give him very specific tasks to do to begin to understand the concept. Once he had done the work, we could then discuss the principles involved so that he could speak from experience rather than from a philosophical point of view.

Getting people to stop talking on behalf of the people they wanted to serve was a very difficult task. Without this step, we were the biggest obstacle to development. We were arrogant in our ignorance of what people really thought, knew or lived because we thought for them without interacting with them. The simplest methodology I used to help disband these bad habits was to insist on a baseline survey, a set of pragmatic questions about the lives and lifestyles of the people we were called to serve. Getting Brian to do this took unbelievable energy on both our parts. He did as he was told and the process got easier as he understood more about the people he wanted to serve. But it was not an easy process. Brian told me how he felt. "A servant is someone who loves another person so much they'll do whatever it takes to benefit them whether or not it's convenient or pleasant for either" and "A servant is also someone who is willing to honestly consider and learn from whatever another person (servant) does for their benefit, whether or not it's convenient or pleasant for either. Thanks, Janne, for being a true servant to me. On the other hand, you should hand out Tylenol and anti-depressants after development sessions. Luckily I have my own supply."

That was really good to hear. Plus, he wrote out the next step of his work, which actually was quite brilliant. Brian started up and developed a very successful youth program working with children living on the garbage dump, a program that was eventually turned over to others and still runs today.

It was a very busy time with many orders for customers and for our Singapore volunteers. In that business I managed to do myself some damage. I was rushing from one task to another when I snagged the strap from my purse on a door. I was going full steam ahead when I was yanked back as if I was on an elastic band. It was very close to an instant mastectomy! I had a cut from my shoulder to my breast and my ear looked like that of Evander Holyfield, the boxer. My lesson in humility grew in leaps and bounds as I had ripped my dress in the process which the staff thought was the last thing I should worry about but then I figured that it wasn't their breast that was hanging out! It took care of my frustration and frenetic rushing about and put me back on track for a few days.

I had begun working with the Missionaries of Charity helping them place some of their orphaned children into new homes. I still had files of parents wanting to adopt children left over from Cambodia House and so when the sisters approached me about a child or children, I would talk with the potential parents. The word got out and other parents would also apply or go to the Sisters directly.

Menrouen continued to help us with the paperwork so it worked out well. We still scrutinized the files of potential parents but other orphanages would not do so. One file we rejected was from a Canadian couple. Apparently, they had connections. They had the Canadian Prime Minister phone the Cambodian Prime Minister and ask him to intervene. Menrouen called me and asked why we had rejected the couple? I answered truthfully that we did not feel that these parents would provide a good home and we did not want to be accused later of placing a child in an unacceptable home. That answer increased the respect the government had for us and nothing more was said.

A few weeks later Menrouen phoned and asked if I would go the airport to pick up a recently adopted baby from another orphanage that had been rejected by the adoptive parents because the baby had cried during the night and had disturbed the sleep of the parents. That was not acceptable to the new parents. I refused and Menrouen picked up the baby and placed it in another orphanage. The Ministry now began to scrutinize files more intently.

The work with the orphans resulted in a housebuilding team of Canadian teachers from the Canadian International School in Singapore (a team that came each year after that first one). Two of these teachers were adoptive parents and wanted to learn more about Cambodia. What we learned during one of the housebuilding trips was that leeches will go on dry land to suck blood as we built near a swamp and for me, it was a learning experience I didn't want.

My new apartment's renovations were finally finished. The builders spent most of that week wrecking what they had done the week before, so I was not a happy camper. My staff helped to put everything in place, but it was a trying time. Heng couldn't figure out why I wanted the fridge in the kitchen. Khmers buy fridges for prestige and so they put them in the living room so people can see them; of course, they don't plug fridges in because electricity costs money. Heng wanted to know how people will know that I have one. I replied that they are allowed in my kitchen. It was such a puzzle to him but I won out and ended up with cold drinks and ice cubes, a gift in the hot weather.

I went to Siem Reap for a visit. Politically things were still in an upheaval; too many rumors, too many guns but calmer than before.

Elections were coming up and people were very nervous. The last coup attempt had caused so much trauma to surface within the people so I was working hard at keeping life as normal as I could for the staff. Visiting all our projects was one way of insuring a sense of calmness in the turmoil of the country. At the time, most of the roads throughout Cambodia, including Phnom Penh, were not paved but full of holes, dusty and worn.

We visited a group where there were five widows with a lot of very dirty, but cute kids. What business had they set up? Making rice wine in regular stills. They could make and sell 25 litres a day when it was hot and 18 when it was cool weather. Cool weather was never a problem here. They were elated and my staff were elated. I was ambivalent. How do I explain such industry to visitors? I said to Ani, "Let's not show this to everyone." She replied, "But Jesus made wine." (John 2:1-11 NIV) I said, "But not all our visitors are Jesus." She was a bit confused with my reaction but was still excited. They asked me to taste the stuff. I thought we had a brand-new cleaning agent.

On my return to Phnom Penh, I had lunch with several friends. We were chatting about the political unease in the country, when one of them mentioned that the US Ambassador had just gone to Anlong Veng, near to where Pol Pot was. The response was out of my mouth before I had a chance to shut it. I said, then Pol Pot will be dead within 24 hours. Both were very angry at my audacity so we made a bet. I said I would buy them both lunch at the most expensive restaurant if I was wrong, but if I was right they would buy me lunch with no expense spared.

The previous week I had met several reporters at the Foreign Correspondents Club (FCC). Both men were in shambles and both had been reporters during the Vietnam War, the genocide and its aftermath. One reporter was shaking like a leaf while the other was clearly unstable, wearing sets of bullets across his chest and several guns around his waist. Both men were frightening, for they had seen and done too much. One of the reporters had gone and done a last interview with Pol Pot. Pol Pot told him that the genocide for the good of the Cambodian people. Three million people killed, starved, maimed, fled; but it was for their own good.

I awoke the next morning to the news that Pol Pot had died. He died alone with his wife at his side in a shack in the countryside. How he died remains unclear but I suspect that there were forces involved to make it all happen.

The reaction of the staff to this news was horrible to see and hear. Our devotions that morning started with the refrain of I am of no value, I am of no value. The faces staring at me were a mix: some staff were so very angry, some had that lost, glazed look and were somewhere else in their maze of memories. One staff said, "I cannot see", while another tuned out the world by being deaf. We had started our devotions about the reports of Pol Pot's death. The thirteen staff had unanimously agreed that it was not true! My response was to ask them to pretend it was true, what then? The emotions in the room swirled, the responses varied; some were troubled for not learning why he had done it, others said it didn't matter. "I don't want to think about it anymore" said one and then the memories started flowing and anger and hurt became the norm. Sambath was very angry: "There were eighteen children in my family, only three of us survived. My grandparents, my aunts and uncles are all gone, my parents are too old, and they don't feel anymore." The others were nodding and then it started again," I am of no value, I am of no value." It was the phrase Pol Pot used to destroy them, "you are of no value." It was horrible in its intensity, horrible to watch the refrain being picked up by everyone; it was horrible to see themvmetamorphose into emotionless, monotone robots.

"But you told me Pol Pot was a liar," I said. It was my refrain for the next five minutes as my chant reached through theirs and the humanity returned. "You said Pol Pot was a liar, did he lie about this too?" I forced each one to answer me and one after another, they said he lied. With that admission came the tears and with the tears came the verbal acknowledgement that they were of value, and not only were they of value, so were all the Cambodians we worked with. Not only were these people of value but so was the whole country of Cambodia." Our work," they said," is to tell all Cambodians we are of value, we are special people." The blindness and deafness disappeared, the lost looks were gone, and the tears were drying up. "Yes," they said, "that is our job, to tell the truth."

~

Cambodia was preparing for an election. The people were divorced from politics; the past 30 years hadn't given them much to believe in. But they were beginning to ask questions, what is this thing called "democracy?" It was mixed in with a new government directive of paying taxes. I once again explained democracy as something that costs them money, time and good decisions. Paying taxes meant you are the boss and you can demand good service in things like education, health and work. If the service isn't there, then you can fire the government through elections. They were amazed at such a concept and were beginning to formulate questions for politicians about the kind of things they wanted to see for all of Cambodia.

Some of our recipients were being trained in the skills of registration of voters. They had learned much and felt like they are part of the country. There were 43 parties registered and several of our Cottage Industry workers had started collecting information about the leaders of these parties. Who do we vote for, they ask? Do research, I said. Ask them your questions, look at their past, you must decide what is best for yourself. Such a new concept for them, what excitement new learning gave them, and they were taking it seriously.

Elections were set for July. We were working in a place called Kilometre 10 which was a large squatter area on the side of the Tonle Sap River in Phnom Penh. One of the opposition parties used the long-standing hatred for Vietnamese as a tool to gather votes. He called them Youn, a derogatory term. The result was that there was a massacre in Kilometre 10. Twenty-nine people slashed and butchered by an angry mob of Cambodians. These were families we worked with. The staff were beside themselves with disgust and anger and yet fearful of their own lives yet again. They made me come to see and witness these atrocities, a sight that left me retching and so very angry. I stormed to the Canadian Embassy and demanded that the Ambassador come and see but he couldn't. Politically the Western countries refused to acknowledge the offenses committed by the opposition parties because for them democracy was about vilifying Hun Sen whilst ignoring the sins of the opposition. This is democracy, they said. Hundreds of ethnic Vietnamese died during that election, Vietnamese who had lived in Cambodia for a number of years, simply people guilty of being human. What was the difference between Pol Pot and the opposition?

Hun Sen won that election and that changed everything in Cambodia. He made it clear that enough was enough, no more war. Hun Sen set out to unify the country, to re-instate peace and security for all of Cambodian citizens. The country was run by war lords, everyone had guns and it took little provocation to use those guns. Within six months, Hun Sen united the country, not through force but by making alliances with one and all. He was not a man to be trifled with. There was a six-month amnesty for people to turn in their guns which the majority did. Hun Sen had a vision, a vision to rebuild Cambodia from the ashes of the past 40 years. It was and remains an immense task, a task that involves every aspect of life, every aspect of society. He began and continues that process. He is still vilified by the West for he can do no good in their eyes.

Emotionally I was a wreck! The past two years of turmoil had left me running on empty and I needed a break and so I returned to Canada for a few weeks. It was the year of my fiftieth birthday, celebrated by a family reunion. I was wined and dined and lived a fully Western life for a few weeks. I could not talk about what it was like for no one in Canada had lived through these things except those who had lived through World War II and I just reminded them of the horrors they had seen. But it was enough to refill me with energy and a desire to move forward. I returned to my country of sorrows.

The staff survived my being away and we moved forward. The latest horrors were in the villages where the loss of life caused by the scourge of AIDs was beginning to leave its mark. AIDS had been brought to Cambodia with the UN Peace Keeping Forces and the tourists that were began arriving. The AIDS phenomena was non-existent in Cambodia during the years of the Vietnam War, genocide and subsequent isolation by the international community. Its impact was slow and stealthy, like a thief in the night. Its impact now started to soar with a number of villages losing all adults between the ages of

20 and 45, leaving behind scores of orphans and grandparents to look after some of these children.

I was still helping the Missionaries of Charity to place orphans into homes. It was early December when Sister Lillian phoned and said she had just received a new-born baby into the home and could I find adoptive parents. I can try to re-write the story of this baby but I'd rather just share what I wrote on her first birthday, it just about covers it all:

"My wonderful, beautiful daughter, Miriam Rose,

I am writing this because when you are old enough to understand and to start asking questions about who your birth mother was, why I adopted you, why did it happen, all your many questions. I want to be able to give you some of your answers.

I want to tell you how much I love you and how much you have changed me and made me a better person. I want to tell you about all the lives you've touched, about the fact that just being you has brought so much love and laughter, so much hope and joy, so much pain and suffering, so much about being alive, to so very many people, some who know you as a person, and some who have never met you but hold you in their thoughts and prayers.

I want to tell you how God is such an integral part of all of this, how He made you a wondrous little girl, how from your first day of life He has surrounded you with people who loved you and cared for you and how He chose me to be your mom and He chose you to be my daughter.

Today is November 1, 1999. It has been a year since your birth mother died; it is almost a year since I first met you. I don't know much about your birth mother. I wish I had met her, but I only knew about her after I met you. What I do know is that she was ethnic Vietnamese, living and working in Cambodia.

Your birth mom was a prostitute and we don't know who your father was. Before you become sad and angry over what your mother's work was, let me say that your mom lived in an era where wars upon wars displaced and hurt so many Vietnamese and Cambodian people. She lived at a time of great suffering, in two countries that are age-old enemies. She lived during a time when human life was considered cheap, and people from both nations were considered dispensable. Your birth mother was a displaced person with really no place to call home. Your birth country of Cambodia did not consider her a citizen and her ethnic country of Vietnam didn't want any part of her. That's what wars do, they make ordinary people non-existent and unworthy to be called people. Wars would not happen if ordinary people were considered to be of value.

Your mother was very ill with AIDS when she gave birth to you. Despite her work and her lifestyle, she wanted you and she loved you very much. She wrote a letter saying that she was dying and asking that someone take you for their daughter. I can't tell you much about her last days on this earth, other than that she was surrounded by love. She was under the care of the Sisters of Charity in a place called Chum Chou just outside of Phnom Penh. I know that Father Jim Noonan from Maryknoll knew her. I know that, when your mother died, you were brought to another Sisters of Charity Centre in Phnom Penh, where you came under the care of Sister Lillian.

Sister Lillian and I are good friends. I had helped to find homes for other children at the center, who were orphaned. When you arrived, Sister Lillian called me and asked me to help find a home for you. That is when I first saw you.

You were so very tiny as you only weighed 1.2 kilograms at birth. Lillian had you swaddled in lots of blankets and you were covered in purple gentian, because you had a rash, probably an HIV rash inherited when your mother gave birth. Even then, you had a zest for life. You had the most beautiful eyes and you looked at life very seriously. What a tiny little person you were.

In December I had prospective parents in town looking for an infant girl to be their daughter. They were Christian and their file looked very good. The next morning, I took them to meet you. You were wrapped in a towel, because the Sisters didn't have access to incubators. The most striking thing about you was your eyes, which were so very, very big in such a tiny body. Sister Lillian and I were talking about how you had come to the center; she talked about your birth mom, how she had died of AIDS. I asked if you had been tested for HIV and she said no. I said I would pay to have you tested and so they took you off for that to be done. The prospective parents were a little nervous for they had heard our talk and felt that they could not care of an infant that might be ill.

The next morning the test results indicated that you were HIV positive. The prospective parents were horrified and left. Sister Lillian and I looked at each other, and then the struggle began. Sister Lillian said that she could not keep you because you might infect the other children there and asked me to please find parents for you.

The next few days were days of frustration; I could not find you parents. My nights were filled with your eyes looking into mine; I didn't know what to do. Each day Sister Lillian would phone me and each day she pleaded for parents for you, "We cannot keep her", was her refrain. The Madame, who had owned your mother, came and said that she would take you, but she would throw you into the river. Sister Lillian told her to leave.

I was at a loss. Your eyes haunted me so much and I prayed to God to help me. His answer was clear: "You take her, He said. Like most people, I don't always like to hear what God has to say "How can I take her? My work is too consuming, I will not have the time to be with her? How will I pay for all the things she needs, I have no money? I am too old, already 50 years, and I am not married. I cannot play with her as I should? What if she dies, how will I handle the pain?" My doubts went on and on, but God's voice never changed: "Take her. She is my child and you must take her." I turned to my staff at Tabitha and shared your story. Soklieng said, "You must take her." Srie, Vutha, they all agreed, except for one, who was afraid that you would make me ill and then both of us would die and she was not ready to lose me.

I said, "For this to happen, I need a bigger house, with cheaper rent; I need to have a crib and clothes," and so on. Soklieng said, "Come with me." Twenty minutes later we had a house. I went back to Sister Lillian and said, "What if I take her?" Sister Lillian's mouth fell open, her response was not what I had expected: "What, you? Where will you keep her?" I was astounded and replied, "Where do you think, in my house, of course." Her response was, "What, you?" I became a bit defensive. "What's the matter with me?" I asked. She answered, "She is HIV positive, are you not afraid?" My answer was simple, "I need a crib and some clothes to start, will you help me?" Without blinking an eye, she said, "Yes."

Both of us looked at you with your big eyes which never left mine. "How did she get the name 'Miriam'?"

I asked Lillian. She told me that you were very ill, near to death several times and that she had baptized you and given you the name Miriam, and then had administered the last rites. You were a fighter; you always survived. Sister Lillian said to me, "You know that the doctors think that she is blind and deaf and probably mentally retarded?" I looked you in the eyes and knew you could see, and you didn't look retarded to me.

So, the process of making things ready began and the time to take you home approached. It wasn't easy. When I told people about you, I was challenged in so many ways. Some said that you were not welcome in their homes for fear of what your HIV status could do to their children. Others said, "What do you know about raising a child? Who do you think you are?" Others said, "What a poor child to not grow up in a 'real' family." The negativity made me question what it was all about.

I will be honest; I was so afraid that you would die from AIDS. A part of me refused to listen to my heart and instead listened to all the negatives. I said to myself that I would keep you until you were healthy, but only until then. I was afraid that I was not good enough to be your mom. I was afraid that I would lose you, that the authorities would not allow me to keep you. I was afraid that what everyone was saying might be right. Yet God spoke each night in the stillness of my heart: "Take her, she is yours."

On January 17, 1999 I took you home. Oh, what a day that was! Your Auntie June was my support. She stood with me in every way. We came to the center at 10:00 in the morning to collect you. The Sisters had you ready to put in my arms. What a moment that was! This tiny girl with the big eyes, completely swallowed up in blankets, and wearing a huge, bright orange hat. It was the hat that had me wanting to burst into laughter and your Auntie June wasn't much better. I left holding you in my arms, amazed at the miracle of you and stunned by God's gift to me.

Later that day we went on the boat to celebrate your homecoming. Oh my, what an afternoon that was. You never closed your eyes, you kept staring and staring at all the new sights and you never stopped looking into my eyes. You seemed to be forever in need of a clean diaper! I couldn't believe that you were really mine. I was so afraid I would lose you.

Our first night was almost our last night. You cried every hour, and I so love my sleep. I thought, "I can't do this." But we survived. The next morning all the Tabitha staff came to meet you. Each one held you in their arms for a moment and each one gave you their blessing. Then I shared the story of our first night. Soklieng, in her wisdom, had brought along Tuit, a new cleaning girl I had hired. Poor Tuit had her own tale of woe for her life had been so hard. Soklieng said, "She will stay with you and take care of Miriam." I thought, "No, no. This girl is not very smart and she cannot speak English." But Soklieng persisted and so I said, "Yes." God, in His wisdom, had given me two daughters, not just one.

Our first week together was very difficult. The Sisters had given us medicine for your incessant diarrhea but it was so strong that it left you befuddled. You didn't sleep more than two hours straight. By Thursday, I decided to take you off this medicine; I felt that, with the weekend coming, I could be with you through the hardest times. By Friday afternoon, you were constantly in pain, and by Saturday morning the diarrhea was constant and your crying hurt me so. I lay on my bed crying with you in my arms and I asked God to help us both, and I heard a voice as clear as a bell say, "Change the formula, she is lactose intolerant." I phoned some staff and your Auntie June and asked that they go and look for some soy formula. All afternoon I kept you off food, with just a little water now and again. You began to sleep. At 5:00 in the evening we had 63 cans of formula on the table, but only one was soy-based. I fixed you a bottle and you slept and you slept and you slept. At midnight I called a doctor friend for I thought I had killed you because you were still sleeping. Dr. Margriet reassured me, "No, she is only sleeping." For the next two weeks you slept 22 out of every 24 hours, you stayed awake just long enough to have some food and a change of diaper. At the end of that time, you opened your hands for the first time, up until then you kept them tightly clenched, as if in constant pain. For the first time, you looked with interest at everything around you, for the first time, a loud noise would startle you, something that had never happened before.

I had you christened by Father John; what a special day that was. It was a celebration of life. My best friends were gathered around us, both Khmer and foreigners. It was a promise before God to do my best for you and it was God's promise to us both, to hold us safe. I christened you Miriam Rose, Miriam from the name the Sisters gave you, and Rose after your grandmother, a woman I loved and admired. You were mine.

The rest of the year was a time of living and loving. We had you in a walker when you were four months old. You couldn't even see where you were going, but you had to move. You gave me your first laugh when we had a holiday at a local hotel when you slept all night long and, in the morning, you began to laugh. What a joy to hear! You would babble and babble every time I held you. You began putting on weight. You were the joy of my life.

In April I took you to have you tested for HIV yet again. I was praying for a miracle, even though I knew what the result would be. When I got the result, HIV Positive, I began to cry. I cried and cried and cried. I cried all the way back to the office. Soklieng and Heng were standing there; they wanted to know why

I was crying. I sobbed that you were still HIV Positive. Soklieng took me by the arm into the office and she said, "You listen to me, now is the not the time to cry, you must be strong, that is the only way that you can help Miriam." I learned that day that compassion and love mean not crying but being strong.

As you kept growing and developing, I kept my tears to myself. When you developed a rash or a cold or a tummy ache, I cried myself to sleep because I did not know what it was that made you so ill. But you never stopped growing, you couldn't learn things fast enough, you were so full of life. You were my joy and my inspiration.

You are now a year old, still very short, with just fuzz for hair and no teeth as yet. You still want to be wherever I am going, doing whatever I am doing, and that is so very good. You have made me whole, you have strengthened my faith, you have helped me to love even more than I thought was possible.

I love you, my Miriam Rose"

⁓

Menrouen and the Ministry of Social Affairs asked that I do something about orphaned children who were living with AIDS. So, I invited a number of people to come and meet at my house every Saturday morning to talk about what to do with these AIDS orphans. Amongst the group were Mu Sochua, Minister of Women's Affairs, the Minister of Health, and Father Jim Noonan from Maryknoll, a Catholic relief organization involved with the caring of many of the handicapped and AIDS adults in Cambodia.

Initially we talked about the AIDS epidemic that had children attached. When I adopted Miriam, she was part of these meetings. Her presence in our meetings changed our focus. Our talk changed from focusing on the disease to focusing on the child who was affected by the disease. When we talked about the disease we talked of treatment. When we began to focus on the child, we started to talk about the child who happened to have AIDS. The end result was that several homes for children living with AIDS were created.

The year 1998 was so full of happenings, of doom and gloom, of excitement and thanksgiving. The people we worked with showed unbelievable courage. Despite all the doom and gloom, they stood fast. They kept their dreams intact; they kept their businesses despite being told by others to close and run; they placed their children into school; they built their homes, little by little. They gave us what we needed, courage.

The staff worked so very faithfully, despite their intense fear. They never failed the people. They witnessed atrocities, they helped bury the dead. They saw several little ones starve to death and were devastated. It made them more determined than ever that it would not happen again. Where there was fear, they gave courage, where there were tears, they wiped them away; where there was hope, they rejoiced; where there was faith, they built a church. They developed faith in themselves and the people they reach. They have faith in their country despite all attempts to destroy that faith. They teach me so much.

# 1999

The year started out with the christening of my daughter Miriam Rose Ritskes. The ceremony was held in my apartment, an apartment too small to hold all that came for this important moment. June and her family, all of the Tabitha staff, and many friends from both the expatriate community and from my Cambodian community. It was so good to dedicate my girl before them all as God's child. It was so very good to have each of them dedicate and welcome Miriam into their lives. One by one the Cambodian staff knelt before my little girl and blessed her as only Cambodians can. It was so very good to have June stand by my side and bless this new godchild of hers. What a wonderful way to start the year.

The work year started out with planning for our third project to be opened in Prey Veng Province. Hang was made the manager there and received a motorbike so he could travel from Phnom Penh to Prey Veng. We hired Phat as his staff and the work there began. Prey Veng was considered to be one of the poorest provinces in Cambodia but then, from my viewpoint, poverty was severe throughout the entire country. In the villages where we chose to work the incidence of severe poverty averaged about 90%.

A trip to Prey Veng at the time was always an adventure. The main highway was poorly constructed, often necessitating a detour through rice fields, bumpy and insecure. The 100 km trip normally took four to five hours. Crossing the Mekong on the ferry was a delight. It was a big boat, overloaded but safe.

We met with a survivor of the bombing of Neak Leoung, the main entry point into Prey Veng Province and where Tabitha was stationed. He was an older man, sitting under a tree. His description of the bombs landing on the town during the Vietnam conflict brought tears to my eyes. He was describing what I had seen on TV so many years ago, with the journalists being unrestricted in their movements and reporting. I remember the journalist pointing to body parts in a river that ran red with blood. I remember knowing then, that one day I would come and work in this country of sorrows.

We, as a staff, had decided to move towards straight savings, eliminating the group loans and savings. We agreed to continue loans for another year and a half but the change went much faster than that. Problems had developed in a number of groups where the strongest members of a loan and savings group would always take their turns first to get the loans and then no longer put their share or repay their loans into the group funds. Tabitha was in the habit of picking up those lost funds so that all members of the group got an opportunity for the money they had put in. But these incidents were unsettling for participants and staff so we made the move to change to straight savings, savings made by each family and returned directly to the family.

The result of the growing Cottage Industry program was that our market expanded to include several shop owners from Australia. Mary was especially wonderful at ordering the bedding and encouraging us to buy whole bolts of silk at a time. We were not yet financially stable enough to do so but that would come in time.

For our workers, their life changes were amazing. When we first started Cottage Industry, the workers would come in on Fridays to deliver their goods and to be paid. The smell in the office would change as the morning wore on. The women had been unable to wash themselves or their clothes with clean water so the smell of earth permeated throughout the building. Now with a regular income, their sources of water changed to clean water and the smell improved. The women were also not used to western toilets; they were used to squatting in the villages, which left for some very filthy washrooms, something that caused me to yell at staff to clean the toilets. This problem was resolved when we installed a squat toilet. Embarrassment ceased and we were all happy.

The making of bedding created a new problem. We now needed to find an office space large enough where we would be able to lay out the bedcovers on clean flooring. The search for another office began.

It was not always smooth sailing. We paid our workers cash for their labors; a fun task every other Friday. In the early years, we would occasionally have a worker steal from other workers. The first time this happened, our staff reported it to me and then asked for permission to seek out the culprit. I agreed, pleased that they would take this initiative. The doors to Tabitha were closed and locked.

The girls invited each worker to come and be searched. They did a complete body search and then they went through the belongings of the worker. Bags, purses, whatever they had brought. It wasn't long before they caught the culprit. It was in her purse where she had cut a slit in the lining to hide the money. I asked her why? Her reply was simple; I needed the money, so I took it. There was no regret other than the regret of being caught. She was dismissed immediately. It happened one more time, same process and the culprit was found. This time though, the worker was very distraught at what she had done. Her child was sick and she needed to buy a lot of medicine. She was very sorry. This time, I did not let the worker go as she showed regret for what she had done. I believed that with true regret people need a second chance and a second chance she got.

This incident led to another change in our operations. We made a fund available for any worker or member of staff who was having severe financial issues because of a family problem. They were granted a short-term loan which was repaid through deductions from their salaries or work earnings. We had very few incidents of theft after that for people had recourse other than stealing to solve their immediate problems.

All of our workers were paid by piece work. Workers who were fast and efficient earned a fair amount of money while those who worked slower earned less. We set limits for earnings. Our good workers were cut off at $200 a month initially for the average wage for teachers at that time was $35 a month. There were no factories yet and we set the minimum amount to be earned at $100 a month. Today the limits have changed from a high of $500 to a low of $200 monthly. Today factory workers earn an average of $160 per month as I write and teachers $250 per month. This was very good money as the cost of living was comparable. When we started, a person could get a complete meal for less than 50 cents and today its $1.50.

A byproduct of women earning a steady income was a change in the dynamics of their households. Ninety percent of our workers were in abusive relationships, verbally, physically and emotionally. The women were extraordinary women. They put up with the abuse until it affected the children, then the women started to fight back. In many instances, the women would go to the local chief asking that their husbands be expelled from the community. It said a lot about the Cambodian system of justice as the chiefs were very aware of what went on. It was the woman who had rebuilt the home; the woman who fed and clothed the children; it was the woman who added to the community. The chiefs required the woman to pay her spouse a certain amount of money, usually, 100,000 riels or $25 dollars, and the spouse was then escorted from the community and forbidden to return. This was strictly enforced, leaving the woman to raise the children with a sense of peace and stability.

Miriam finally tested negative for the HIV virus. We celebrated with several sets of parents who were going through the adoption process. Their gift to us was three days in a luxury hotel in Phnom Penh. The first morning there, Miriam woke and laughed out loud. What a day that was, me doing everything to make her laugh and she laughing with every trick I pulled. That evening as we sat down for dinner, Mu Sochua, Minister of Women's Affairs, walked in with her husband Scott. It was the first time they had met Miriam. Sochua touched my soul when she said she thought I was the bravest person she had ever met to take in an HIV positive child. What a lovely evening we shared together.

~

House Building taught me how to explain why I loved Cambodians so much. Whenever we had a team coming, we decided which village the team would build in. We went and talked with the families in our program and asked: who should we build a house for? The families were equally poor and equally deserving of a home. It was their answers that made my love for these people so clear. The families would look around and say, that family, or this family and then give the reasons for that choice. As one man so clearly put it, me and my family will one day build a home but that family won't be able to. You see, she is a widow, has 5 children and no other family so she needs the house more than we do. You build for her first.

We had a British team coming to build four houses. The process of selecting the families could be very painful. We chose a lady who had worked with us for four years and, during that time, had saved enough money to finally buy a small piece of land. She had saved $200 for materials for her home. The team was bringing $700 for the rest of the materials and would provide the labor to build. She was very excited by the possibility of having a home, but she was also burdened by her past. She was afraid to hope, because if she hoped for something as big as a home, the gods might get angry and punish her. For her, the few days left before her house was to be built was a time of tension, tension fluctuating between excitement and losing hope. It was very difficult.

Her husband was a miserable person. After the materials arrived for the construction of the house, he beat her physically. She was heartbroken. We all talked and decided it was better to wait until he was more stable before building her home. So, instead, Sokkun got her house. She and her husband had been waiting for two years. To see their joy was very touching. They kept bringing food and water for the volunteers as they helped build the new home. It was almost too much for the team to be a part of such gratitude.

---

One of the most important happenings this year was the process of becoming a Cambodian citizen. Miriam was granted to me as a foster child by the government but not as my adopted child. Menrouen decided that I should get Cambodian citizenship. He decided that this was the best way the Cambodian government could show appreciation for all that I had done. He went to the Prime Minister to fast track this process. The BOSS looked at him, started to laugh and said, Janne will not accept that from me. He was right; I wouldn't because if anything politically went wrong, my citizenship would be questioned.

Menrouen then started the official process of my applying for citizenship. What a long process it was. It started by getting permission from the village chief, then the Khan, then the City, then up to the Ministries. Menrouen arranged all the appointments and paid all the fees for he was adamant about this as this was the Government's way of showing appreciation for all I had done. It was at the Ministerial level that things went a bit awry. None of them could understand why I wanted citizenship. I couldn't understand why I had to see every Minister. Ministers of Justice, Social Affairs, and Interior I could understand and then came the ones where I started to rebel a bit. Minister of Education? Okay. Minister of Agriculture, that's where I really rebelled for what did agriculture have to do with my citizenship? Menrouen started to laugh and he said they are all fascinated by your wanting to become a citizen and they all want to meet you. I declined that privilege gently but firmly.

It took several months and finally it came before the Ruling Council of Ministers. The heads of both parties signed approval and it moved up to the office of the Prime Minister. It was a Friday night about 6 o'clock. Menrouen worked as an advisor to the Prime Minister. He put my file before the Boss who smiled when he saw it and signed the final decree. The last step was the signature of the King who was out of the country at the time, so his representative signed. My citizenship was official! I received my Cambodian ID card and my passport followed quickly with the most important paper of all, Miriam's adoption decree. My girl now had legal protection and I had received the honor and privileges of being a Cambodian.

Miriam had stopped thriving. She was a very active little girl but she was no longer gaining weight. A nodule grew on her neck. Our landlord lived downstairs and we had become good friends. Bophea kept saying you need to take her to a doctor. I had very little money at the time but finally I took her to an expat clinic. The foreign doctors looked at her and said they could do nothing as it looked like a tuberculosis nodule and was too close to her brain for them to do anything. I was in despair. Finally, Bophea said, okay I will take you. We went to a Khmer doctor, a man who took one look at Miriam and at the lump and said, you are a bad mother! That made me feel a lot better! He said, I will remove the tumor but you have to pay me top dollar. I asked him how much that was, $5.00 he retorted. I agreed. He took Miriam from me and had a nurse hold her and without preamble he pierced the nodule. Miriam was screaming, I was crying, Bophea was wailing as a dishfull of gunk came out of the nodule. Finally, it was over but he left the wound open so it would drain. For a moment, silence reigned. He looked at me and realized I was a foreigner so he wrote out a list of twenty medicines for her, a list I would not fill as it was too many for such a small child. I paid him $10.00 and I asked that he help another child with the same problem which he did. Sadly, he left Cambodia soon after and went to France. Cambodia lost a very good man.

In the meantime, friends rallied around us both. Miriam was x-rayed for tuberculosis for free. She had TB in her lungs and in her lymph nodes. I went to the new TB hospital set up by the Japanese where treatment was free. The Japanese were a bit wary of this foreigner with a child but they agreed to treat her under one condition: Dr. Bo would come to my house each morning for 8 months to ensure that Miriam took her medicine. And so, it happened that my girl was cured of TB. She never looked back.

We met as a staff to talk about our progress this year. Vutha shared her vision of working in a new community where "dreams and hopes" were the basis of the work. "I want to do development with the poorest but I want them to believe they can do. Before I thought, maybe they can do or maybe they cannot do but just in case, I must give them a loan, otherwise they will be unable to do. But I have learned that it is not the loan that helps them so much, it is giving the people the power to decide their own "dreams" which changes things. Vutha told us about one of her families, a woman called Rom Touch.

Rom Touch was a woman in her late thirties. She had three children, almost grown with one daughter who was married and lived with her. Rom Touch got married right after the Pol Pot years because she was afraid to be alone. Her husband was not such a good man for he liked other women and he couldn't hold a job. Eventually he just up and left. Rom Touch had heard that he was living with another woman. She was left to raise her three children by herself. She had a small piece of land given to her by the government for settlement. Life was difficult and often they went to bed hungry and for many years the children could not go to school because she had no money for school fees. Her house was a simple one of thatch and mud floors with little protection from the sun and rain.

She met Rom Touch two years previously when we started our new community in Choupouk Eke. She was a very sad person! She earned an income cutting grass for cows to eat. Sometimes she could find grass but many times she could not. I asked her about her "dreams". All she wanted was a good house. She told her how she could one day have her house if she saved her money. She listened and she started to believe. She gave her a loan for a small business and she and her daughter started selling vegetables. She saved her money and the first thing she bought was pots and pans.

That first step was enough to start the neighbors teasing her, laughing at her for even thinking she could have a better life. Her son-in law joined in the derision. How much that hurt. But she was determined. With her second loan she started growing and selling flowers; her third loan was to start a small grocery store on the outside of her shack. With her savings she paid off her debts; she bought a bed and mosquito nets as her income increased. So, she stopped her from getting any more loans.

Rom Touch said, I still want my house, help me. Vutha put her into the savings program and every week she saved between 5,000 and 10,000 riels. The taunting of the neighbors got worse, we told you so, you cannot have a house! In the next year she saved enough to buy cement foundation posts; wood for the floor and tin for the roof. She never complained and she never got tired but she was sad to hear her neighbors and her son-in law tease her so. She was so lonely.

In July, we had volunteers come to build houses for people who had worked so hard for their dreams. The team brought enough money to buy the wood for the last wall and they did the construction so she didn't have to pay for labor. Her house was beautiful, her dream had come true. But you know Janne, she could have told her neighbors, see, you were wrong but she didn't. She is helping them now to "dream", to save their money, to believe in themselves. She is still saving her money for she has another dream. Her dream is one day to have tables and chairs, one day to have a bed of her own. No one laughs at her anymore.

All the staff were anxious to share because there were so many stories to tell. Dara spoke of how his life had changed with Tabitha. Before Tabitha, his life was sad and I had no freedom. He could not get a job, he could not earn money, he was always asking his uncle for money if he wanted to buy something or try something. He was so ashamed of myself. He thought he was no good. Then he started to work with Tabitha and started to save and could choose to do what I wanted.

Now he is giving that freedom to others. It is liberty that we give, liberty to choose how we want to live.

Kum Chuy was one of the first people Dara worked with in June of 1997. She was in her mid-twenties, married with two small children. She and her husband were very poor and could not afford to live away from her family. So, ten of them lived in a small house of thatch and mud. She was very discouraged and sad. Dara said to her "start your own business and save to build your own house." He gave her the first loan and she started a small business selling meat. Over the next two years, Kum Chuy built her business to the point where she was able to buy her own stall in the market. She saved to buy a used motorbike. Her husband became a motodop taxi driver and bought pigs to raise and sell.

She bought cheap land because it was always flooded. She bought landfill and then saved money for materials for her new house. She built the house last October. It has cement foundation posts, wooden floors and walls and a tin roof. Then she saved her money to dig a well for water. She just finished her new toilet. She has pots and pans and they bought a battery and a second-hand television. The children are in school. Dara stopped her loans a year and half ago because the income from her business was so good. She stayed with us because she had more dreams, Dara said.

Before, Kum Chuy was afraid of life. She was very depressed and very worried about her life and that of her family. She had no hopes, just fears. Now she is free, free to choose how she will live. She and her husband work hard together. They don't work just for themselves; they help seven other families now to also be free. You see, Dara said, that Tabitha gave me the freedom and liberty to choose how I want to live and I am so lucky that my job involves letting so many other families have the freedom to choose how they will live. Maybe one day all the people in Cambodia will be free, do you think that one day we could help everyone?

The staff meetings are over and our fifth year has ended, our sixth year is beginning. We are thankful for the liberty and freedom to reach out; we are in awe of the strength of giving freedom to others; we stand in humility that we are privileged to be a small part of such a wondrous gift; we are free to bask in God's grace for such a life.

# 2000

The year 2000, the Millennium Year, started with a lovely phone call from the Philippines. I talked with my former employees, Manang, 73 years old now, Mila, Remy, Melly and a few others. What a shock that was! It was a fun phone call as they told me about the Savings Program. The Quezon City government had taken over the program with all of them as part of the staff still running the savings. They had over 20,000 families with more than 60 million pesos in the program.

The best part was that several families who had started in savings while I was there asked me if I remembered them, if I remembered telling them that if they saved eventually their young children would be able to go to college. They were so excited as all of their children had not only gone to college but had graduated and got decent jobs. The poverty cycle was truly broken. What an affirmation of my work there and the importance of savings. What a way to start the new Millennium!

In Cottage Industry we had started a relationship with a woman from Australia, Karen Harley, who really liked our emerging line of housewares: bedspreads, duvet covers, and pillow cases. The line had been developing through our bi-annual sales in Singapore but Karen brought it to a new level. We worked out a dozen color combinations and then she placed her order for 40 sets of bedspreads and duvet covers complete with contrasting pillow cases. This brought Cottage Industry to a new level. Suddenly we needed a lot more silk weavers, not an easy task as all the silk was hand woven and each weaver had their own style.

In my wisdom I decided that we should design our own line of printed silk: color coordinated stripes! What a challenge that turned out to be as the warp of the silk determined the weft color. What should have been navy blue turned light blue, what should have been red, turned pink and what should have been light green turned dark green and on and on. Still more difficult was to have several weavers producing the same color stripes. Our line changed from under 50 to over 100 colors. It was a nightmare. On top of that, to ensure that we had enough silk on hand to meet orders, we had to buy silk in bulk, a huge challenge as money for capital was always scarce.

---

We had started to work in Prey Veng province, a province that was considered one of the poorest mainly due to insecurity, flood and drought. People lived in deep poverty. In one of these stricken villages lived a man named Tout. Tout had a unique skill for he could make silver and gold products but he didn't have a market for his goods. Phat, our manager in Prey Veng, asked if Tout could sell his work through Tabitha. I talked with Tout for some time. It was clear that the village was extremely poor but I knew we would not be able to sell very many of his products as they were of Cambodian myths, not appealing to Western shoppers. I was very much into the mindset that once we started working with Tout, it had to be for the long term. I asked him if he would be willing to make Christmas ornaments and perhaps some jewelry. Tout, didn't know Christmas. I asked are you willing to try. His answer was a firm yes.

We continued to talk and I asked him, if we did this, how would this help his village? Tout came to life as he answered me, I will promise you that all the villagers will have better homes, they will have water; they will have cows for ploughing and money for seeds. I promise I will change the whole village to prosperity.

So, we began to work together. The first task was to choose a few designs for Christmas ornaments. We started with the standard ornaments like balls, stars and snowflakes. The process was difficult as Tout had to make a mold out of wax and he carved each mold by hand which was a very intricate and time-consuming process. Then we had to decide the materials to be used. Initially we chose pure gold and silver, well, 90% pure as we had to add an alloy to give strength to the ornament. Tout was able to buy bronze and iron very cheaply. When we first started silver and gold was inexpensive and available, but over time, the cost of both these alloys increased and then our ornaments changed to silver and gold dipped ornaments. The drawback of using pure silver and gold was that both metals tarnished so it meant customers had to polish them, a task very few were happy with. Now our ornaments no longer need to be polished.

Tout kept his word. His home village had been transformed. Ninety percent of the villagers have strong, sturdy homes. They all have wells for water, cows and chickens, crops that can be grown year-round. Tout was able to buy a small plot in Phnom Penh and had built a modern home. He bought a car and he still produces ornaments for Tabitha.

———

The constant worry about funds was wearing me down. So many needs, so many dreams. It wore me down to a point where I became weary. I would get weary thinking about what else we could we do. I finally remembered that the Bible says "Come unto me all who are weary and I will give you rest." (Mathew 28:11 NIV) When I rested, I felt better again and, besides, it kept me thinking and trying all the time.

Most often the answer to the weariness was to expand our programs and so we did. We opened up in Kompong Som. Vutha was appointed the manager there. Within a very short time, Vutha had selected several communities in the port area of Sihanoukville. Once again, the poverty was striking, misery abounded. Many of the groups she developed were young ladies sold into the sex trade, young prostitutes whose dreams of returning to a normal life were nil, for once in the sex trade a girl was no longer considered to be of value. She was considered to be spoiled goods, a cultural norm in Asia, one that Cambodia fully embraced. These girls had been sold for a price. Their families were in some desperate need and selling the girl enabled the family to survive the current crisis. The girl was now the property of the person who had bought her. She needed to work long enough for the owner to recoup their investment in the girl. This was always prolonged as the girl's earnings were taxed by rent, food and medical costs imposed by the owner.

The savings cycle started to change this for the girls. Vutha had gotten permission from several of the owners of the girls to do savings. The owners believed that this would be welcomed by the girls and cheer them up. She asked that I come and visit the groups. I came and brought Miriam with me. We spent the day talking with many of these girls. I would share Miriam's story, the story of her birth mum, my love for this little girl. The girls opened up and shared their stories and then I asked what they dreamed of for the future. They spoke of returning to their villages with enough money to start a business, of buying land so that a man would marry them because they owned land. All of them spoke longingly of one day having their own child. It was a very poignant afternoon.

Miriam's circumstance in life touched a great many lives. We had a film crew come from Star TV to talk about HIV positive kids. They filmed a little five-year-old who was so very sick and so very thin, struggling to feed himself. Then we went to a village where, in three months, there would be 94 orphans for all the parents were in the final stages of AIDS. Miriam's story resulted in other parents willing to adopt an HIV positive child; one of whom has turned into a beautiful young lady just like Miriam. The Missionaries of Charity were miracle workers, taking in these children on the brink of death and turn them into healthy young people. I was so very privileged to be a part of all of this.

The housebuilding program continued to grow. Teams were now coming from Singapore, Australia, England and the United States. Then we had the team that angered me beyond words. It was a team of 20 students and five teachers. They came for orientation on the first day which was a mandatory exercise and visited The Genocide

Museum and the Killing Fields. Problems started to surface that day when the teachers rebelled at the prospect of having to get up early.

The team was late. We arrived at the housebuilding site at 9 o'clock and by at 10:00 the teachers had had enough and they wanted to quit because it was hot. I got angry and said go but the students were crying. So, I compromised. I told the students to continue to build and I told the teachers to go sit on the bus and wait. Later that afternoon, there was a lot of shouting and cheering from the back of the village. The teachers ran to see what the fuss was. The villagers had caught a 15 foot python. I was shamed by the reaction of the teachers. Kill it, they screamed. I screamed as well, get back on the bus! I was so angry, that they did as they were told. The house was finished but the teachers wouldn't allow the presentation of the house to the families. I thanked the students and they left.

The next morning, they wanted a meeting with Soklieng. They wanted to have a discount on the bus fares as the bus was only being used for a half day to bring them to the airport. Poor Soklieng argued long and hard but finally gave in and said ok, we would pay the rest. The teachers felt good and then handed Soklieng the extra half day payment and said this was their donation to Tabitha. I finally came to her rescue. The teachers greeted me with their gift, which I rejected. They then asked if they could come again in six months' time. My answer was firm, no; I don't think this is a program for your school. Every year they ask, and every year I say no to the one and only team that I continue to refuse.

The following month we had another team come to build houses. The US Ambassador wanted to come and see as the team was a group of Americans from Singapore. We had a handing over ceremony where the Ambassador cut ribbons on the six houses and then presented the houses to each family. One of the recipients, a grandfather with 11 children, told us: "We thought we had been forgotten. For 30 years nobody cared about us. We live far away from the city. We gave up hope of anyone caring. Then you came and you found us. You helped us to begin to hope. You have given us new life. May the gods bless you." The old man insisted on giving me his blessing and so I was on my knees in front of him as he laid his hand on my head. It was a wonderful moment because he had seen it all, the war, the genocide, the insecurity as he spoke for all the families. As the Ambassador said, "They have true joy in their eyes. These people are no different than all of us. They want the same things that we do, safety, honest work and healthy children. It is good to be here with them."

We had outgrown our office space yet again. It was time to find another building to call home. We found our new place very quickly but there were problems. We had only five days in which to pack, move and set up again. The old landlord was being difficult; the new one was quite amenable; the staff were in a dither; the workmen hustled to finish the alterations to the new building; and our workers were delivering their goods.

We got it all done in record time. Now there was plenty of showroom space and room to grow. The customers liked it as well. For two days in a row we had customers buy $600 worth of goods. The silk bedding was a big hit, but we also sold a wide variety of products because people could now see it on display.

The staff coped well with all of this. They kept their cool most of the time, and when they lost it, they shrugged it off rather than getting angry. We were tempted to ignore the little repairs as we were so stressed but I decided not to let that happen. It meant that all the toilets would flush as they were supposed to, all the light bulbs actually worked, all the flowers and plants were in place and the garbage was put out before we moved in.

My next site visit to Siem Reap was a special trip as our newest staff member, Mari, had asked me to come and see her work. Mari was an orphan, her parents killed when she was six years old. Mari lived with her aunt and uncle and her grandmother who were all very poor. Every time Mari wanted to buy something she would have to ask for money from her uncle but there was so little money, so she was often frustrated and unhappy. She was 21 years old and her future looked bleak.

Two years ago, she heard about Tabitha. She came to our office and talked with Ani about becoming a sewer. Ani saw something in Mari that she liked. We needed someone to clean and help supervise Cottage Industry. Ani asked Mari if she would be willing to do so. Mari agreed. Like so many orphans, Mari had very low self-esteem. Over the next few months, that self-esteem began to change.

Six months ago, I had asked Ani to give Mari a community to work in. Her job would be to encourage the very poorest to save money. This money was to be used to do things like pay school fees or fix their houses, in short, to give the poorest the belief in themselves to change their lives. It sounded impossible and yet Mari knew what we were talking about. She had known that feeling of despair and hopelessness, of wanting to buy and do things but not being able to see how she could do it. Over the two years, Mari had a regular salary, not a big one but a good one. She had been able to buy clothes and personal things she needed. She had saved for a bicycle, she had saved for a television, and she helped her grandmother each week. Now she was saving to buy land. She had dreams and she could see, how, in time, those dreams would come true.

It was not an easy job, so for several weeks, Mari talked and talked with people. And then it happened. Her first group of twelve people, then a second, and a third and a fourth. She desperately wanted me to see what she had done. She was also very nervous, would I like what I saw, did she do well?

Mari, Ani and I walked through the fields. I was struck once again about the stunning beauty of the countryside, the blues, greens and browns sparkled and flowed. In the midst of this beauty lay poverty, so deep and so entrenched. It tore at my soul.

The first family we met was Lon Wing, a widow. Her husband had been killed nine months ago when her baby was 10 days old. She had two more children, a six-year-old and a twelve-year-old who looked about eight. I looked at her house. It was terrible, there were scraps of thatch left on the roof and on the walls, and the floor had a few pieces of bamboo. There were two new sleeping mats and a spoon. There was nothing else. What my eyes saw, my mind could not grasp. In my horror, I asked what they did when it rained. The twelve-year-old spoke sharply and clearly, "We sleep in the rain."

I asked Lon Wing how she could save. She answered in a low voice, "When my husband died, I lost all hope. I have three children that

I must support. I cannot even give them a safe place to sleep. Then Mari came and she talked about how I could begin to change these things. I listened and I saved. Three weeks ago I got my savings and look; I could buy the sleeping mats. My next step is to buy thatch to repair the roof. It is good, isn't it? Yes, Lon Wing it is very good. As we walked away, Ani asked, "Can we build a house for her with a team?" I think so.

By now, we had gathered a crowd around us. We continued through the fields to the next house. This was the home of Bun Kun. She and her husband had eight children ranging in age from seven months to twenty years of age. Their home was four by six meters made of thatch. Although life was hard, they were full of fun. Bun Kun and her three oldest daughters wove baskets for extra income to their farm. Their story of savings was a delight.

Bun Kun had saved first and after ten weeks she had enough to pay school fees for her younger children. The three oldest girls saw this and decided that they too wanted to save. The problem was, all their basket income went to their parents. A family discussion was held. The girls had their own dreams and they wanted their own money. Their mother would have to give them some of the income from the baskets. The parents agreed and each girl started her own savings. What were their dreams, I asked? The two girls were very clear with their answers: first, we will buy and raise a pig and then when we sell the pig, we will then buy our own bicycle. The youngest one wanted the bicycle so she could go to school; the older one wanted the bicycle to be able to cut her own grass for basket weaving. The twenty-year-old said very little; her dream she said shyly, was to save so that she could get married. All of us were excited. It was so very good to be with them for they cared and shared with each other

As we were talking, five women came and surrounded us, listening to our chatter. All five women were in savings. They too shared their stories. One had eight children. I asked what she wanted. She was mischievous, oh, she said, with eight children I am always tired and we never have clothes. With my savings, I am buying clothes for all of us. I know I will be beautiful and my husband will see me and want another child. For him I will buy a pair of pants that he cannot open but he will be handsome. All of us were giggling. Then the four women said, "see Im Ni, she's been married for ten years now and she has no children. Now she is pregnant." Im Ni smiled bravely, with my savings I will have everything I need for the baby when it comes.

The sun was beginning to set and it was time to go. I looked at Mari and Ani; both of them were glowing from the friendships and dreams they had helped to make. I was also beaming, what a good day it had been. What a privilege to spend just a few hours with these people. How blessed I am to be here, to have such amazing staff, to live within God's grace."

We received a cheque from a donor for $11,000, a princely sum meant to buy silk stock. The timing was perfect since we had received several big orders for bedding and pillow shams: 115 bedspreads, 460 pillow shams and 1200 silk stars. This meant work for everyone plus a few new workers and an additional 100 silk weavers. I was afraid that we would have to look for a bigger place yet again and none of us were ready for that. A month later, we were thrilled to learn that our bedding was featured in a three-page spread in an Australian home décor magazine.

We opened our fifth province in Takeo, close to where the silk weavers all live. Phum and Chrieng were made staff under the supervision of Pon and Srie. We worked closely with the weavers now numbering 650. The colors of silk were amazing and deciding which silks we needed was difficult. We met a 70-year-old bent over grandmother, who showed off the bright red silk that she had woven. I could not say no to this wizened old woman for she touched my soul.

We had made a special bedspread for an order. As we spread the finished cover over our showroom bed, one of the King's daughters walked in, took one look at it and said: this cover must be for my father, the King. All of us stood with open mouths, for the KING! Whoa, that was a thrill. The princess came often after that to purchase many of our housewares to grace the royal palace.

An Asian based company decided that their CEOs from various Asian countries should come housebuilding. As usual they needed to do orientation day, an orientation that I conducted. In that process I told the group, the vast majority who were in their late 50s, that Cambodians didn't think they could do anything physical, much less complete houses and they had to prove Cambodians wrong. A group of young Asian women were responsible for the logistics. They booked the team into in a five-star hotel, but that didn't bother me. The young ladies had everything sorted in advance of the team's arrival. However, they were going to work with the poorest in a crowded area. The first day of house building didn't get off to a good start. The girls had ordered several circus tents to shade the heads of CEO's that were to build. I said rather vehemently that this would not be suitable. Back went the tents!

Building was going well for the executives were out to prove Cambodians wrong. At lunchtime a huge truck from the hotel arrived, filled with lunch boxes. I stared at the young girls. They said it was lunch but not to worry for they had brought enough for all the staff and for me. I opened the box. Soklieng and Heng were doubled over laughing as our first course was caviar followed by lobster and salad and finished with fruits and pastries. I was mortified at this luxury, so embarrassed I could hardly speak. Heng being Heng, made joke after joke: fish eggs instead of real fish, he chortled. I made it clear to the young ladies that the next day was sandwiches and little else.

The second day went much better, the houses were completed and sandwiches delivered for lunch. That evening we had a wrap up dinner at the hotel. I was rather tired and just wanted to stay home and relax. I arrived at the hotel and was met by some of the housebuilders. They were of many Asian nationalities. So many of them were in tears. I was so uncomfortable, what's the matter I asked? One after another said, I grew up in this kind of poverty and I have forgotten how awful it all is. Thank you for reminding me. Thank you for being our leader. It was a very emotional evening with tears flowing freely and emotions running high. We finally said farewell with promises of returning the following year to build again.

A year passed and I heard nothing from the company. I was in Singapore on a speaking tour. At one event, I ran into one of the young ladies. We talked and I asked her what happened to the team? She looked at me with wide eyes, you haven't heard! No, I said, what happened? On their return to work, the vast majority of CEO's had resigned. They all wanted to return to their countries of birth and give back by working with the poor. The impact of housebuilding on these gentlemen made all our efforts worthwhile. I will never forget them.

I made Heng the House Building manager as this program was growing so very fast. He and the staff handled their first team by themselves in Siem Reap. Poor Heng was overwhelmed with the responsibility involved. He phoned me and said, "I never want to be boss again. We only handle one team and we are already exhausted from making sure that everything is ready and they haven't even arrived yet. Can't you come?" I laughed and said: you all will do fine. I will do the orientation and make sure they are ready to behave properly.

When we said farewell to the team; they were overwhelmed and very emotional. Heng and staff had done an excellent job. The team had a tremendous experience. Bringing grace to people who have never experienced grace in their lives is always a heart wrenching experience. They also left with diarrhoea, caught the day after they finished the houses. So, memories were mixed.

In the midst of all the work, I was still helping the Missionaries of Charity to place orphaned children into adoptive homes. Adoptions were again being questioned by the government for good reason. The custom in Cambodia was that orphaned children are cared for by extended families. Suddenly there were a great number of orphanages where children were "found by village chiefs under trees". Adoption had become big business and made some people wealthy. I was thankful the government was beginning to act but sad that legitimate orphans would no longer have the option of being adopted. Having said that, we were able to place another twenty children in homes before the adoptions were closed.

~

This was a year of exceptional flooding in Cambodia. It happened every ten years or so. The country was inundated with two to three meters of water. I travelled to our Prey Veng project. Highway Number 1 was a mess. The corps of army engineers had blown up several sections of the highway in an effort to divert the water from Phnom Penh. It meant that I had to lower myself into the tiniest of boats to circumvent the blown highway several times; then travel by motorbike to the next blown area. We arrived safely and Hang and the staff took us by small boat to several of our villages. That trip was horrific as several times we had to push bloated drowned victims out of our way. The families we saw were huddled on the only dry land; shoulders of main roads, living in horrendous conditions. It was so terribly sad.

When we thought that things couldn't get worse, it did. The Prime Minister was quoted saying that he was dizzy after one month of non-stop relief work. I could sympathize with his feelings. The heavy rain continued and plunged the entire country under water to a depth of several meters. All the major highways were now impassable except for one and it was in danger of breaking apart. Fears were real for more flooding in the coming weeks.

For Tabitha during this time, the task ahead seemed daunting. Our families in Siem Reap were heavily battered and our staff were housebound for a week as floods surrounded the entire area. Our Cottage Industry workers were living in chest deep water and found it difficult to work. Our silk weavers were cut off from Phnom Penh. Our families in Prey Veng continued to sit on road shoulders as the waters stayed unusually high. It seemed never ending.

Then, when I think, just what can we do, I went with staff to Srei NaLaom. The road was potholed and water logged. We got out of the van and the staff half carried me to meet with ten families because they thought I would fall in the muck that surrounded us.

We talked in a circle in front of four houses that didn't deserve the name "house". Each was several meters in size, with missing walls, no floors, and broken roofs. One of the women broke into tears. I am upset and ask the staff "what have we done"? In broken sobs, she said that for so many years, I have never had a real house, my first husband died leaving me with two children and my second husband is gone leaving me with two more children. When Tabitha came and talked about saving for a new house, I believed and I saved. My neighbors came and said, you are too poor to lose your money, how can you trust them. But I so want a home for my children and so I believed. Today you come to see me. No one ever came to see me before, no one ever cared. I cry because you gave me new life. I never thought I would have a new life but that is what you give me." I am silent before her and before the others for I am overwhelmed with a deep sense of humility. I look around me, surrounded by unbelievable and grinding poverty, by women and children caked in poverty and surrounded by muck. It will be many months before things change in a material sense for it will take an effort of the heart and mind but these women will do it. What have we done? We have brought hope but, oh my, it is so hard to see them suffer so.

Afterwards we met with the staff from Prey Veng. Discussions revolved on how best to help families. House Building was a major concern and we talked about how many houses we could build with our limited funds. We are careful not to make promises unless we are sure we can do it. Creativity soars for getting teams to the area will be a task in itself. Costs of building materials are soaring so how can we cut those costs. In the end, we are renewed for we have options and we are excited to explore each one. It was good to end the year on such a positive note despite all the sorrows.

# 2001

The New Year started with my all-time favorite housebuilding team arriving, our adopted Cambodia House children accompanied by parents, friends and siblings. This team would come every couple of years to house build, to renew relationships and to create new ones. The adopted children knew each other. It was fascinating, as children were being raised in various countries around the world. It was a wonderful way to watch them all grow. Miriam, of course, was accepted and adopted into the group as she became the little sister to all of them.

We built in a community I had visited with Srie and Tharry late last year. There we met a number of families they were working with. Ly Soy was the spokesperson for the community. Ly Soy and his wife had seven children, the home they lived in was two meters square, had a roof and a floor but no walls. Ly said that the poorest folks, like him, were very afraid of loans for, several years ago, another group like Tabitha had come and given loans to some of the families. They had charged interest plus had required collateral of land and houses on the land. The families had been unable to meet their repayments and had lost their land and homes. This, they could not do.

We said, but what about savings. Ly and his group listened but they couldn't believe that their money would be safe so Srie brought them to our office in Phnom Penh. I met Ly and his 23-year-old son. I showed them my toilet. Beside the toilet were two filing cabinets. Inside the cabinets were envelopes filled with people's savings. They could not believe what they saw! This is good, said Ly; this is what we must do.

And so, they started to save. Each week Srei and Tharry collected 500 or 1000 riels (about 10 cents) from each of 80 families. Ly's son talked to everyone he knew and encouraged them to join. Soon we had 120 families. At the end of 10 weeks, Ly and his group got their savings plus we paid them 10% interest on their savings as an encouragement. Ly bought a water jar which was big enough to hold 30 gallons of water. For the first time, his wife and daughters did not spend hours each day walking several kilometers to collect water.

Several of the savings families were tormented by their neighbors for daring to better their lives, a common occurrence in all the areas where Tabitha worked. At first the taunts were about losing their money but when the savings was returned in ten weeks those taunts stopped. Then Pech Nea, a widow with six children, said she was saving to build a house. This caused much grief in the village and late one-night angry neighbors came with torches and told her "Don't believe you can do this!". Why would they speak so because for the past thirty years all had lived desperately hard lives with little hope? Now Pech Nea, Ly Soy and the other families were making a mockery of the fear and hopelessness they all lived with.

Then came the floods and life became very, very hard but the families had continued to save. Our Cambodian House children were to come in January to build three houses for Ly Soy, Pech Nea and Nong Ri. The team arrived. They had brought $800 per house for the cost of materials and the cost of the local contractor who built the frame of the house and they brought their strength to build. And build they did. Children as young as eight and Grandma Shirley who was 76, all chipped in with sawing and hammering, thatching and nailing. At the end of the week these families had new homes, four meters by five meters, which was three times the size of their old houses. The houses came complete with walls and floors which was unheard of in this village. The laughter and cheers of the team were new sounds in the community.

Nong Ri's mother was paralyzed, a left over from the Pol Pot years. She had lived too hard and seen too much but at the end of the housebuilding, she finally spoke, "I have prayed to the God for help but I thought He never heard me but I was wrong for He sent me you, His angels."

⁓

I had applied for Canadian citizenship for Miriam the year before. The process was rather daunting to say the least. I did all the things required, got all the papers, made endless entreaties. It had been a difficult couple of years for me because my little girl lost out on knowing her extended family and I lost out on the support I needed while she was so young and fragile. This loss for her first two years caused me much pain and sorrow. And then the moment arrived when she received her Canadian citizenship papers and her passport. God is good!!

To celebrate this gift, Miriam and I travelled back to Canada to meet the family. It was a wonderful visit. Miriam was a wonderful traveler.

The long flights brought tears just once and the pleading of no more planes, no more planes. Promises of meeting wonderful people at both ends kept her content for most of the time.

Wide open spaces, grass, trees, birds, dogs and squirrels, buses and loud noises kept Miriam on edge for the first few weeks for she was quite frightened by it all. By the end of our holiday, she walked the dogs and chased the birds but never quite liked too many trees all in one place.

The countless stores brought her to a standstill. Our first shopping trip left her awe struck and immobile as she tried to come to grips with the wide array of goods for sale and people of all shapes and sizes. McDonalds was quickly discovered and known.

Miriam now had an extended family. She no longer looked with awe at others as they talked about their grandparents and aunts and uncles. She had her own. Grandma was a surprise for she was no longer able to recognize us and she struggled to communicate. For Miriam the first meeting was fraught with confusion because her grandma couldn't pick her up and hold her like her friend's grandmothers could but grandma sure could give wonderful kisses and gentle touches. Grandma was so happy to have us for company so by the next visit, Miriam kissed and hugged back freely. All the other grandmas we met in our travels were soon told that they were not Miriam's grandma for she had her own.

The highlight of the trip was "Tami's marry", as she refers to her cousin's wedding. We shared in the preparations, the actual event and the aftermath, bringing what it means to be family into a wonderful and memorable experience.

It was wonderful to meet with our adopted family and adopted Cambodian cousins. Boreth, a nine-year-old, confronted me in the midst of the reunion. Why did you adopt Miriam and not us? Because, I answered, I found moms and dads for all of you but I could not find one for Miriam for she was quite ill when she was born. He seemed satisfied by that and then asked, who will take care of her if something happens to you? Who do you think should care for her, I replied. We will take care of her, he said, I promise you, we will take care of her. What a precious promise that was. A trip to remember! How good it all was.

———

Deth Dara died suddenly on April 4th. He was just 37 years old. Dara was a man after my own heart. I loved him so. Dara joined Tabitha in 1996. It soon became clear that Dara was an ordinary man with an extra-ordinary compassion for the poorest people of this land. He was a man of curiosity and intellect. Our discussions focused on how things happen in life, why the genocide here, why the suffering, why the pain. He was intensely interested in how politics worked and how the future of this country was being shaped.

His life story, like so many he touched, was one of pain and anguish. He spoke of how he watched his two brothers, a sister and his mother starve to death before his eyes. He felt so helpless. Only a handful of rice a day was all we wanted, he said. But I could not get that handful of rice and so they died.

He took this burden and turned it to hope for so many of the families he worked with. Each visit I made meant another trip with Dara on his motorbike to another destitute and suffering family. We must do more, he would say.

We'd talk about the future, about his dreams and Ani's dreams and Apo's and Sarouen, of all our staff. Save your money, I said, buy land, I said. This country was still in turmoil and land was cheap. And so, my visits then included looking at land, land that Dara and Ani bought and sold until they bought the land where they would build their home. Dara made sure the families he worked with saved their money to buy land and hundreds of families did.

Their son was born two weeks before I got my daughter Miriam in January of 1999. We rejoiced together. You must name my son, Dara insisted. I could not do so but I did give a list of ten names from which they could choose and so Zachary and Miriam became part of my monthly trips.

We must build a home for our son, they told me. Dara pulled out the blueprints and asked me what I thought. It was a big house, 12 bedrooms in all! Too big I said. No, said Dara. The upstairs is for you for one day when you are too old, you will need a home. This will be your home. They paid for the materials from land that they sold and the house took shape. Now each trip included watching the progress of their dream house being built.

Dara contracted malaria last summer and he was ill for the month of September. He spent that month in Phnom Penh to be close to the medicine he needed. I think he knew that he was very ill but he did not say anything. Each time I saw him after that, I would ask him how he was for he failed to regain his weight. He was often tired but his spirit remained strong. The last time I saw him was a week before his death. He was ill and I brushed his forehead as I asked him how he was. I just need some sleep he said and so I let him sleep.

On the weekend, Dara was well again, he laughed and teased as was his way. He talked of his families and he talked of his son. We all rejoiced to see him so happy. On Wednesday morning his fever was back and Wednesday evening he went to his rest.

Ani was devastated. Her grief was painful to see. It was so quick she said. We brought Dara to the place for his cremation, as was the custom here. His final trip was through the community he loved so much, down the dusty paths through the unrelenting heat. His mourners were the poor whom he loved. They lined the pathways where he worked, paying homage to the man who cared so much for them. We stopped under the mango tree where we stopped on each trip and Apo handed me a Coke because that's what Dara always did. As we gathered there for the last time, I thought, how like him this is, the very poorest kneeling around us, the lowing cattle, the dust and the heat, the startling beauty of the countryside surrounding us, the Coke and the sharing of our thoughts and tears. Goodbye my friend, we miss you so.

Ani phoned a few days later, her voice still marked with unshed tears but her words brought hope. Apo's baby was born she said, it's a little girl. Apo, who was so strong for Ani in her grief, who with Sarouen and Mari made all the arrangements for the funeral, who stayed by Ani's side both day and night, whose first child died in stillbirth a year ago, came on the phone and spoke with joy. You must name this child, she said. I never named a child, but I always supplied a list of ten names and they would choose from that list. She named her daughter Nancy.

We had our first and last Cottage Industry event in Bangkok Thailand. I couldn't make the first day as we had several housebuilding teams in town so Soklieng and Chanthou went ahead of me. They were met at the airport by the organizers of the event who showed them the Tabitha space. Then they were brought to the hotel and shown to their room. I arrived early the next morning and went straight to the hotel. As I got of the elevator, I was surprised to see Soklieng and Chanthou standing there looking downcast and worried. I asked them what was going on. Soklieng spoke and said, we get into the elevator and push the button, and then wait until the door opens and we are in the same spot all the time. I didn't dare laugh but asked the girls to show me what they did. We got on the elevators and they pushed the button for the floor they were on. Of course, they went nowhere. I showed them how the elevator worked which relieved both girls for they had stayed in their room without food since late the previous day. It made me realize that so much I took for granted in today's world that neither of them had experience with.

It reminded me of several months before when I had taken Miriam and her nanny, Tuit to Singapore with me to celebrate Miriam's Cambodian passport. We stayed in a hotel with an escalator. Tuit was terrified of it but we needed to use it to get to the main lobby. An hour of cajoling and threatening finally got her on it. Later that day we went to a supermarket. Tuit had never seen a supermarket before. As I was going through the aisles, I could hear Tuit calling me. I went over to the aisle she was in. She was so excited, mum, we have to buy lots of these cans of food, they look delicious. I followed her pointed finger and started to laugh. We were standing in the pet food aisle. The cans of food that looked so delicious were cans of dog food. I was not sure how to explain this but I did. Tuit's eyes grew wide with wonder. Oh mum, she said, dogs eat better than people. This became a running mantra for the two days we stayed in Singapore; it became the story of the week on our return to Cambodia. It left me wondering where we, the wealthy, had gotten it all so wrong.

—

We held our annual staff meeting. This year the floods had arrived early for a second year in a row. I truly thought this meeting would be all about how difficult the community development work was. But it was a very different meeting. The meeting started with my asking the managers how the floods had affected their areas of work. Phat talked of how his areas in Prey Veng were flooded again and that the waters were continuing to rise. Vutha spoke of how the floods and bad weather were preventing large numbers of her families from being able to fish or farm in Kompong Som. Siem Reap staff spoke of how the flooding had come with very high winds and a very rapid onrush of water. Sarouen and Mari spoke of families who had lost their homes and possessions as the waters had come too fast to save much. Pon from Takeo province spoke of different problems, she spoke of the drought that prevented so many from planting rice.

As we were talking, the usual sense of utter despair was missing. What was the difference? Phat, one of our quiet staff for he thinks much before he speaks, spoke. The difference this year is the savings, he said. Last year, when the floods came, many people still had loans from us and with the floods, they couldn't pay us back and so when we came, the people were ashamed and afraid and they would hide. Many voices chorused in support of his words. Obviously, he was saying what they all wanted to say.

154

Phat continued; we helped them pay back their loans but then we told them they must save instead. At first, I felt like this was not good because these people are so poor. They only save a few hundred reils every week, (about 10 cents), what could that do? The chorus began again as one after the other echoed his words, each in their own unique way.

The strange thing was, Phat continued, suddenly we could help many, many more people. The very poorest wanted to join in and save, just pennies, but it was so important. Then, he said, when they got their savings in ten weeks and we payed interest, everything changed. They bought things that were so important to them. One family with nine children was able to buy clothes for each child! It was like a miracle for they bought second hand clothes for just pennies! The clamor in the room rose as each staff member wanted to share their own version of similar miracles.

Phat was not finished, his confidence soaring as he was encouraged by the others. When I go to the people now, they wait for me at the road and they call me their friend. No one is ashamed, they are so proud. Now laughter filled the room as one and all shared their joy. You know, Phat continued, even the local chiefs now talk to the people, before they wouldn't even look at them.

Now, the troubles are back! This is the second year when the people can't plant their rice. It's the second year when their houses are soaked and to eat every day is a problem, Phat continued, but the difference is so striking! Do you know that everyone is still saving, just a little bit but on the day when they know we are coming, they catch a fish or two or a snake and sell it just so they will have savings? Now the rest joined in as the unique efforts of each family to continue to save each week is worth writing a book of hope. Phat was not finished; you know, we have new families who join each week, never before have I seen this for their lives are very, very hard. One family lost their child to drowning but they all want to save because it gives them hope. Do you think we will be able to help everyone who wants help? They all look at me with hope and expectation. I think so, I said, for how can we not help? The meeting ended with a goal of 6700 families for the next year, about 53,000 people that the staff want to touch. It took a few years for the staff to fully understand how important savings was, how important giving dignity and respect to people was but we finally go there.

———

Our regular Christmas season was upon us. We had added a new dimension to this. Many volunteers and friends kept bringing us clothing items. The managers wanted to distribute these to their families. This was okay but I felt we needed to add some food items so each family would get 20 kilos of rice, a carton of sardines, cooking oil and fish sauce. We had been doing this for several years but it was never enough nor did people have a choice in the clothing they were given. We tried to match clothing for children to the number of children a family had but we didn't distinguish between sexes.

The first couple of years, it wasn't too bad but it became clear that we never had enough for there were always families left out which left feelings of resentment. This particular year, the work of putting it all together for each project was enormous. We were in Siem Reap distributing the packages to families, where one little boy of about 12 years of age stood in wonder holding a bottle of fish sauce in his hand. I have never tasted fish sauce, he said, how rich I am today.

Beside him stood his friend with tears slowly rolling down his cheeks because there was no fish sauce for him. I was so sad and said to the staff, we cannot do this anymore, for every person we bring joy to, we leave many in sadness and that is not right. As I was speaking a mother of six walked up to us and handed back her bundle of clothes. I would like these all in blue because I don't like these colors. She just added insult to our thoughts and feelings.

We carried on to deliver parcels to our next village. The roads were just mere tracks. We came to a handmade bridge. I said, we cannot cross this but all the staff argued and said it was safe to cross. I knew it was not! The pick-up we had hired was very heavy, loaded with goods. I said, fine but I am walking across, see you on the other side. The truck almost made it, the front wheels were on safe ground when the bridge gave way and the back of the pickup hung into the abyss below. Several of the staff had been sitting in the back and slid not so gracefully over the packages and caught the tail of the truck. There they dangled, holding on for dear life. I was a bit put out to say the least. We were able to rescue everyone and people from the neighboring village came and helped us pull the truck from danger.

With the deliveries of all these goods came the opportunity to talk with villagers from all our projects. I met Samath an eleven-year-old orphan, who lives by grace with 15 young ladies were of the night. Two years ago, Samath started to save with us. He collected soft drink cans to sell and he saved enough money to buy a bicycle, then to enroll in school, then to buy his school uniform. He stood proudly as I took his picture standing beside young Rosa, a 16-year-old service worker. She was busy sewing special clothing for her friends. Rosa had also saved for two years as she put herself through sewing school and bought herself an electric sewing machine. The brothel owner had been paid off and she no longer serviced men. But she had no home to go back to, so she stayed and sewed beautiful clothes.

We stopped by Meng Sarouen's house who was grandma to all of us. Meng was 72 years old and cared for nine grandchildren, orphaned and abandoned by her grown children. Two months ago, Grandma's house was just one meter by two meters of rotting grass but now she lived in her sturdy home, given through the grace of our volunteer housebuilders. Grandma was so very thankful, "you are angels", she said, "I prayed to the God that I would be able to die in a real house and He answered my prayers."

We stood by Lay Pouve's house. He and his wife had nine children. Two years ago, they had no home, no clothes and no one was in school. Now, they have a home they built themselves, the kids are in school and they are proud of what they have done. This brought me joy but it wasn't all they had accomplished that was so special. Lay Pouve shyly took me to his neighbor's house. Srei Neang was a widow with five little ones and she too had a new house; three of her children were in school and she beamed when we came. "Lay Pouve helped me to build my house; he helped me to believe my children could go to school. He is a good man". She then took my hand to show me the family that she was helping to save and believe in a better life for themselves.

It was what Tabitha was all about, sharing the good news about living a better life through savings and dreams coming true. It was about walking and sharing with your neighbor who in turn walks and shares with another. It was a phenomenon that had been repeated endlessly throughout the years. It was about Christmas, the ability to give of yourself in a way that allows others to receive and choose to do and then share with another. What a good way to end this year.

# 2002

I had a miracle happen over the Christmas holidays. Tabitha was struggling with funds yet again, yet despite that, I still held our annual Christmas celebrations and lived on faith that all would be well but I was oh, so tired in many ways. On Christmas morning as I walked into church, I was met by Sister Regina. We hugged and I wished her a Merry Christmas. Her face was radiant as she looked at me and asked: have you heard? I was truly mystified by that question. She then told me that Maryknoll has decided to give Tabitha a sizeable grant. Tears sprung to my eyes; my head could not comprehend but my soul soared. That Christmas morning, the celebration of the birth of my Saviour was a celebration of life itself. What a miracle it was!

The year started out with a grand opportunity for us, a chance to have a shop at the airports in Siem Reap and Phnom Penh. The airport authorities had seemed very positive so we had ordered special shelving and signs ready to set up if and when the authorities said yes. As each month passed and the answer was not forthcoming, I became discouraged. Our shop was in a mess from the Christmas rush so I decided we needed to clean it up. As we started to reset up our store, I said to Soklieng, "We'll never get the airport, go get our shelves we ordered for the airport for the office." Soklieng was properly horrified, "don't give up," she said. But I did give up and the new shelving looked so nice, we made big investment and bought enough shelves to give the entire shop a professional look.

Several days later, the airport authorities phoned to tell us we could have a space in Siem Reap domestic airport and we had two weeks in which to make it ready. Soklieng just grinned and grinned. We had a housebuilding team in Siem Reap so we had to wait until they were finished before we could set up.

Finally, the big day arrived and it was time to set up the showroom space. The space was against the wall, about the size of a small bathroom. As we were setting up, passengers started opening boxes and pulling things from our hands. It was a good omen. There were three one-hour time slots each day when passengers were in the airport. Our space was so small that only four people at a time could shop comfortably but that did not deter the customers and these three hours were hours of mayhem and excitement. We hired 12 more workers which was a prayer answered. The authorities told us that if we did well, they would give us space in the Phnom Penh airport which would be an added bonus.

## The Water Program

We officially started our water program. Water like so many things in life is something that I take for granted for the simple reason that I have access to it wherever and whenever I want it. I never realized how many people in life do not have access to water. Water is essential to life. Being unable to wash on a regular basis, a person develops body rashes, poor eyesight, hair that is lifeless. Without water, bodies fail. Without clean potable water, water-borne diseases result in the needless deaths of many children.

In Cambodia at that time, over 80% of rural dwellers did not have ready access to clean, potable water. Often the main water source for a village was many kilometers away. The main task for children in a family is to fetch water, often long distances away from their home. They are not the only ones fetching water. Hundreds of people wait in a long line for their turn to get water. A child may leave home as early as four o'clock in the morning, carrying a pole over their shoulders with two pails attached on each end. The long line means waiting your turn at the tap or the pond which may be up to four hours, then the return walk home. Being young and full of life, they sometimes stop to play and in the process spill some of their water while other times they trip over a stone and lose what water they had collected. One of the most serious ramifications of this lack of water is that children are unable to attend school as fetching water takes up a good portion of the day.

The amount of water collected does not cover all the needs of the family for not everyone can bathe; nor is there enough water for cleaning dishes. If a family by chance has any animals, then they must be watered first before family needs are met. Growing a small garden is impossible during the dry months.

The most common thing people saved for initially then, and continue today, was water jars which are large clay pots capable of holding up to 50 gallons of water. Cambodia does have a saving grace for the rainy season can be as long as six months. During the rainy season, families would devise ingenious methods of collecting rain water, sufficient for all their daily needs but too wet for several months to have a garden. Animals would thrive during this period as long as the annual flooding of the land did not exceed six inches. Flooding caused great discomfort but was needed to replenish the water tables and renew the soil with deposits of silt on the fields.

I resisted putting in water sources in the early years because wells cost money and money was something we did not have in plentiful supply. Besides, I had all the water I needed so I did not feel the pain of those who did not have this saving grace in their lives. We opened our Water Program in Siem Reap which has had lifesaving impacts for thousands of families throughout the country.

When Dara died I shared his passing with friends in Singapore who raised money as a memorial for him. Tabitha had taken care of all the funeral expenses so I asked Ani what she wanted to do with the money. Ani said, "Let's use it for the people, they desperately need water so can we dig wells?" I went to see the impact of these wells. I saw 23 families, people who suffered destitution. Many of the families lived in grass huts, several meters square, the poverty stark and painful. Near their shack was a new well with a cement patio. Each family was already growing vegetables beside their homes. I shared this with other partners and in January, these partners came forth with money for another 25 wells.

Despite the initial success, I was still very reluctant to start a Water Program. This cost money, money we did not have! My faith failed me for I did not trust that God would give us enough to do this.

A few months later Ani phoned me at three o'clock in the morning in a panic; you must come and come today. I caught a flight and arrived by eight o'clock. We drove to a village and arrived by nine o'clock.

The sight that met me was worrisome. In front of the small huts the villagers had gathered. There was no chatter, no joy at my arrival. Under a nearby tree lay a young girl of 12 who was severely battered and bruised. What's going on, I asked Ani.

The villagers were all in savings. Yesterday the cycle had ended and everyone got their savings. The problem was that the young girl under the tree was also into the savings program for herself. She had earned a few riels each week by cutting grass for the neighbors and she had put that money into her own savings account. When she had received her savings, her mother had requested that she give her savings to the family because the older daughter was getting married and the money was needed for the wedding. This was the normal cultural way of doing things, all the members of the family working together to make things happen.

The young lady refused to hand over her savings. She held her savings book in her fist as she showed me her dream, her dream of attending school. Every day she watched as other children passed by her house on their way to school. She overheard snippets of what they had learned; she envied the students their uniforms, their friendships. She envied their ability to play and chatter. Ani had talked of savings and of setting dreams and how dreams happened. She had been heard and understood and the young girl had a dream, a dream of going to school and was determined to make that dream happen.

The mother was very angry at her daughter and waited until the father returned from the fields. The day-long argument was overheard by all the neighbors and they were all worried. The girl needed to obey her parents otherwise all the children would rebel. Reluctantly the father asked his child for the savings but the child refused and so he did what he thought was right, he began to beat her. The neighbors watched and encouraged him yet the girl would not turn over her money. All night the battle of wills went on, all night the father would beat his child, all night she refused to turn over her savings. Ani had been called in the night to solve the problem, to stop the beating, to stop the rebellion of this one lone child.

Her solution was to call me. Who was right and who was wrong? The parents were right to follow the custom of all members of the family working together to make things happen, a family dream of a wedding for their oldest daughter. The young girl was right to dream of getting an education, of learning to read and write; to learn numbers and their value; to dream of a better life.

I asked the father, what would be the one thing that we could all do together to make both dreams come true. Without hesitation his answer came, if we had water, if we had a well, we could grow food all year long and we could raise animals. This was what would make both dreams come true. The villagers murmured in agreement. Ani looked at me long and hard, okay, I said, let's get a well in. I didn't know where I would get the money from but let's do it.

I returned to Phnom Penh, exhausted and wondering where the funds would come from so I spoke to God the only way I know how. Show me the way. God, as usual, answered before I asked, for when I opened my computer there was a donation to cover the cost of five wells. A further justification of our water program.

As other staff heard of the wells going in to Siem Reap, requests came for wells in their areas. This was not as easy as it sounded as each are had its own unique issues with water. Our first task was to determine a fixed cost for wells. We based this on the needs in Siem Reap where pump wells were the best solution. Heng and project staff researched the options. Our first pump wells were $200 which included the drilling, the pipes, the pumps and a one-meter cement skirt surrounding the well. We learned about getting water tested when we dug. Ministry of Rural Development was very helpful with this. We learned of the issues with well water; the threat of arsenic in the water at very deep levels, or the overabundance of magnesium and iron.

As we did with housebuilding, we searched for a local well drilling contractor, a person who was very knowledgeable about soil in the area and where to find water. All of us learned about water divination, using a metal rod to find water. We all learned what small plants grew in the soil above the water table so we would look at soil that appeared desert like and there would be this tiny little plant signifying where the water table was. We would draw up a contract with the contractor to do all our wells in an area at the same price.

The wells could not be donated free for then the families would believe the wells were ours, not theirs, a lesson we learned from the first three wells we installed. As soon as the flange in the pipe would break, I would get a phone call from the family demanding that I come and fix the well. When the families had to donate a small amount towards the cost of the well, the phone calls stopped and the families would fix the flange. We also learned that we needed to be able to cap the wells during the flood season, a trick we learned at the outset of the program. Flood waters damaged the quality of the water and so the wells needed to be capped.

Beginning our Water Program of wells and ponds did not sit so well with some of the volunteers on Tabitha Foundation boards. At the time we had three: Canada, USA and Singapore. One board volunteer insisted that we could not do water as he had read about wells in Bangladesh which were contaminated with arsenic and had injured large numbers of people. My response was and still is, it is for us to decide what programs we will do and it is for you to decide what programs you will fund. It was and still is a painful process. I started Tabitha Cambodia so that I would be able to be free to help the poorest in ways that would most benefit the poor. The Foundations are volunteer organizations set up in support of our work, not set up to determine what that work should be. Their role was and is to hold us accountable for what we do both in terms of progress with our families and in terms of how that money was and is being spent. Their role is to ask the hard questions in what and how we do our work; their role is not to decide what that work should be. It's a very fine line, a line that must be respected on both sides. We were going to do water. This particular volunteer resigned. Many other volunteers stood behind us in our work. Water helped to transform whole communities and thousands upon thousands of families' lives were changed in wondrous ways.

As the Water Program grew so did our knowledge of the various ways to provide water. It became clear that in a number of areas, pump wells would not work as the salinity of the water was too high below a certain depth. Dig deeper than ten meters and we would have salt water. The solution was to dig ponds. We dug ponds that were seven meters long by three meters wide and five meters deep. This allowed people who owned small plots of land to have water for all their family needs as well as growing crops and raising animals. To prevent animals from entering ponds and polluting the water, ponds were built with a two to three meter high dyke all around. Families were ingenuous in devising ways to transport water to their fields, buying water pumps and hoses through savings. It dramatically changed the landscape of our villages as vegetables and animals began to dot the landscape. Ponds were more expensive than pump wells so we needed to come up with a new explanation of the varying costs to our donors.

We also dug open pit wells in a number of areas. Pit wells were wells that were dug ten meters deep on average, and these holes were dug by the families. The walls were supported by cement rings which were one meter in circumference. They were completed with a one-meter cement skirt poured around the bottom to keep the area clean. The cement rings needed to be at least 1.5 meters above the ground to prevent small children from falling in.

I received another special blessing as my family came to visit for several weeks. My two sisters, Theresa and Nancy, and Nancy's husband Wolf came to see what Tabitha was all about. What did my family see? My family saw poverty that was appalling, grass shacks with a cooking fire and a pot; undersized children with runny noses and spartan clothing; old people bent double with the strain of living. They saw glorious smiles and shy laughter; they saw families in newly built houses; they saw pride in the silk produced. They felt the heat of the day and were covered with the endless dust found in every nook and cranny. They rode the pot-holed roads and side tracks; they went on the river and wallowed in the mud of the Mekong; they ate the food of the rich and the food of the poor; they saw the pain of AIDS and saw the joy of a young prostitute making her way out of poverty.

No matter where they went, they saw the strain of poverty in the faces of those around them. No matter where they went, they saw the pride of those making their long, slow process out of poverty.

It was not without its funny moments. We went to visit Siem Reap and Angkor Wat. As we were leaving, waiting in the airport, watching customers shop in our little kiosk, Wolf needed to go to the washroom. Miriam, being Miriam, followed Wolf into the washroom and watched as he did his thing. We were doubled over laughing when Miriam came out and walked up to me, Mama, she said, I need one of those things Grandpa has! It was so very good that they were here. I miss them although Nancy and Wolf would continue to return on a regular basis in the years to come.

———

Like all countries, Cambodia has a mixed population and with this mix comes prejudice. I see all people as having the same value in God's eyes even though I don't understand nor necessarily approve of how different groups live but their intrinsic value as God's children requires that I must respect and treat all people with dignity. Working with minorities in Cambodia was a mantra I voiced strongly, whether the people were of ethnic Vietnamese background, Muslim, Cham or other minorities, made no difference. The staff resisted at first, prejudice is hard to break but all of them began working with minorities as well as native Cambodians.

Vutha had started working with a small ethnic tribal minority called the Saoit. They are considered to be less than human by most Cambodians. Prejudice is alive and well in this country just as it is in all countries. Why are they considered less than human, I asked? The reasons given were as follows: they are hunters and gatherers; they don't wear normal clothes; they don't live in houses but rather the tribe sleeps around the fire at night; they don't understand money or the power of education; and they hide in the bushes when we come to visit. These are all the reasons why these people were feared.

I asked Vutha, why work with them if they are not the same? Vutha's answer came boldly, they want to change, they want to have houses and clothing and put their kids in school. They want to do this step by step and we can help them without hurting them. They are just like us but they just say it differently. Such confidence!

I met these people and by our standards, the destitution was appalling. Twenty people sharing a grass hut two meters by two meters with their spartan belongings strewn around the houses. They were malnourished and shy, yet spoke with boldness about what their dreams were. It was hard to distinguish who belonged to what family; they were just one homogenous group of people. What impressed me most was that they knew what they wanted, they knew their dreams. Vutha was right for they were no different from all of us, their dreams are the same but they use different words to say them.

⌒

One of the benefits of living in Cambodia was that we get to celebrate the New Year several times each year but Khmer New Year is the one where we close Tabitha for a week and all of our staff and families get together to celebrate and then the staff depart to celebrate with their families.

My little family went native this year. Yes, we spent several days on a small farm close to the city where it was very hot, in the 40 C's. Going native meant that I swayed under a tree in a hammock, lazily fishing with a bamboo pole dangling from my hands, surrounded by 20 children from one year to 13 years of age, each one seriously contemplating my efforts, screaming with delight when I caught a fish, a novelty that did not wear out all afternoon. Cambodians fish with nets not with a pole like the silly foreigner.

As dusk began to settle around us, we moved to the road and threw water and baby powder on all passersby, a New Year's ritual that is good fun but messy. Our little band of 20 grew to 50 with young people of all ages joining in the fun and laughter. Older people looked on benevolently and were amused by the antics of this old lady, me! They surrounded me with towels and mopped my hair which was an opportunity not be missed. Is white hair real? Is the hair on my arms real? Can blue eyes really see?

This fun with water was so meaningful as I travelled to Prey Veng where 19 families had received wells. It was so very hot and dusty for most of the families had no access to any water at all. The children bathed only once a week. When I arrived the throwing of water took on new meaning as scores of children sat near each well, carefully filling buckets with water and then giving each other a shower. The showers were done in such a way that the water could be collected and reused to water the newly sown vegetables and to wash clothes. What a joy on the faces and what a celebration we had. I was liberally showered at several homes but I didn't mind, the water was a miracle of life, something to be reveled in and enjoyed.

I was invited by the British Ambassador to have lunch with Her Royal Highness Princess Anne from the United Kingdom, who came to Cambodia for a visit. This luncheon was to be held in Siem Reap. Being me, I thought that a thousand people would be there to meet the Princess and I would just be one of the many. I worked all morning with the staff in the project areas. I showed up in time for the luncheon but was a bit puzzled, where were all the cars and all the people? It wasn't normal for foreigners not to attend such an auspicious occasion. Besides I had on working clothes and was hot and sweaty from my labors.

Boy was I wrong! I assumed that there would be several hundred people at the luncheon and that I could come and see her from a distance while I hid in the crowd. To my dismay, there were only 18 of us invited. There was no place to hide and peek. To my delight and honor, Princess Anne spoke with each one of us individually. We spoke for twenty minutes. It was so easy for she knew all about Tabitha and me; she knew about Cambodia and its poverty. I felt as if she really cared. What a gift that was.

Her entourage were a delight. They had purchased silk products from a competitor and had found our shop afterwards. Our prices were much lower for the same quality. We spent several hours discussing the discrepancies in price amongst many other titbits of information that they were fascinated with. It was truly a fun and relaxing time. I learned that the British are actually quick of wit and very kind for not once did my dress or behavior attract their attention, at least not in my presence.

The House Building Program continued to expand. We had a team come from the Canadian International School in Singapore. They brought a reporter along with them from the Canadian Broadcasting Company (CBC). The reporter had questions that so many volunteers and visitors had. His concern was that we would turn young students off if we confronted the students with the history or the poverty of Cambodians. This was part of the orientation that I did and was mandatory with each house building team.

The format for house building has remained the same from the very first team. The first day of house building is orientation at Tabitha, explaining the recent history of the country and the impact on the people. People who are deeply traumatized and suffer severely from post-traumatic stress syndrome, even today. This is followed by a mandatory visit to The Toul Sleng Genocide Museum and the Killing Fields. The purpose of this was to make sure that volunteers understood the recent history of Cambodia and the people they would meet, people who were survivors of this regime.

Orientation was also to explain some of the cultural differences between the two cultures. For example, small children did not wear diapers or panties so that when they had bodily movements these would not soil their clothing. The volunteers were taught the simple gestures for greetings that would be culturally acceptable and basic phrases.

I made it clear that house building was not about the volunteers but about the people they came to serve. Servanthood is putting yourself in someone else's shoes, putting the needs of someone else before your own. This message changed the attitude of volunteers who often came with the attitude that this experience was all about them and their needs. "It's not about you", is the phrase which became internationally known and accepted amongst our volunteer house builders. The truth was, and is, it was all about them. The life changing experience for thousands of volunteers was a testimony to their needs being met in unexpected and wondrous ways simply by putting the needs of others before themselves.

We were and still are quite dictatorial about our expectations of our volunteers, which can be a shock to many of them. Simple things such as getting up early to travel to the building site, using local toilets which was often a hole we dug with a waist high wall, doing hard physical labor in some very hot surroundings, water breaks where heads were cooled by pouring cold water over their heads thereby preventing heat stroke, wearing appropriate clothing, shorts as long as their knees, t-shirts with sleeves, gentlemen keeping their shirts on, were just some of our clear expectations.

Culturally, we made it clear that no one should hold babies as this was often a signal to the villagers that the volunteer wanted the child. Over the years, several people have phoned me in a panic from a village asking what they should do as they could not give the baby back to the mother. In my anger I made it clear that this was their problem to solve and solve it they did.

We forbade people giving small items to people in the villages, especially to children as this caused great grief for all of us. Several times I was called by a provincial governor to come and take back whatever item was given. Poverty is a harsh task master. When one person receives a trinket from a volunteer, the others in the village become jealous, causing disharmony and anger throughout the village. It was made clear by the governor that I personally had to come and retrieve the trinket. My guess is that the governor thought I needed to learn a lesson, a lesson I learned well. Passing this on to volunteers is not always gracefully received for there is a perceived emotional need on the part of the volunteer to have a feel good experience without bearing the consequences. Thankfully the vast majority of volunteers have listened to our rules.

Volunteers were also given warnings about their behavior outside of house building sites. We expected volunteers to abide by the laws of Cambodia, to not use any prohibited substances such as drugs and to not solicit sex from Cambodians, especially children. Cambodia is sadly one of the target countries for pedophiles to come and abuse children. We would advise volunteers not to talk with children on the city streets as they were automatically perceived as pedophiles. Volunteers were encouraged not to physically touch anyone except from someone of the same sex for this was a cultural taboo. Over the years and thousands of volunteers we have been fortunate to only have a few instances of people breaking these rules.

All of these rules bothered the reporter. My answer was simple: if we denied either the history or the poverty; we would be denying the dignity and the life of Cambodians. We would also be denying volunteers the right to know and respect Cambodians not as people to be pitied but as people to be admired and respected for their capacity to survive such horrors.

~

We had our Cambodia House team come to build again. I wanted to have the store in perfect shape for the visitors and everything was finally done. Thirty minutes before they all arrived, I was working with Chanthou and some customers when it sounded like war had broken out. The floor tiles in the big showroom started to explode! Well, all of us dived for cover, some in my office, some in the silk room and some in the hallway. When we thought it was all over, two women came out of the office and boom, ten more tiles exploded. They screamed and made a dash for the hallway. Then one of the racks in the silk room came crashing down. I thought the building was collapsing, but, no, as June tells me later, it's quite common for tiles to explode. It's happened twice now in her house and once in her office. The Khmers tell me it's because the tiles were laid too tight. But God is good and in less than thirty minutes we had cleaned it all up although the floor now had ugly scars where the tiles were missing, and the rack had been replaced.

There was an incident in our apartment that really affected Miriam. One night our landlord started shooting into the air to scare the neighbors over a personal dispute. The shooting was on our balcony and was terrifying. The poor girl stopped trusting our little home so we moved again, this time to a small bungalow surrounded by mansions. There was a garden to play in, room to play in and a place to have friends safely. It was a good move in many ways.

There were others that needed a new home as well. I ended the year by visiting families who were hoping to get a new home. Three of the families were tribal families, still frightened when they saw strangers, even more so when one of the strangers had white hair. It was hard to overcome their fear yet they came trembling to show us where the houses would be built.

The next three families lived in a beautiful setting. We walked through rice fields and shaded valleys. Their homes were humble, the people meek. One was a grannie in her 80's and she so much wanted a home, but we could not do so because she had not saved enough.

The chosen three families listened carefully to her sadness; in one family the husband was unable to walk; in another the older boy was blind and in the third family, another grannie was taking care of her orphaned grandchildren. They said very little. Their expectation was marred by the need of their 80-year-old neighbor. They asked me for a little time to talk with each other. Their decision touched us all: each of the families would help give wood to the grannie who was without and she, too, would have a new home made from old wood. It is this caring for each other that makes me love Cambodia so.

# 2003

The year started out with a little drama in our house. Miss Miriam received an aquarium, complete with fish from friends. She was dismayed to see several little bodies floating in the water the next morning. I tried to explain to her that she couldn't keep catching the fish in the net and taking them for a walk. She was a bit puzzled by this; then what do I do with them? Well, I said, talk with them and feed them. The next morning, more little bodies. Miriam was a bit put out and the fish were very put out. I asked her what she had done. I talked to them mom, I caught them in my net and talked to them one by one. More explanations about how to care for the fish. We now have a number of baby fish and one big one left but they are no longer being walked or taken out for a talk.

Some of us old-timers, people who had been In Cambodia for a long time, went out for dinner one night. In our usual fashion we shared our various opinions about the state of Cambodia. Foolishly, we came to a consensus that life had become rather boring in the past year for there were no gunfights or coup attempts, just endless chatter. In a strange way we all missed a bit of the living on the edge, the constant state of awareness and tension that comes with living in a war zone.

We commiserated and laughed about the near-death experience of several of us flying to Siem Reap for our work. That fateful day, the toilet had blown out of the plane. A huge hole in the body of the plane left us gasping for air and saying a great many prayers. The pilot was excellent and God was merciful as we descended safely and we got to share our tales.

But, we all sighed, it was definitely boring. We went our separate ways. As my little household settled down for the night, we heard gunfire and grenades. I grabbed Miriam and put her in my bed. As I did so I looked out the window and to my dismay saw an armored personnel vehicle outside our gate. Apparently, the rumor mill was working overtime that the Thai authorities were killing Cambodians in Bangkok. Needless to say, Cambodians were out to defend their countrymen and had attacked the Thai Embassy and all businesses and homes belonging to Thai residents. And we had foolishly said that we were bored, never again!

When we started our Water Program, Phat and Ponluck, our Prey Veng staff, insisted that people in Prey Veng did not know how to grow vegetables. I struggled with them for a year about the importance of water and how that could change the lives of our families. They were just as insistent that people in Prey Veng had never learned about vegetables or growing rice year-round and that I was just being a silly foreigner. I countered in anger that they both had a choice: either put water in or lose their jobs.

We had this argument while driving through a village. We had stopped to talk and as we were talking, we watched another vehicle come in and stop their car about 500 meters across the field. A man got out and opened his trunk. Clearly visible were all kinds of gadgets like televisions and batteries. As we watched in horror, he approached an older woman and chatted and within ten minutes he had given her a television and battery and she had given him two small children. Phat just said this is where they buy children for the sex trade. I was horrified and repeated to him that water and growing food would change this behavior.

In pure frustration, Phat installed a well in a village and then went to the market and bought vegetable seeds. He threw the seeds in different small village plots with no soil preparation, no planning. He just threw the seeds around and then he told the villagers, water them and grow vegetables.

A few weeks later, Phat and Ponluck insisted that I come and see. What a visit that was! As we went from one garden to another flush with growing vegetables, Phat had the grace to look sheepish and confess that we were wrong when we told you that people didn't know how to grow vegetables.

The vegetables were grown and sold, and the gardens were planted again. The second time around the vegetables were all in neat rows. Each garden had a different vegetable, from winter squash, to beans, tomatoes, lettuce, cabbage, and more. As we were walking from one garden to another, I came to a garden where the lady looked familiar. I knew her. I started to laugh as she grabbed and hugged me. She had been a beggar on the streets of Phnom Penh. With the gift of water, she was no longer begging but was living a happier life by earning money from her garden. What a gift that was for both of us, both of us laughing and hugging each other.

2003 was another election year. It made everyone uneasy. There were 23 parties vying for power. Lots of noise. Traveling to the villages was difficult. There was a traffic jam from the various parties coming to woo the votes of the people. Each party brought its own version of vote buying through the handing out of t-shirts, rice and 10,000 riels, a small fortune to the poorest. The people were not mindless; they attended each party's rally and took all the handouts. Savings was not a problem during those months.

One of the benefits of elections was that roads were repaired during the campaign period. I loved it because travelling to our projects became so much easier. We had expanded to Kirivon, a project near the Vietnam border in Takeo province. The trip had become a true test of endurance. The first 100 kilometers was over relatively good roads but it was the last 38 kilometers that took some three bone jarring hours to traverse. I am not a person to become car-sick, but car-sick I was on those trips. Every part of my body hurt and I learned that bras have very little use on such bad roads. The people came out in throngs to meet us for our program was well received and within a month of the staff starting there, 160 families had been enrolled. Then came the election campaigning and the various party members stamina rejected the "road from hell" and repairs began. Unfortunately, we then had detour through rice paddies while repairs were ongoing.

The election results did not leave any one party holding a majority, which was the usual outcome in Cambodia. It wasn't until June 2004 that the elections were finally resolved and The Cambodian People's (CPP) party, headed by Prime Minister Hun Sen, took over the ruling of the country. Finally, some peace and security for this country of sorrows.

Around the same time, the SARS pandemic broke out. Most foreigners left Cambodia and tourism and house building teams did not come. It significantly affected our local sales and our house building program. The solution to all this unease was to send the staff out to visit each other's projects. The community development staff spent two weeks traveling to each other's work sites, learning about how we are all the same and learning how we are all different. I asked them what they had learned. They all started to talk asking me if I knew these things, coming in the form of questions. The excitement was in the variety of impacts on families who had been saving for two years. Did you know you can grow vegetables a meter up from the ground on bamboo platforms? Did you know that a family can have four pigs instead of the usual two? Did you know that people with secure housing can earn double the income because all the adults are able to work? Did you know the number of orphans who are able to pay their own way through school? Did you know how many healthy babies were born this year? Janne did you know all this? Actually, yes I did as I got to see everyone's work throughout the year. The staff were amazed at their own results. It's hard to see when you are doing the work because you are too close. But to see it through the eyes of your peers, what a gift that was.

There was sadness too. In several of our projects it has become obvious that the impact of AIDS was unrelenting. Where two years ago, the number of two parent families averaged around 80%, now it was down to 50 and 60% with most of the deaths attributed to AIDS. What was comforting and sustaining is the number of orphans being raised by grandmothers and being supported by everyone in the community, even the poorest.

The Cottage Industry program received a huge boost as Tabitha Singapore held its first bedding show. It was decided that it would be good to have a large sales event twice a year in Singapore. Gerry very kindly donated the use of her furniture store to display our goods. Her store was in an old black and white, spacious with a large garden. All the volunteers made and brought snacks; invitations were designed and sent out to the expat community.

The display was stunning. I was the speaker for two days of the sale. We had no idea of how well the show would go. It went extremely well as women and men came early and waited for the shop to open. Once we opened the doors, the customers came and bought and then bought some more. It was unbelievable. With coffee and snacks, people stayed and talked with each other and then they encouraged new shoppers to shop. It was amazing. On the last night, close friends came and we had champagne and talked till two o'clock in the morning. We had our biggest sales result ever in those two days: $30,000 worth and orders of over 400 bedcovers between Singapore and Australia.

That sale changed the way we worked with Singapore and Cottage Industry. I carried back over $30,000 in cash, a bit unnerving. It was time to set up a banking transfer system. It was also time to do away with volunteers carrying goods back to Singapore in black bags and set up a shipping system. The benefit with Singapore is that it is a small city state and volunteers could easily meet with each other and plan events. Shipping required that we needed a secure space to store our goods. Once again UWCSEA stood up and gave us a room. Later that space would be transferred to the Singapore American School (SAS).).

It was during this sale that I learned of my mother's failing health. She had gone into a coma and her future looked bleak. Good friends,

Audrey and Andy, had gathered to be there for me when they told me. Later on, after composing myself, I said that Mom would be very proud of what we had done, but then she would say to me, "It's just like you, you can't sew on a button but you can get others to make things, and you make them enjoy it as well."

On my return to Phnom Penh, I shared the news about my mom with the staff. Life was very difficult for me. I was torn between my birth family and my adopted one here; their need for me at the moment was very great. It had been a difficult year for us in many ways. The month of September is about Pchum Ban, remembering those who have passed away. It was always a time of great sorrow here because none of my staff were able to say goodbye to their parents or even know where their parents died. Mom's illness was allowing all of us here to grieve, so many tears were being shed for all our mothers, for all our fathers, they were one with me in my grief. The days were strange as we started in tears and ended in tears and cared for so many others in between. It was as if their grief at not knowing and never being able to say goodbye was now being allowed and my Mom had become their mother.

Most of all I think of what Mom would have said, "Don't cry for me. I am going home soon, I will be safe. Look after your daughter, take care of each other and raise her well so that one day, when we are together again, we can all sing our praises together." Miriam had a sixth sense and knew there was something wrong with Grandma. She had dreams of Grandma talking with her and was very upset.

On December 8, my mother passed away. I gave the Missionaries of Charity a Christmas tree full of our teddy bears and dinosaurs and wrapped 100 gifts for the children as our memorial to Mom.

The Sisters actually cried, and that was unexpected. Tabitha USA collected donations in Mom's memory to build a house for another mother here. Flowers and special touches came from friends. It was all so weird, because every time I wanted to cry, my Mom's face was there and she was young again and laughing and she made me laugh. What a God our God is.

Mom was a good friend to me. We became close friends when I moved back to Brockville, where she lived. We laughed a lot, like the time she broke her leg and didn't tell me until after my sister Francis and Hans had gone home from one of their visits. The cast was put on, but it seemed that the cast was bigger than her. She was afraid to walk, so she sat all day long until my brother John brought her a secretary's chair. Well, we said, time for a bathroom run. I had her moving at quite a clip when we hit the ledge of the bathroom floor. The chair stopped but Mom didn't. I think we both peed our pants from laughing so hard.

When I left to go to Calvin College, Mom came up one summer for a month to work with the street folks. She was a bit leery as all their talk was a bit silly. We took everyone on a hayride, Mom on the back between these two big guys. She started talking like them, which tickled everyone's funny bones. Then these guys decided she was okay and started treating her like a queen. She couldn't do much as they were so much bigger than she was. Pretty soon they were physically carrying her everywhere. Both of us were caught between being scared and laughing.

Mom came to my graduation from Calvin College. The first thing she said to one of my professors, who complimented her on her bright daughter, was, "What did you teach her here that she has to go so far away?" Both of us were a bit deflated after that comment.

For all the years in the Philippines I wrote to Mom and she wrote to me on a weekly basis. When I came home, she said, "No wonder you like it, you have others to cook and clean for you; that's just like you." Mom was never impressed with my housekeeping skills. We would talk about the work and the conditions of those so poor, and, as usual, her wisdom was astounding. She shared her years as a youth in poverty and often told me what to do when people were sick with typhus or cholera. Her remedies worked.

While I was in Kenya, Mom's ability to write every week diminished, but I continued. When I came home she had all the letters wrapped and tied together: "Here," she said, "Before I forget, these are yours." During that visit her memory lapses were becoming obvious. We had one awful afternoon when she insisted she had no panty hose and we had to go buy some. So off we went and bought a dozen pairs. Once we were home and had a cup of tea, she started to cry for she had forgotten where she put the pantyhose. We went back to the store for another dozen. We came home and I opened the fridge and there was our first dozen! We were both a bit exasperated, but then, as usual, we started to laugh.

When I came home for my 50th, we had lunch together. She had aged but there were times when she was quite lucid. At that lunch, Mom and I talked for several hours. Her mind was clear and so we shared our love for our God and our love for each other. I asked her forgiveness for my foolishness. She said, "Don't cry. You are my child, I love you. There is nothing to forgive."

Go in peace, Mom. I miss having you; I thank you for having me. I am so blessed.

# 2004

Miriam and I had traveled home to Canada to grieve with our family and to celebrate my mother's life and the life she had given to all of us. It was a time of excitement as Miriam discovered snow and all its joys; she discovered what cold is and all its trauma; she learned about grief and that it is okay to be sad; she learned that family is a source of renewal and hope.

On our return, we were met by our Cambodian family. There were hugs and tears, and there was joy and excitement, and above all there was a sense of relief that we had come back.

Som was our handyman, our security guard here in Phnom Penh. He was 46 years old and was married with five children. Som never said much, never did and probably he never will. He watched all of us and helped where help was needed. My return brought a big smile to his face, a gentle hug and a welcome home coffee. Som, my quiet one, spoke "It is so good to have you back." We grinned and I wished him and his family the best of 2004.

Som began to reminisce. You know Janne, before I met you and Tabitha in 1995, my life was very hard. I had a very poor house; only two of my children could go to school. My wife was very unhappy because she had no work and she would sit all day and think of bad thoughts. These thoughts would make her ill and then she would cry. She grieved because the children were jealous of each other because only two could go to school each year and the other three had to stay home. Our children would be angry and ask us why they couldn't go to school. My wife and I were both so very sad and we had no hope. I could only provide for twenty percent of my family's needs. It was too hard.

Then I met you and you hired me as a guard. Tabitha was so different for you made all of us take care of our own needs but also the needs of the people we work with. You made us all equal and it made me feel like I was a somebody, that I was just like everyone else. You made me save and think of what I could do and not about what I don't have. You kept telling me that a good home was possible, that my children could all go to school, and that my wife and I could laugh again.

Then in 1999, we built our house together with you. Later that year I dug a fish pond and my wife had work to take care of the fish. She doesn't cry anymore, she no longer thinks about sad things; every morning she sings as she gets the children ready for school. Then she takes care of the fish; she feeds them and makes sure the pond is strong. Every day she brings fish to people in our community who don't have enough to eat. The fish we sell every month help pay for 30% of all our needs and she is proud of that.

Then you helped me buy my motorbike and I can be with my family each week-end. Before that, it was hard to go home because everyone was unhappy and I couldn't do anything to make it better. Now I enjoy going home.

You know the best thing I like about Tabitha is the house building. I get to go all over the country and meet people who were just like me, a nobody, and now, just like me, they are somebody. I am so very proud that I can help myself and my family but I am even prouder that I can help others to be just like myself. I know that God blesses you and that He blesses me but I want you to know that I bless you as well and all those who help us. I and my family are so happy to be a part of Tabitha and all the people that we help. My blessings are not just for this year but for all the years that lie ahead. Som made my homecoming to Cambodia feel right, a time to remember why I was doing what I was doing. Mom would be proud of that.

Starting in new provinces always involved a lot of work. Staff spent days traveling throughout a province, meeting with the local chiefs and talking with the people. Discussions were held with me and other staff and more questions and more traveling and more answers until we think we should begin.

But before we began in a big way, I was requested to come and see for myself and to give my final stamp of approval. I approved the opening of Banteay Meanchay province, a province whose location is contiguous to Siem Reap and was a natural choice for expansion. Let me share my two days that I spent with Ani, our manager in Siem Reap and Tim Kameak who is our new manager in Banteay Meanchey.

Kameak joined our staff in 2000. He was a close friend of Dara. Dara, I suspect, knew that he was dying, and so he quietly trained Kameak in the work. After Dara's death, it was natural to hire him as staff and to take over Dara's work. Kameak was just 30, single and women were a bane in his life. He was the youngest of five children; his parents and oldest brother killed by the Khmer Rouge, leaving his four sisters and himself. He was another quiet one, putting up with the constant teasing of the female staff in Siem Reap and the hugs and kisses from me, his boss. But he liked it for if we didn't do all these things, he'd think he has done something wrong.

Monday morning started early. I flew out of Phnom Penh at seven o'clock and arrived in Siem Reap 45 minutes later. Ani and Kameak had the car ready and off we went. Kameak was the driver and he took his vengeance out on us. The road was tarmacked for 30 kilometers. On this section he drove no faster than 30 kilometers an hour so my patience was tested, but I said nothing. Then we hit the dirt roads and speed crept up to 120 kph and both Ani and I were white faced and perspiring. Slow down I would say as we hit another crater and he smiled and just went that much faster. I smacked him on the arm and I got the grin. By this time, Ani had her arms around my neck; her breathing came in gasps and groans so I smacked him harder. Then we saw a bridge and he slowed down to 10 kph, a breather except the bridge was in horrible shape with gaps in the girders and spikes all over the road, but we made it. Sadly, it was the first of 77 bridges. I came to love them and hate them at the same time.

An hour later we arrived in Banteay Meanchey province. At first it looked like Siem Reap and then became flatter and flatter with huge expanses of seemingly endless plain dotted occasionally by a community. Kameak proudly drove us to the office he and the staff had chosen. I was horrified. It was a shack of broken wood with mud floors. Ani saw my face and quickly assured me there was nothing better for twenty dollars a month. I said: we can afford more but then she said: we looked. The $100 ones are the same and she then showed me one which on the outside was done nicely, colored tiles but inside it was wood and mud. This will not do, said I, you must fix it with cement floors and new walls, a bedroom and a kitchen and a toilet. Ani laughed, I knew you would say this when you saw it. Kameak grinned again and I gave him a hug.

We went off to see the potential families. We met several of the 650 families all of whom broke rocks into small stones for a living. It was hard to imagine breaking rocks for a living. The morning was hot and women, men and children all sat in makeshift shade breaking rocks. None stopped as we talked. They worked seven days a week to crush one truck load of rocks. Their homes were mere shells of bits and pieces of grass and plastic, mud floors, little else, a lifetime of misery for so very little. Yet none complained for then Kameak showed me the ones with no homes and no work, hundreds of them and I was appalled. Breaking rocks, the people said, is much better than having no work and no food. Poverty is a hard task master. I am humbled by the quiet strength of those who work so hard for so little and even more humbled by those who desire to work but cannot find any. Their will to live is so very strong.

At 2 o'clock, we left for Poipet, the border town with Thailand. Here my culture shock re-asserted itself for we stayed in a five-star hotel with a casino. The price was $30 a night which included two meals and a $10 chit to gamble with. I was horrified but Ani said: you need to see this. As we stood at the top of the hotel we saw horrendous poverty next to the wall of the hotel, where 850 families lived in shacks with no water, no toilets, no anything. Then we drove around the town where behind the front row of respectable businesses were thousands of families living in poverty. On the outskirts of the town were entire suburbs of families living in poverty. Everywhere we went there were more, and each place had its own unique mark of dirt, filth, and limited space. Oh Kameak, I kept saying, lots of work, lots of work. I kept getting the grin. With such poverty, security is often an issue so we discussed all our options and decisions were made.

The next morning, we stood at the border and watched people streaming across the border to find what work they could. Kameak was mesmerized and forgot he was driving, people were honking and screaming at us to move our car out of the road but he just couldn't absorb it all. Finally, we were off again, this time to find the silk weavers. Three hours later we were on a dirt road without gas. We were saved by a wizened old man who showed up with 10 pop bottles of gas and off we went. In the silk weavers' villages, the poverty was much less as they were making a living growing the silk worms and showed us the process which was fascinating. Most of it was sold to our weavers in Takeo and other places.

We returned to Siem Reap and by 4 o'clock we were at the airport. Ani, Apo, Sarouen, Mari, Chrisom, and Vath all said good bye. Kameak stood before me with his grin, both of us were hot and dirty and smelly and then he gave me a big hug. I held him close for a minute and then said, well done, son, well done. Our two days together will never be forgotten.

While I was in Banteay Meanchey, Miriam had an incident at home. A friend had come over to play in the yard. Her driver had a cyclo which Miriam thought she should push around. The cyclo started to gather some speed and ended up crashing into the gate with Miriam's arm caught in between. She screamed with pain, but the nanny thought it was all okay. She checked with teachers the next day and they said it was all okay. I came home to hear Miriam's version of what had happened and then the nanny's reassurance that all was well. We went swimming as my penance for not being there to help her, something she loved to do, but wouldn't use her arm to come out of the water.

I took her to the expat medical clinic. Miriam was not happy. When we got there, they kept telling me she was fine and that it was probably a sprain, but I forced them to take an x-ray. Once that was done, everyone came running. Yes, she had broken it and I was told that I would need to take her to Bangkok for specialist care. They couldn't put a cast on here. What? Come on! It's a broken arm for goodness' sake! Instead, we had to go to Thailand to get a cast, money I couldn't afford, plus a hospital and doctors and a night in a hotel! I was thoroughly disgusted.

Our hospital visit in Thailand took a total of 40 minutes for x-ray, cast and all. Then back to the hotel where Miriam made up for lost time by doing handstands and backflips chortling: no pain mum! I was worn out with it all and wondered what Cambodians do when they have a broken bone.

———

Cottage Industry kept growing with more product lines. We had volunteers come from Singapore and helped us put together color coordinated sets of bedding as well as hand bags. Karen came from Australia and together we designed another twelve lines of bedding using striped silk as the feature of each set. Our silk room expanded to new heights and oh, how beautiful the silk looked. I loved that room. So did the customers; one woman walked in and bought $3000 worth of silk. We were blown away.

One night I awoke to find a man standing by my bed, shining a flashlight in my eyes! Good grief! Without a murmur, I closed my eyes while I registered the fact that this was not good. I didn't cry out and I didn't move because we all know that to cry out or move would result in death which was the custom with robbers in Cambodia. In the 30 seconds it took to think about the situation I received the wisdom to turn on my bed light and jump out of bed, easier to fight while standing, I thought. The bed light was dim, but it gave out enough light for me to see that my bathroom door was slightly open. I walked quickly to push it just a little, enough to know that it was not my imagination for the glass in the window was gone.

I wasn't frightened and my thoughts were quite clear. I had to make sure Miriam and Tuit were safe. So, I left my room with the door open and went to their room. I told Tuit there was someone in the house and to call the security man next door. Tuit, in a confused state, said, "Don't worry, I'll kill the cockroach." I grabbed her and said, "It's a man, not a cockroach, call the security next door!" I stood in the living room with a flashlight ready to take on the intruder should he come out of my room. At the same time, Tuit opened the backdoor, she didn't call out, but she slammed it and came back breathless and badly shaken for there was a second man standing nearby.

We went into Miriam's room. She didn't cry out, she didn't say a word. She just held her arms out to be held. I had bought Tuit a mobile phone for Christmas and she grabbed it "Call Soklieng", I said. Another miracle, Soklieng answered after the first ring. She said, "Don't leave the room and don't make a sound, I'll call the police." Meng Wan, our second nanny, was sleeping in the outside guest room. We phoned her to tell her what was going on and she, too, stayed quiet.

Fifteen minutes later the police and Soklieng arrived. Meng Wan walked across the yard in slow motion, deeply traumatized by what was happening. As the police entered the yard, I held my door shut while Tuit opened the main doors to the house. At first, the police thought I was just a crazy foreigner until I took them to the side to show them the missing window. It was only then that things happened quickly, guns and more guns, and a thorough, professional search of every inch and nook and cranny of the house, the garden and the roof. One of the intruders had left his shorts behind, a fact that left Miriam wondering as to why.

There were so many police and they were so professional, it was very comforting. I started to shake and then they asked me what happened. I told them everything. The police were astonished. "Why didn't he hurt you?" they asked me. "They always hurt people if they know you are awake." I was still a bit numb and my mouth opened before I had time to think. "I think they were after one of the pretty girls, and when they saw I was an old lady, they decided it was too much." The laughter eased the tension, but all of us were beginning to tremble from the fright.

In the morning light the police returned to take the fingerprints; the chief of our commune came to make sure all was well; and the landlord sent workers to fix the windows, put on iron bars, and install razor wire and spotlights. Soklieng and I decided that this was a message sent to make sure we were safe and so we hired a night guard, something I had resisted for a long time. At the end of the day, all of the staff and workers came, about 90 people just to touch me and make sure all was fine. We shared, we hugged and we laughed, so much comedy in the midst of it all and we thanked God for keeping us safe.

—

I took Menrouen out to see a housebuilding team. We arrived earlier than the team so I walked him through the village to see what people had accomplished through their savings. Family after family proudly showed off their gardens and pigs and small shops, lots of talking. I heard the team hammering away so I told Menrouen it was time to see the team at work. As we walked up to the building site, Menrouen stopped dead in his tracks, his jaw dropped and he was speechless for several minutes. I was busy talking with the builders, giving advice and teasing them. Finally, Menrouen spoke. This can't be, he said, these are foreigners! Yes I said. You don't understand, he gasped, foreigners don't work, they talk a lot but they don't work. I looked at him speechless, his angst at all this activity by foreigners came as a shock to me. Foreigners are good time people he said, they never do anything physical! I never realized how we white folks were perceived by Cambodians. Both of us were stunned by this revelation. I will make you the Mother of Cambodia, he decided that moment. Nobody can get foreigners to do physical labor to help Cambodians. It just doesn't happen. It's a miracle.

I told Menrouen about some of the problems of housebuilding. Our biggest issue was the scarcity and difficulty of getting materials, particularly wood with which to build houses. We had changed from thatch and wood frames to wood frames and wood walls. He explained that many people were cutting down trees everywhere in Cambodia and exporting the wood. This was being done illegally and was causing a shortage of wood within Cambodia. The government was beginning to cut down on such activities and to check where the wood was being moved to. Heng, who was in charge of housebuilding, was stopped innumerable times by both legal and illegal check points on the roads leading to where houses were to be built. It cost a lot in the way of payments at each checkpoint and took a lot of time to move the wood. Menrouen commiserated with me and said he would do what he could to make it easier.

Water, wells and ponds were a big hit with our donor community and for this of course we were very thankful. We had opened up a project in Kampot and I went to see how it was all going. Roads in Cambodia were atrocious and the main highways were a joke to say the least. These visits game me time to talk one on one with all the development staff and seeing what they had done. On this site visit I went with Srei, Tharry, Pon, Soklieng and Heng. There was lots of time to talk with each of them and time to talk all together and even some time to meditate for the roads to Kampot varied in degrees of horribleness. On a scale of one to ten, with ten being the best, we started on a six and rapidly decreased to a two. I am a seasoned traveler but this time, even I was beginning to fade with the bouncing and jolting and the terrible snail's pace we kept up for hours at a time.

The seven of us were delighted to finally arrive and meet our new staff member, Sokha. He was a gentle and unassuming man and took all of us in stride. People kept finding us and pulling us to come and see what they had done. Within six weeks of starting, 320 families had joined our program. The poverty was ameliorated by the enthusiasm of the people. We were able to visit several homes before our vehicle ended up in a rice paddy, in mud up to the axles. We left the boys to free the van and we girls went off to see the wonders of the wells.

We met a group of five families. They had plowed several hectares of land and had planted cucumbers (about 6 cm high) and lettuce. There was such excitement as they showed me scrub land that had been like theirs before and then they showed me more hectares that other families were tilling to plant their vegetables. "We have water, we can do so many things" they all said. I was a bit dubious about it all and asked: did you not plant before? No, they chorused, for no one ever came and talked with us; no one ever shared ideas with us. We couldn't think anymore but now we can think of so much that we can do.

The government had finally resolved all the election related issues of the 2003 elections. Prime Minister Hun Sen was now firmly in control. He asked all government officials to decide which party they wanted to be a part of. Mu Sochua, who was Minister of Women's Affairs, had to choose as she was member of the main opposition Party, Funcipec. Sochua and I were friends and she asked me my opinion. I advised her to think of how she wanted to impact the people of Cambodia. If she wanted to help change the country then she should choose the Cambodia People's Party but if she wanted to advocate for western style democracy then she should choose for the opposition bearing in mind that her efforts to help the people of Cambodia would be minimized considerably.

It was a terrible choice for her to make as an individual. On the day she chose to be part of the opposition she phoned me and cried and cried. I was deeply saddened for she was a good person and could have done so much for the good of the people.

Sochua's replacement was Dr. Ing Kantha Phavi. The government had been in such turmoil since my arrival that I struggled about what to do. I didn't know her or her reputation yet we had our Memorandum of Understanding (MOU) with the Ministry of Women's Affairs. I discussed it with staff and decided against sending her our congratulations and best wishes.

Several months passed and it was time for our renewal of our MOU with the government, beginning with renewing our MOU with the Ministry of Women's Affairs. I sent Soklieng with our file and request for renewal to the Ministry. The response was swift; I was requested to present myself to the Minister forthwith.

My initial meeting with Phavi started with a very angry Minister asking why I had not presented myself to her after the election. She was not happy. I told her in my typical Janne way that I didn't know who she was. There were many in the government who served their own needs rather than the needs of the people. I thought she might be one of them. Within 30 minutes both of us had learned to respect each other. I invited Phavi to come and see what Tabitha was all about. She agreed.

Several months later, one of my favorite teams arrived, the Margaritas. It was an all-woman team comprised mainly of Australian mothers living in Singapore and their friends. Their first house building trip had occurred several years before. At the end of their first house build, we had a debriefing lunch together. What a lunch that was! Sharon, Lisa, Sue and so many others were in tears. They cried for what they had learned about the history of Cambodia, they cried about the poverty Cambodians lived in, they cried because they could do so little despite the ten houses they had built. We became friends, friends who have stood beside me and beside Tabitha ever since and in so many ways they became my soul mates. They returned every year since their first house build in 2001.

They were also a team that put up with a lot. I often asked them to build in difficult locations, staying in village hotels that left a lot to be desired. In one hotel, when someone flushed the toilet on the top floor, the waste emptied into the room below. They ate in village restaurants where they watched rats as big as dogs compete with beggars for food. And they did it all with good grace.

This particular year I had asked them to build for landmine victims; men and women who had lost a limb to the scourge of landmines in the countryside. The government had granted each one of them land in a far-off place. They took it but had no homes. I needed 50 houses so they came with 50 women, and each woman had raised enough money for a house. We put them up in a resort which I had nicknamed Jurassic Park because of its propensity to the weird and wonderful nature in which it stood. The rooms consisted of cabins dotted in the wild.

One poor woman went to her room and encountered a Tokay lizard on her door. The Tokay is a rather large lizard with a propensity to be still for long periods of time. In Cambodia it is believed that when a Tokay croaks seven times it will bring the listener good luck. They were also known to bite anyone who touched them with a ferocity and intensity that boggles the mind. It hadn't moved during the time it took to unpack, have a dinner and time for bed. The poor woman had become convinced that the Tokay was an ornament so she reached out and grabbed it. The Tokay bit her which caused a great deal of panic amongst the women. Now everyone was upset and very few slept the night through as electricity was an expensive commodity and the resort turned it off at 9 o'clock. Every rustle in the night caused dread and angst amongst the team.

Phavi's first visit was to see this housebuilding team. As we walked through the village and saw the land mine victims, saw the women building, Phavi remarked she had never seen anything like it. Then I took Phavi to another village we worked in, one where the road was just a path and we drove though rough terrain. There, we were greeted by family after family bearing gifts of fresh vegetables grown because of wells.

Afterwards she took me to one of her villages beside a beautiful pond and we sat and had a Khmer meal. I am not fond of rice and even less fond of some of the Khmer food. We talked and shared our lives with each other. We became friends that day, a friendship that would grow and blossom into a sisterhood of shared lives and shared dreams for the people of Cambodia. I thank my God for Phavi and her gift of life.

———

October was our tenth anniversary month and so we celebrated. Of course, we didn't do it the normal way by having a big party instead, we decided to build as many houses as we could for as many families as we could. The result was nine volunteer teams that came with 183 people and built 62 houses. The teams brought their own brand of excitement and of grace which was infectious and so we were all excited and were surrounded with grace. What a way to celebrate!

Our orders and sales were also phenomenal; in fact, we were able to hire more workers. Two of these workers were young ladies, sisters actually; one was 17 and the other 19 years of age. Their home situation was one of extreme poverty. Their mother had been ill for several months and the medical bills were paid by borrowing funds from money lenders who were not too happy that these could not be repaid. The family of eight was down to one meal of rice per day, their home nothing but a simple hut made of grass. It was rainy season and so all had fallen ill from being wet and unable to sleep through the night as the rain fell inside as well as outside.

Neither one of the girls had any sewing skills but what they did have was determination. Their first few weeks were a trial for everyone. It was hard for them to sew even a straight line. They earned a few riels but not much. And then I let it be known that if their skills did not improve dramatically, they would be out of a job. Several of the workers lived together and invited the girls to share their home. Each night they worked with the girls. As the orders increased, the pressure was on to work hard. Then one Friday, there was a lot of chatter and laughter. I walked through the building and both girls were standing in the hallway looking very distressed. I asked what was going on. The girls were struggling with their pay for in their minds they had been drastically overpaid. They had never seen so much money in their lives and they wanted to give some back. Everyone was enjoying their disbelief. We were all deeply touched with their thankfulness and joy when they realized the money was all theirs. What a way to celebrate our tenth anniversary!

I traveled with the staff to meet two groups of families in one of our new districts, Kirivon. Now Kirivon was one of those places that I do not rush to visit because the roads were a bit bone jarring to say the least. The request had been presented in August but it took me three months to find the time to come. Srei, Tharry, Phon, Cheiring and Pow were all delighted. Actually Cheiring and Pow were a bit nervous for they are relatively new staff and I had a reputation of asking the hard questions.

Both groups were very poor, with their main source of income was from carving bricks from volcanic rock. It was an onerous task requiring much skill and strength. An improper sized brick would not be purchased. An average family could chip out five blocks a day earning on average 2500 riels or roughly 55 cents per day. Their houses were made from scrap thatch, their clothing bare and their food subsistence.

As we stood talking about their labors, they proudly showed me their new pick-axes and hammers they had bought from their savings. The staff, as usual, didn't tell me why they had wanted me to come so badly; they waited until I was properly enamored with these people. Then they said to the leader of the group, show her what you want. We walked to the side of the road and they pointed at something and asked if Tabitha would help them clear their reservoir. I looked for the reservoir but found it hard to see as it was covered with bush and thistles. I took a few tentative steps in the right direction and sure enough there was a pit about eight meters square with water in it. I asked the story. The families told us how this had been dug by their grandparents 60 years ago to keep water for the village. There was a second one a half kilometer away. The reservoir had fallen into disuse despite having water in it. Things had fallen in to spoil the water. I asked what things? People were not so anxious to answer, children, cows they murmured.

I didn't say much for I had an inkling of what had really happened. The Pol Pot years tended to use such spots as places to dispense with those they murdered. I turned and asked Cheiring and Pow what they thought. They just shuffled their feet and looked away. Srie looked at me with beseeching eyes, please understand, she begged. I asked the people, why do you not clear the bush, why do you allow it to be this way? Again, much shuffling of feet, obviously, my inkling was right. What do you need, I asked? Money, they said, money to put cement and steps and to drain the water and to clean it. How much, I asked, $300 they said for each reservoir.

I said little, kept looking at the bush and picked a few thorns out of my leg. I said, okay, this is the deal, you must clear the entire bush and the water and you must do this yourselves. When you have done this, then Tabitha will give you the money. If you do not do this then Tabitha will give you nothing. The leader, a wizened old man, agreed to do this. You have one week to clear and clean both reservoirs, I said, I will see what you do.

The next week, the staff proudly showed me the pictures of the cleared reservoirs and I released the money. The following week, the staff returned with laughter in their eyes, Oh Janne, you should see it: the cement and the poles, and the ceremonies. They are no longer afraid of the ghosts for they are laid to rest; they are no longer dirty, they can now wash; they are no longer thirsty, they can now drink. It was so very good.

I ended the year with the regular Christmas celebrations and a special visit to Prey Veng. We went to see the wells we had put in memory of my mother and the houses that had been built in her memory.

It was a difficult visit in some ways. Our first stop was to a community in a district that we started about six months ago. The surroundings were very beautiful. The fields were all colors of green, filled with what I thought was good rice. We started talking to some of the families. There were only moms and children and a couple of grandfathers there. I asked how things were and they started to share their stories. All of the husbands had left and went to the city because the beautiful fields were full of useless stalks of rice. There had been very little rain and they didn't have wells. The rice stalks bore no fruit. They were very hungry and the husbands had to go and find work in the city so that they could survive until next year. The village had 126 families: 25 of the families were children who were orphaned, whose parents had died of AIDS and five more families had parents who were now sick with this disease.

I was sad when I left that village, wondering how we could help these people. Our next stop was ten kilometers away at a village where we had worked for the last two years. This was the village where we had placed my mother's well and built six houses a short eight months before. Here the families were excited to see us. The ingenuity of the villagers was amazing. As the contractor was drilling the well, the families asked him to drill a second well two feet away but with no pump. They paid for this with their savings. A few weeks later they had saved enough as a group to buy a diesel pump. They hooked the two wells together and then turned on the pump and the water just gushed forth.

These families had never grown rice because they never had water. They took us out to their fields. We were stunned as each family had grown three-month rice twice in the past six months and the yield had been very good. They were now starting their third planting, something that had never been done before in the district, a historical moment. Then they showed me the vegetable gardens that each family had. The gardens had a variety of vegetables and spices growing. What was so very good was that the husbands were all there, doing the work. It was a wonderful way to end the year with new challenges and rejoicing in what had been achieved.

# 2005

The year started out with a reminder that life is short and not to be taken for granted. The tsunami that hit the neighboring countries of Thailand and Indonesia caused us to pause and think about those families who had just suffered tragedy in their lives. The waters in our ponds and wells rose and fell that day, initially causing panic in several Cambodian provinces as people tried to come to grips with what had happened. At first, they believed that there were evil spirits and then as the news spread of the earthquake and the resulting tsunami, people settled down. Our thanks to our God for reminding us, yet again, to make each day of our lives count, to appreciate the gift of life, to remember to say I love you to all around us.

It was also a reminder of how silly donors sometimes are. I got a phone call from one of the agencies involved in the provision of AID to these countries. The request was sincere, would I like to have a container of breast implants. I was dumbstruck and asked several times what the container was full of? Breast implants! I actually had a crazy moment when I thought that perhaps we could use these to build someone a house. Thankfully wisdom prevailed and I turned down the offer.

We were privileged to open up a new office in the province of Kampot. My site visit to approve the office was an eye opener as to just how many ways people managed to make a living in this country. We visited salt fields near the border, a thousand families making a meager living from gleaning salt from flooded fields. The road, as usual, left a bit to be desired, and the poverty was so very striking. What bothered me most was that at the end of the day no one had any water to clean their salt encrusted bodies. Life can so be hard.

For Cambodians, having a house to die in, is one of their most sacred needs. Over the years, all of the staff were able to purchase land and a home. Every time there was a serious threat of insurrection and war the prices of land and house tumbled and every time, I would encourage my staff to buy. Most of them did so but the only one who didn't was Heng. Our poor Heng was deeply traumatized by the past and every sign of trouble put him on edge. See, he would tell me, it's happening again. It wasn't till the last few years that Heng had saved enough to buy but by that time, land and houses were truly expensive.

This year, we heard of some land near Phnom Penh that was for sale so Tuit, Ming Wan, Soklieng and I went to take a look. It was not far from the city, electricity and city water were to be installed, the land was legitimate with legal papers and the price was so very cheap at $400 a lot, compared to the inflated prices of land around the country. Should they buy? The lot was not large and although relatively inexpensive, two of the women still needed to borrow money from Tabitha, to be repaid within ten months out of their salaries. Could they buy they begged? Yes, I said. Their joy and their deep-seated contentment was always a lesson for me, a reminder that our staff, all of them, needed a place to call their own.

Life wasn't always dramatic. The staff have a fine-tuned sense of humor at the ridiculousness of life. We laughed a lot. I had a trip to Siem Reap early in the year. All of the staff were there, even Kameak, our manager from Banteay Meanchey. This was unusual so I knew that something was up. They all giggled and finally said that Kameak wanted to marry! He was 34 years old and he'd wanted a family for so many years. Now his time had come. He was a rather shy man but like so many of the staff, he saw me as his surrogate mother. I asked all the motherly questions: what was the girl like? She was younger than him but she was ugly! She was a hard worker and she liked his dreams for the families he worked with. She would make a good wife. Ani got the giggles for she was now to be his surrogate mother, like I was for her marriage. Ani said, he has a picture of the girl but he wouldn't show it, instead Kameak showed it to Zach, Ani's 6-year-old son. Kameak needed to borrow money for the wedding itself.

I looked him in the eye and told him if I can't see her picture then I can't help you. Ani squeezed herself with delight and Kameak knew when he was beaten. He gave us a quick glimpse and I said that was not enough. Kameak finally let us hold her picture. She was not ugly at all but Kameak believed in the old customs of Cambodia. If he had said something nice about the girl, then something bad would happen. Kameak, like everyone I knew here, was afraid of wanting good things. His life had been too hard. I smiled and he gave me a real hug. Kameak will have a family to call his own.

Khmer New Year brings out the occasional electricity problems. I'm not sure why, whether it's because the country shuts down as everyone goes to their home villages, including those who work on electricity or it's because the weather is always at its hottest and the electricity use is at its peak. Whatever the reason, my home was without electricity for two days and nights, an experience that tested me to the core of my being and resulted in a schizophrenic personality that swung from utter despair to elation and unusual bonhomie to one and all when restored.

I received a disturbing phone call from one of the provincial governors where a team had built houses. Someone on the team had given a few trinkets to several village children but there had not been enough for all the children. Jealousy, exacerbated by poverty, had caused a furor amongst the villagers. I needed to come and take back the trinkets so that peace could be restored. What a horrible day that was. The governor was there on my arrival and gave me a much-deserved dressing down in front of the villagers. After I was appropriately humbled, I asked the haves to return their goodies so that they could become have nots like the rest of the children. It was a sobering hour for everyone involved. At the end, all the children gathered around me in commiseration of my humility, a trait that is common in Cambodia and which makes me love them so much. I started the fun by throwing water on several of them and the afternoon ended with a full out water fight, which I lost of course. After that episode I became an ogre with house building teams. DO NOT GIVE ANYTHING TO ANYONE! You don't know the problems you can cause, especially for me!

I had a site visit that brought tears to my eyes. Srie, Tharry, Pon, Pow and Cheiring asked me to visit a village in Kirivon. The trip was long and hard and had several roads that defied description. We had received our first rainfall after six months of drought in Phnom Penh and felt refreshed but the farther we drove, the less the elation as the drought in the countryside left us feeling bereft for the people we saw.

We arrived in Kirivon and were met by several hundred people. They were gathered around the only well in the area where all kinds of containers were lined up in a row and people were bickering with each other over whose turn it was. Many had been waiting for several hours to get their water.

The water was good for washing but was unsafe to drink. I asked, where then do you get your drinking water? From another well about three kilometers away, they answered. How many families does that well serve, I asked? 489, I was told. We must use this well for water for washing and cleaning and we must use the other well for drinking water. Most of us spend up to five hours per day, just getting water. That is why we asked you to come.

They led me to the back of the village and there they showed me what they had in mind. In front of me was a reservoir that they had dug. There were 226 families in this village and every night after work 201 families sent a member of their family to help dig. The original reservoir had been dug over 60 years ago by their great-grandparents and then came the Khmer Rouge years and everyone was forced away, and many were executed. Most of the families had returned since then but the reservoir had filled with dirt and only a small pond remained. The drought each year had caused much grief for these families. They had heard about the other two reservoirs that we had helped with in 2004 so they only knew that we expected them to do their fair share of work before we would help. They had not seen the other reservoirs because these were 50 kilometers away. They had begun to dig where the top step was visible and as they dug, the steps kept going down. They dug three meters and still the steps went down.

Our staff, Pow and Cheiring, had taken the leader to the other reservoir to see what we had done. The leader came back to the village and shared the news with the families. We must provide the stone, he said, and then Tabitha will help with the cement and sand to make the walls. This was good, the villagers said, because that is what we do, break stones into gravel and we sell the gravel to others.

Now, they not only divided into teams to dig, but also divided teams into going into the surrounding hills to collect stones for the walls. Even the children were part of the teams, doing an adult portion of digging and carrying. The children refused to stop doing their share of work while I stood with the elders and we talked. I asked the children why they worked so hard. They giggled and shyly hid their faces. A tiny ten-year-old finally spoke. We have no water and our parents work so hard. We can do this to help all of us and we can see how much we have done. Next year, we will not be thirsty and our parents will not be so tired.

The elders, staff and I talked about how big this would be. The elders said we want to dig another two meters, making it eight meters deep and we heard that you wanted us to make it square so it will be 18 meters long and 15 meters wide. That way, we will have water all year round. Will the water be good, I asked? They replied that the water would come from the hills around us during the rainy season and it was very good water for drinking. The cost would be $600 to make the wall all around for the wall would be one meter high. It would keep the reservoir clean. How long would it take to finish, I asked? By June, we will have it done.

I thought about the days of no electricity and water that I just had; the heat and the inability to do anything about it. Here was a village of people who were doing something about it. They were doing so with sacrifice and hard work, and they were doing so together, from the youngest to the eldest, and they were doing so with joy. Could we start this week, with the wall? Yes, you can, I said. The staff and elders remained behind to purchase the cement and sand and the children returned to collecting stones and I returned home. I thought that this is what it is all about. The reservoir was completed several months later. It has provided life-giving water to so very many ever since.

There were times this year when I didn't feel so well physically. It was my menopausal year. I didn't have funds for a doctor so I just lived with the ups and downs associated with the change of life. Site visits were a panacea to my discomfort. One particular bad week I went on a site visit to meet with 60 families who had been in the savings program for about a year. The families wanted very much to show me what they had done. I went rather reluctantly because I was not feeling well, I was on a special diet and my body hurt and ached. The visit pulled me out of my self-pity. As we went from home to home, people ran to show me the things that they had bought, things they thought they could never have, things, they said, that only rich people can buy.

At one house, Ly's family hurried to show me the pots and pans they had bought. Oh, said Ly, now I can cook. Sopheak grabbed her clan and she showed me her dishes. Her sons were so very proud, these are not plastic, said the oldest, real porcelain, just like the rich. The family next door said, but we have even better, we have drinking glasses. I marveled at how good it is to take joy in these things.

The widowed families were not to be outdone. A single father showed me the sleeping mat that he and his children were sleeping on. Now the floor is not so hard, chirped a daughter. A widowed mother proudly showed me a sack of rice that she had bought. The baby will not be hungry this month, she said. An old woman showed me her ice chest that she had bought, it will help to keep my daughter's medicine longer, she said.

My self-pity was rapidly disappearing for it was being replaced by wonder. What joy, what pride each family had. Not to be undone, a family showed me their new mosquito net; we can all be safe now from malaria, said the mother, we all can sleep under it. Another mother proudly showed me the pigs and chickens they had bought. This year, she said, we will be rich for my pig will help us to buy many things. And yet another proudly brought out the chair they had bought. Now grandma can sit in comfort, laughed the grandson. A young man showed me the blanket he had bought, we will no longer be cold at night, he said.

The visit was a long one, sixty families are a lot to see. Each had their dream to share with us, each was so very proud of what they had accomplished. Each shared about their next dream to achieve. I came home exhausted but refreshed. The diet was no longer a burden for I had a choice of whatever I wanted to eat. My water was cold because I had a fridge, my bed was always soft, and I had enough blankets. I marveled and was thankful for these families who had taught me so much, to be thankful and to take joy in all the things that I took for granted.

Like most parents, I worried that Miriam would learn to appreciate and be grateful for what she had and that she would learn to be compassionate with those who are not as fortunate as her. Sometimes I got a glimmer that my desire was taking fruit.

Our adopted Cambodia House children returned for another house build. This year there were 16 children with their siblings and parents in tow. For the first time, Miriam, my six-year-old daughter found a soul mate, seven-year-old Chanta. Their histories were very similar as both girls were born positive for the HIV virus; both girls had lost their parents to AIDS; both girls were adopted by single moms. The other adopted children were all in their early teens. It was an honor and delight to see how well they were doing and how they absorbed the girls as their little sisters into the group.

Our first days together followed the normal pattern, getting acquainted and re-acquainted and then I did orientation. This time the difference was marked. The young people understood what was being said about what happened historically in Cambodia; an understanding of those years began to awaken. It was such a privilege to be a part of that awakening. The adults answered as many of their questions as we could. Their visit to the Genocide Museum and the Killing Fields brought a new awareness to each of them.

The next day we were off to Kompong Som and the beach, a four hour journey that left us all ready to splash in the waves. Unfortunately, the rains had come early and the surf a challenge for swimmers.

The next morning, we left for our village. The trip took an hour and a half but nobody minded as there were lots of people to talk to. We arrived at our destination ready to work and everyone began to hammer with the early morning burst of energy. Suddenly the skies burst forth with rain and wind. At first, we all tried to shelter to keep dry but it soon became clear, that no houses would be built if we did that for too long. So, one by one the workers came out and renewed their efforts.

For the first time, the young people formed their own group to build a house, with no assistance from the adults. As the wind and rain lashed their bodies, they hammered the walls and the floors. Miriam and Chanta rapidly became cold and were shivering. With the cold came the need to go potty. The latrine was a very simple affair off in the field. Both girls were very nervous but managed to walk gingerly through the mud and the rice paddies to relieve themselves. Once they knew they could do it, it became an hourly adventure. Two little girls, walking hand in hand, always one standing on watch so that no cows would come near, while the other did their business. Both girls spent much of the time watching the children of the village and their families.

At the end of the day, the young people had completed their first home. Everyone was soaked to the skin and filthy from the mud in the rice paddies. We went back to the beach to once again to swim in the rain.

The next morning, Miriam woke to very wet and muddy shoes. She began to cry, "I am not poor mom! Poor people have only one pair of shoes and they are always wet and they never have dry feet. They only have one set of clothes and those are all wet and dirty and now they can't get their clothes dry. I hate living like a poor person, she cried, I hate it that they are poor." I was speechless. Miriam with all her exposure to those less fortunate than her, had never expressed how bothered she was with this. I said nothing, just helped her put on her shoes as she needed to cry. And then a big hug and a tickle and she went forth to another day of building in the wet and cold.

In the bus trip down to the village, Chanta began to cry. She was crying because the people were so poor, they had so few clothes and little food to eat. It wasn't fair. It could have been her. Chanta's mother couldn't say much either; she held her close and let her cry. And then together, we talked of other things so that Chanta could regain her composure. Then Chanta went forth to another day of building in the wet and the cold.

Miriam and Chanta did well that day, no complaining, hammering nails like big people. The latrine was still their fascination, the village children an education. The young people built their second house. They did it with humor and compassion for each other. They beat the adults. They were a proud group. I could say with great pride, well done, well done.

When we returned to Phnom Penh, we took the girls to the orphanage where they came from. We came laden with toys made by some volunteers and clothes the girls had outgrown. Sister Maripol was delighted to see them. She took them by the hand and showed them off to the others and then she prayed with them.

Chanta's mother and I were privileged that week to see our girls grow in wisdom and strength, to develop the values we hold so dear. The girls' desire was that one day no child in Cambodia would be poor, no child would have wet shoes or wet clothes. Something that I too pray for.

I became aware of the lack of medical care for many people in Cambodia. Chanthou had her second ectopic pregnancy. It had burst while I was out of town on a site visit. She walked around with the problem for several days. I was really upset when I learned about it. How could you walk with such pain and discomfort I asked her? She hung her head and said you were not here to talk to when it happened. I didn't know what to do until my fever was very high and the staff took me to the expat clinic. They gave me medicine for my infection. I no longer want my own baby, she said, I am too old. Can you help me adopt a baby, one just like Miriam?

Several months later, Chanthou adopted a baby girl. Like Miriam, she named her Rosa after my mother. Several other staff also adopted baby girls; all named a version of Rose. Several families in the neighborhood we lived in adopted baby girls too, again all named a variation of Rose, after my mother. It touched me to the core of my being.

Heng came one night to my home. He was in tears. His wife had given birth to a son but he had died. The hospital didn't tell Heng or his wife of the baby's death, they just cremated him along with the rest of refuse in the hospital. He was heartbroken. So was I. He was not a young man anymore, nor was his wife. They had had a baby girl two years before and she was gorgeous, a boy would have kept his lineage going. We cried and held each other for a long time that evening.

---

We had several high government officials come to one of our housebuilding sites. Menrouen was determined that these officials knew what Tabitha was doing. The Minister of Agriculture was very impressed with the Savings and Water Program, the Minister of Education was profuse in his praise.

Menrouen had told them about the House Building program but, like Menrouen, they thought that local contractors built the houses and the teams just came to see what had been built. Their excitement and disbelief at seeing foreigners with hammers in hand, sweat pouring from their bodies, finishing these houses had an impact that is rare. "Foreigners don't do physical labor," I was told, "you know they are all tourists; we have never seen anything like this" I will be honest; I had an attack of pride which rapidly developed into a sense of humbleness and thankfulness for all the volunteers who had come and stood with our people here.

It was not only the prominent officials who were impressed. The local village chief had mocked the villagers for believing in us and for believing in themselves. His harsh words and mockery were something that Pon, Srie and Tharry had borne with good grace for several years. When we had arrived with the officials, the village chief had hidden himself in fear and shame. Our visit was short and then we left. The volunteers remained and built the houses. The chief came out of hiding and he didn't know what to say but Srie did, she made him laugh and asked him to join. The chief, like so many others here, had learned that people can be very hurtful. The Khmer Rouge taught him to lose faith in all people but the staff's faithfulness over the past years, the work of the volunteers and Srie's open arms taught him that maybe Pol Pot was wrong. He joined our program that week.

Water Festival came with several million people arriving in Phnom Penh. I loved it because it meant that the country was at peace and that people could come to the big city and marvel at all its offerings. They all had opportunity to see the Royal Family, to see the Prime Minister and his cabinet; to be a part of the cheering that came with the dragon boat races: each province, district and commune had a boat. So much to cheer about.

I also hated water festival when we had house building teams in town and the logistics of moving the teams in and out of the city was a nightmare. Often teams were stranded in the throngs of people and traffic couldn't move. I hated it for the staff who needed to work during this time: orientation, sales, and more logistics kept us in a constant state of anxiety and grumbling.

In the midst of the busyness and grumbling, one of our Cottage Industry sewers walked into my office. She was very nervous. She stood before me twisting her hands. I asked her what she wanted. She shyly turned and presented me with her family of four boys and three girls, all of whom were twisting their hands and giving me scared glimpses through downcast eyes. Each face tried desperately to hide little smiles. Each child was wearing new clothes. How beautiful. Their eyes were shining then there was a giggle from the smallest and it became infectious. The sewer said softly, my children will celebrate Water Festival this week for the first time ever. I wanted to come and show you the clothes that I could buy them. Do you not wish to join them, I asked? She shook her head, no she said, tonight I will join them. Today, I want to work and earn enough money so that next week I can pay for each one of my children to go to school. I am so blessed, she said, I never thought this would happen.

I returned home and stood on the street with Miriam and watched as so many people had come to celebrate. So many people were in ragged clothes, clutching a few riels in their hands, so many who walked for hours just to be a part of the celebration. I watched and saw the children stare at all the many new things to see. I watched as they tried to decide what little tidbit of food their money could buy. Miriam's hand was in mine and she was staring. She was watching a young girl with a little one on her hips snatching scraps of food off the food stalls. Miriam asked me, can I spend my pocket money on whatever I want? I said yes. She went to the owner of the food stall and ordered rice and fish, soup and chicken and a fruit shake. I asked her if she was hungry. Her face was ashen but she said nothing. Instead she went to the girl and took her by the hand. She made the girl sit on a stool and the little one got her own stool as well. The little one couldn't sit still as her bottom beat a tattoo on the stool. The girls ate and ate. Miriam didn't move as tears slipped down her cheeks. She said: I am so happy mom, that God gave me you as my mom. Miriam touched my soul as we quietly slipped through the crowds that night.

The year ended with a visit to Kampot and our families living with AIDS. Srie, Ti, and Mara, our staff there had asked me to come and see how our ten families living with AIDS were doing. The drive out was beautiful although some of the roads were not so beautiful. We walked through rice fields to meet these families. There they were in a clearing, a member of each family standing and waiting. As we began to talk, I shared Miriam's story with them, how her mother had died of AIDS, how Miriam had tested positive for the HIV virus. I showed them her picture and one of the men said, my daughter was put up for adoption when my wife and I knew we had AIDS. We were saddened by his announcement but it opened the doors to be able to share.

Their story was one of poverty and loneliness. Each of these people owned just a small plot of land, not large enough to grow rice, not large enough to feed their families. Each husband had left to work on the Thai border and in the long absences from home, had slept with taxi girls and contracted AIDS. In the several months when they could be home each year, they had passed on the virus to their wives. All of them fell very ill. Their neighbors held them in scorn, they feared them, and would no longer allow them to be part of their communities. Their children were taunted at school, to a point where they no longer attended school. They were unable to work in the markets, and so they began to starve.

Ti was a volunteer in our program in Kampot at the time (later he would become staff and then manager) when we had started there two years before. He had asked Srie to come and meet with these families. Srie did, and they joined our Savings Program. They couldn't save much but Tabitha talked to them and this was enough to get them started. All of them had started on retroviral drugs given by an AIDS NGO but the drugs were not enough. The continued isolation from their community, their inability to feed themselves, kept them in despair.

After a year, Srie and Ti decided to install three wells near the homes of three of these families. The families were too poor to pay even the small amount of money required by us. Things changed dramatically for them. Each family began to grow vegetables near their homes. It was amazing to see: one meter for limes, a meter for morning glory, several banana plants, mango trees, guava trees, chili peppers, sugar cane, etcetera. Each fruit or vegetable had its allotted space of a meter or two. Soon they were earning and eating on a daily basis and they began to be able to purchase simple things such as pots and pans, dishes and glasses, blankets and mosquito nets.

But the thing that changed the most was the gift of water to their neighbors. Clean water was available three kilometers from their homes but now the wells brought clean water to within 50 meters of their neighbors. They came and asked our families if they could also use the water. The families gave their blessings and with the gift of water came reconciliation and forgiveness. All our AIDS families were now an integral part of the community, their children were once again in school, no longer being taunted.

I asked them if they were angry with their neighbors. No, they said, for Tabitha gave us love. We were so long without love but now we give our love to our neighbors. The water is plentiful and clean and cool and there is so much love to share. We can provide for our families every day, we can share with our neighbors every day; we can tell others how to get help every day. There are 600 of us in this district and we all need your love and to share this love with others.

I then asked, are you afraid of dying? They answered with joy, no we used to be afraid of dying, it took all our energy just to get through each day but now, with the wells, each day we think of what else we can grow, what else we can teach, what else can we share with others around us.

What a wonderful way to end the year.

# 2006

This year my sister and her husband came to visit for the month of January; a rare occasion, and one that Miriam and I celebrated with thankfulness. One of the questions they asked was how do we decide on where to work, a question often asked by our many visitors. Let me share how the process worked to open up in our newest province of Svay Rieng this January.

Part of the vision of Tabitha Cambodia was to reach out to the very poorest throughout every province in Cambodia. During our annual staff meetings in July, Phat our manager in Prey Veng asked for permission to open in Svay Rieng this program year. We all had heard stories of the poverty of this province so the staff gave him the unanimous support to investigate the possibilities.

Phat, like all my staff, knew they needed each other's support to convince me and to receive my permission to open in a new area. In December, I was invited by Phat and his staff, Ponluck and Choeun as well as Srie, Heng and Soklieng to please come and see the work in Prey Veng. I knew in my heart it was going to be one of those days.

They brought me to a village of Prek Sneu, an area that I had seen two years before. The poverty had been agonizing to see then, with people full of despair, little income or food, and pain and suffering etched in the faces of young and old. This time, there was no pain as the faces were etched in joy and in anticipation of what they had wanted to show me. A team of house builders from our local international school had come and built houses there two years before. We had put in three wells and the families had put in another two. One after another, the families showed me their work. For the first time in remembered history all the families had grown three crops of rice. Half the families were raising pigs while others raised ducks and everyone had chickens. They had formed groups of five families and each group had set aside a quarter hectare to grow vegetables. Most remarkable of all was that each family had dug their own private fish pond. They were all raising fish, 1500 in one pond, 2000 in another, 1300 in yet another. Fish were cheap during the rainy season but became very expensive during the dry season when the water from the wells kept the ponds full.

I laughed at their joy and asked how much income they made each day. The average was 10,000 riels a day, about $2.50 per day and they had all the food they needed. What was wonderful to see was that the men folk were all home, working hard to make a better life. Their smiles said it all.

And then the staff took me to Mesang District which was on the border with Svay Rieng. Here we met the village chief and as we walked through his village the poverty was painful to see. The houses were decrepit, the children were malnourished and dirty, the women with downcast eyes and the men, well, the men had all left to find work on the border with Thailand. Then we saw what we had seen before in Prey Veng. There was a car with its trunk open and women and children gathered around. In the trunk were gifts of clothes and pretty hair bands, enticement to take the children away to work on the border as sex slaves. We were deeply offended by what we saw. This, said Phat, is what we have in our new district in Prey Veng and then he pointed to a line of trees in the distance; that, he said, is Svay Rieng. In that area, there are more than 2000 families living in poverty. Please, may we start there? I looked back at the car and the torn expressions of need and despair on the faces of the mothers as they struggled to say no to the enticements and to keep their children. I said yes.

Ponluck was appointed the new manager in Svay Rieng and rather than take his annual holidays, he and Phat went and opened our newest province. In less than 6 weeks, Ponluck had enrolled 200 families in our savings program.

The AIDS epidemic was in full swing in Cambodia leaving entire villages without any adults between the ages of 20 to 40. It also affected us in Cottage Industry. Eighteen women living with AIDS had been trained by another NGO to make quilts. This NGO was unable to continue and asked Tabitha to take on these workers. I agreed. I talked with Chanthou and all the workers, explaining the situation of these women and that they would be coming to work at Tabitha. I was very fearful of the reaction of the current workers for AIDS was a frightening thing.

The day of the AIDS women arriving was a bit of a torment for me. I wasn't sure how they would be received. I should have known better.

Chanthou, Sina, Che and the workers were busy all morning cooking food. When I brought the ladies in around noon, Chanthou got up, gave the women a warm welcome and invited them to come and sit and join the others in a meal. I was in tears. Such kindness and grace were evident that morning. Before the afternoon waned, they had all become fast friends.

I asked Chanthou why? Why did all of our workers do this? She looked me in the eye and said, you don't understand, their story, their pain is our story, our pain! They are our sisters.

A year later, one of our AIDS women shared her story as we sat together enjoying some beautiful weather. She was born in Kompong Thom. When she was 14, she was sent away to live with her grandmother here in Phnom Penh. Grandma decided that she should be married and so she arranged a wedding with a man that she did not know and never loved. The marriage was an unhappy one and ended when she became pregnant with a child her husband didn't want. Her pregnancy was a short lived and tragic one. The baby was an ectopic pregnancy and so she was operated on. It required several blood transfusions, blood that was not tested for the AIDS virus.

Several months after the operation, she became ill. She had no money for doctors and she lived on the streets. A kind family picked her up and she was happy for a couple of years and then the illness returned. They brought her for tests and then decided she could no longer live with them but she could join a Women's Association. Srey Peu fell into a deep depression; she didn't want to do anything.

In 1996, she once again became very ill. Once again, she was tested and the truth was finally told to her. She had AIDS. It was a time when

AIDS was not yet talked about and people with AIDS were scorned. She no longer wanted to live. She ended up with other women living with AIDS. These women had no desire to do anything else and there was no help.

She married her second husband, a man also ill with AIDS. Together they went from job to job but people were frightened of her. Finally, she broke down and cried and as she was crying, Father Jim (the man I would have married if he wasn't a priest) found her. He brought her to another NGO and she learned how to sew. They gave her support for housing and medicine. She and her husband then adopted a baby girl who was born HIV positive but later negative and healthy.

And then, the NGO stopped the sewing program, and she came to Tabitha. She believed her life was over yet again. Her sewing skills were not very good but she persevered. At first, she earned very little money but her skills improved and now she earns $200 a month.

She came to thank us and she wanted to say how much she loved her life. She said, I have finally come home, you are my mother and Tabitha staff are my brothers and sisters. I have life again. Srey Peu is still with us today and now earns $400 to $500 a month.

One of our biggest problems was how to ensure that all our workers had work year-round. With the arrival of our AIDS ladies, this was threatened if they all started to sew silk. Our answer was innovative. One of the issues in House Building was that the family receiving a home was cold at night. The house moved the families off the ground to three meters high, allowing the wind to circulate freely through the floor boards. I decided to solve two problems at once. We had the AIDS ladies produce quilts for families receiving houses.

These quilts would be hand embroidered squares sewn together. Now our embroiderers also had long-term work. The payment for these blankets was included in the cost of materials to construct a home paid by the volunteers. For the families receiving the homes, this quilt was presented by the volunteers at the end of house building with a ceremony and gift that were and are touching for all concerned. We no longer had complaints from families about how cold they were.

There were new problems with house building. The availability of materials, especially wood needed for the sides and frame of the house, was being restricted by the government. In a number of areas, wood became very scarce and so we had to make some difficult decisions. In some of our projects we decided to use bamboo for the floors. Bamboo was a local material which had some attributes that were attractive. Bamboo was durable, it was locally available and it had a bit of spring in it that made sleeping a bit softer. For the teams that needed to do bamboo floors, it was another story. It required thousands upon thousands of nails to complete one floor. This was excellent for teams with many people as it required a lot of labor. It was not so good for small teams whose labor was doubled.

We began the process of searching for an alternative for the wood walls. The answer was to use galvanized iron sheets that were becoming increasingly available and less expensive than wood. There were a number of colors to choose from. We decided to select green as green was the color of Tabitha. For the volunteers switching over to galvanized sheeting, it was a challenge. The edges of the sheets were sharp and could easily slice an unsuspecting worker. Nailing the sheets to the frame was another challenge. The wooden frame was made from second cut wood, scraps left over from cutting a tree into planking. This meant that the wood included offcuts of various trees, some soft wood which was easy to nail while other pieces were hardwood such as iron wood which was almost impossible to nail. For volunteers, this caused concern and suggestions that we buy better wood. That would easily have quadrupled the costs of the materials, a cost borne by the volunteers, a cost that would have stopped house building in its tracks as no one would be able to raise that kind of funding.

Despite all the challenges involved in the House Building Program, the houses had a huge impact on our people. We had a team come that built in Kompong Som. As they completed their houses, the houses were presented to the families. The spokesman of the families was a lady in her forties, 90% blind and raising seven children. She said, "I have never lived in a house and I thought I never would. Now I have a home. You will not remember us over the years ahead but on the day that I die, it will be your faces that I see." The impact of the House Building Program was immense on both the receiver of the house and on the volunteers themselves.

Our project areas tended to be in areas where our staff had suffered under the Khmer Rouge regime. This year we had opened in Kompong Thom and appointed Apo as the manager there. I went to see our newest project area with Srie and Apo. Srie had come a long way over the years since she had joined Tabitha. She was now the head of Community Development and supervised all our development projects.

When Srie first started with us, back in 1996, Srie was a trembler as her whole body quivered and she was frightened of everything. Over time, she became a very confident and competent woman.

As we drove to our new communities, Srie asked if I would like to see where she had suffered during the Khmer Rouge years. I said, yes, I would like to see. Over the years Srie had shared bits and pieces of the horror; now I learned so very much more.

We drove to the village of Slakor, in Stung District. As we were driving Srie said, this is the village where a thousand families from Phnom Penh were sent by the Khmer Rouge. Out of those families, only nine broken families survived. Mine was one of them.

We stopped at the house where her family was billeted with an "old family", a rural family who lived there and was considered good by the Khmer Rouge. Urbanites were billeted with the old people to ensure that they were being watched. "This is the house where 25 members of my family stayed, she said and only three of us survived, my mother, my sister and myself."

As we were talking an old woman came out of the house. This woman, said Srie, she saved my life. This woman watched the Khmer Rouge come and take away my father, then one by one, my six brothers, my uncles, my auntie and my cousins. They killed them all, one by one. The old woman heard that I was to die next. She felt great pity for me and she said, I will beg for your life, I will cry and I will beg but you, you must not cry, for if you cry they will kill you. For two days the old woman begged and cried for Srie's life. Srie never cried for she wanted to live. The Khmer Rouge relented and didn't take her. I thanked the old woman for her compassion and bravery as her own life was at stake for begging. She grasped my hand in both of hers, "They were bad times" the old woman said.

Srie's eyes were burning red but she did not cry as we spoke, instead she was animated. Come, Srie said, I will show you where they killed my father. Fifty meters away was a Wat. As we walked into the grounds, Srie pointed at three trees; these are the trees where they killed the babies. The Khmer Rouge would hold them with one leg and then bash them against the tree. I could not speak for such behavior was beyond my comprehension. Then Srie grabbed my hand and we walked to the Wat. In this building is where the people stayed for the last days of their lives. If the Khmer Rouge put you in this building, then you knew you would die.

She turned and ran down the stairs to an open pit fenced by bamboo; this is where the bodies were thrown. The government came and cleaned out all the bodies; some are now in Phnom Penh and some are in a Wat in a nearby village. She went on and described her father's death and those of her brothers and of her cousins and her uncles and then her final relative, an auntie. They came for my auntie, she said. My mother told my auntie, do whatever they tell you and don't cry and you might live. Two hours later a dog came running by their home with her auntie's skirt hanging from his jaw.

She turned and pointed to the building where they all were forced to eat together. They killed people every day, she said but one day of the week, they would kill very many. On that night, we were not allowed to come and eat and we would be awake all night long. I could not cry because then I would die. Then she pointed to another tree with an excavation beside it. This is where I saw my father's body or a part of it. When I came back for the first time in 2001, I could not sleep as I felt the souls of all the people who had died around me. Then in 2003, I came back and made a ceremony for my father and for my brothers and now I can sleep here. I come to this spot a lot. Tears were streaming from my eyes for her pain and the pain of so many others. Over 12,000 people died in this spot, Janne and then she cried.

When the tears were done, she continued with her story. She said: we heard that the Vietnamese were in Phnom Penh and chasing the Khmer Rouge away. The old lady came to my mother and said: you must go now for the Khmer Rouge are angry and they want to kill you and your daughters. The villagers gave us a lot of food and then brought us out to the main highway. Go, they said, or you will die. We went along with what was left of eight other families. Later, when the Vietnamese came to bring freedom, the old people killed all the bad Khmer Rouge, all the ones that had killed so many.

I lived, but I didn't know why. Now I do, Srie said. I live so that I can give life to others. I want to put a well in this village in honor of my father and one in honor of my brothers for the water will give life to so many others.

We left the Wat and Apo and Srie showed me several hundred families that we were now working with. The poverty was hard, but the spirit was good. We all want to live, she said. Srie got the wells to honor her family; life giving water in memory of those who had perished during that horrific time.

~

A miracle occurred this year, one that we thought would never happen. The story began last April during the Khmer New Year break and the Easter weekend. A couple of donors had arrived and they wanted to see Svay Rieng as a potential project that they would like to support. Srie, Soklieng, Ponluck and I took the folks out to see. When we arrived at the first village, I was once again struck by the meanness of poverty as family after family lived in houses less than two meters square, made of grass and nothing much else. The houses were unusually close to each other. It was Khmer New Year, a big holiday here in Cambodia. The children and adults swarmed around us, dressed in their best although much of the clothing was the wrong size, dusty and often with holes. They were happy to see us and we were happy to see them.

Despite this, the poverty was painful to see and in one of my moments I blurted out how disgusting it was to see people living in such squalor, living like animals. One of the village volunteers asked Ponluck and Srie what I had said and in a rare moment of honesty they told him what I said. They were standing in front of part of his village where in an area of 20 square meters, 14 families were living in poverty. There was no space, there was no privacy. He looked at Srie and Ponluck and said that he was ashamed that I had seen this.

Ponluck said that he should not be ashamed for we just wanted to help, to change all of this. If they could have wells the volunteer said then things might change. Srie spoke up, if you have a well, nothing will change as these families have no space and no land to grow vegetables or to raise animals. We cannot put in wells unless they can do things with the water to change their lives. Nothing more was said.

In May, local elections were held throughout the country. This volunteer was elected as village chief. His first task as village chief was to go up one level to the commune chief. He shared his story of our visit and he shared his desire to help his people but, he said, we need land. The commune chief listened and empathized and he gave land to the villagers, enough land that each villager could have at least 10 square meters.

The village chief returned to his families and he shared the good news. Out of the 14 families, 12 moved their shacks to their new land. They tilled the soil and planted their seeds and then they said to Ponluck and to Srie "Now we need a well." And wells they got; four for this group of families.

The staff and I arrived a month after all this took place. We visited with a family of six young orphans who were elated because they now had land and they could grow food. We visited a family with nine children, their house was still too small for everyone but they were all busy working the soil, even the baby. We talked with the widows who were already raising pigs. We chased after chickens with the family whose father was handicapped and whose mother was blind. We marveled at the land given by the commune chief, with land still waiting for 50 families to accept this gift.

They talked with the chief, amazed at his courage, amazed at his wisdom. He, in turn, talked of Ponluck and Srie and of their willingness to speak honestly. As the team left the village, the chief spoke again, this time, he said, I am not ashamed for you to come.

The staff came back with new wisdom. We must not give wells unless the families have enough land to earn from the water. We must not be silent; we must speak for land for these families. We must not give wells unless families can show us beforehand, that they can do things. We must give wells only to support three families in growing vegetables so that there is enough water and enough income to change their lives. Then they challenged me, "Janne, we want 1,032 wells next year, can we have them?"?" This challenge would become a constant refrain from all the staff.

We talked as a staff about what had happened, how the chief had gotten land for his people. Several months later, Ani and Vutha came back with similar stories. I got a phone call from Ani, Janne you won't believe this, she said. The commune chief has given land to fifty of our families. Vutha greeted the news with joy, for more than a hundred of our homeless families in Kompong Som had also received land. It was a miracle to be repeated many times over the coming years.

I had a very early morning phone call from Wolfgang Seitz and his colleagues, Ivy and Russ. They as a group were called Lotus Relief,. I had met all of them several years ago when they visited Tabitha. We had talked about the work we were doing. They sat in on an orientation for a house building team; they had visited several of our communities, saw the savings and wells and had bought numerous cottage industry items. They had decided that they would sponsor our work. So, for a number of years they would give us a grant for the work.

The phone call that morning was strange to say the least. Wolfgang asked us all not to speak until he was finished talking. I want to give you a house, he said, a house to call home. I couldn't grasp what he was saying. I said; no, give us the money to build lots of houses for our families. No, he said, you don't understand, this is not about the people you work with, this is about you and my way of saying thank you. It was way beyond my comprehension and so I argued but he would not budge. I could not accept such a gift. I now understood how our families felt when they received a home from us. Grace, receiving without deserving, was so very difficult to accept. Finally, he capitulated, alright he said, we will give you money to buy a house and if something happens to you or you leave Cambodia, the house will be sold and the money we invested will be returned to us. The balance will be split between Tabitha and Miriam or you. Would that be acceptable? This I could live with.

My head was reeling and so the search for a home began. Phnom Penh and Cambodia were just beginning a surge in development. I had seen roofs of new houses going up but I could not find the way inside this particular development. I renewed my efforts and finally found the entrance. It was all mud and dirt except for the model home near the entrance built on a street called Maple Street, a sure sign I thought! The construction of homes was going full tilt. There were a number of houses under construction, but there were still four houses left to be sold. Low was the superintendent of the company and he showed me all four. I wanted the one on the corner, the one that had a planned playground next to it, an empty street across from it and one neighbor on the side. Perfect I thought. Construction had not yet begun because Cambodians believed that it was bad luck to have home at the end of the street. I had no fears of such things and so the deal was made.

Of course, all the staff were involved in this process. There were several small row house developments nearby. Soklieng and Srie both wanted to live nearby and so they sold the homes they were living in and bought a row house near to each other and not far from where I would live. It was all so surreal.

The construction of my house began. The development company had its own contractors. Sadly, they were not very good at it. Soklieng came to me and said the workers wanted me to buy a chicken, a live one that they could use for a ceremony. They needed to get rid of the spirits that were roaming through the house. I had been complaining to Low about the quality of the work and had demanded that several walls be taken down inside the shell of the house. I was incensed with Soklieng's request as the only evil spirits were the workers themselves. She told me their story.

The day before, as the workers were approaching the site, they had seen a very small man all dressed in white. This little man was beckoning them to come. As they drew closer, this little man dressed in all white started to grow in height and continued to beckon them. When they got to the house, this now large man beckoned them to follow him inside. There he pointed at the many errors they had made in construction. Then he pointed at a pile of poop one of them had deposited in a corner. The man in white shook his head vehemently, no! Then he disappeared. The workers were terrified. I, on the other hand, couldn't stop laughing. My guardian angel had revealed himself to the workers!

The workers did not get the chicken. Instead I talked with Low and said that I wanted him to build the shell of the house and little else. Low agreed immediately and refunded the balance left from the materials and construction of the house. I sub-contracted the work myself. The staff all knew skilled people and the work began. Every day I went and checked the progress and everyday Low would tell me what was wrong. Our electrician, a man I called Mr. EDC supervised everything and he insisted on quality. Finding the quality materials was a task in itself as stores that displayed floor and wall tiles would only have two or three tiles in stock. A new German company built the kitchen, western style.

Over the next four months, as the construction continued, Soklieng and Srie's houses were also being completed. It came time to paint. Soklieng asked me to come and see her colors. I was speechless: the walls were every color of the rainbow with bright reds, blues, greens, orange and purple. Did I like it? I couldn't say anything for it was her home. She was willing to share those colors for my home. I stammered and replied that I wanted just one color and I would decorate with color in each room. That was not the Cambodian way! Once my house was painted, Soklieng repainted her house and everyone admired it.

The last two months of this year were tinged with deep sorrow. Som, one of our longest serving staff, was a man who was suffering from heart and liver failure. Som had been ill for the past two years with active Hepatitis B. The doctor told him that he was in heart failure and he should rest and not work so he was sent home but his heart was not at peace for he felt ashamed that we continued to pay him his salary.

Ah, my Som, how could I not pay? It was like a marriage, Tabitha was, it was for better and for worse, it just happened to be a worse time for you right now. Remember when we first met, you, like all the staff, were suffering so terribly from post-traumatic stress syndrome. You could hardly move and how for the first six months I would leave a list of things for you to do and you did them without complaint. Remember how you slept downstairs in the garage and I slept upstairs in the stock room? We both felt safe as long as we were there together. Then House Building began and you came to life as you helped us with our teams, making them strong and feeling good about themselves. You spoke of how that gave so much meaning to your life. Then when Miriam came along you in your quiet way, made sure I did things the right way with her. When she was two, you taught her how to hold a hammer and to hit a nail. Three weeks ago her teacher sent home some work she had done for she had read a story about a fish who granted wishes to a man who had saved the fish's life. The question was asked, what would Miriam ask for if she had the fish. Her reply was a testimony to you for she said, I would ask for money. My mum and I work for Tabitha and we need money to buy lots of wood so that teams can build houses for all our families. You and I gave up working with the teams several years ago as it was time for the younger people to carry on.

You were older than most of the staff and your quiet wisdom gave so much to us. When the staff were upset about what would happen if something happened to me, you spoke and said, that Tabitha would go on because when I was on holidays, you all worked together to make it good. You always liked a good laugh; the bees in our trees were a good example of how you and I could get others to do things both of us knew was not so easy. Our parties were so much fun as you were the first one up dancing and the last to sit down. Every morning you greeted me with a quiet word and a cup of coffee. You always started my day right. I miss not having you here.

You had touched so many lives in so many ways for there were so many people who would not have grace in their lives if it were not for you. You were a model of grace and wisdom and quiet attention to all that needs to be done. The past year, you quietly cleaned every item in the store, making sure everything looked good. No one told you to do so, you just did it.

You were a model for me, your quiet dignity and strength gave me dignity and strength. You were the representative of all who give to us so that we can reach out as so many gave quietly and without expectation of reward simply because, like you, they had faith in us and in the families, we worked with.

I know not what the future holds for us, both but whatever the journey may be, I am with you in spirit and should you leave this life of sorrows then know, it won't be long before we will meet again.

Som was finally treated by expatriate doctors who prescribed the appropriate treatments for his ailment. After six months off, Som returned to work is still with Tabitha.

A number of very close friends were leaving Cambodia for good. June and Father Jim were just two of the many whom I called friends and compatriots. It was so hard.

I got a phone call one morning. Menrouen was dying. He was in the hospital and didn't have much time left. I rushed to the hospital and talked with a mutual good friend, Heng Touch. Menrouen and I had talked the day before; he seemed full of his usual life. Touch told me the story. Menrouen was used to sleeping with a bottle of water close to his bed. That night someone had accidentally placed a water bottle of clear insecticide beside his bed. Menrouen had woken and drank from it. He was now unconscious and close to death. I lay down beside him and held him. I knew that he knew I was there as he struggled to wake. I kissed him farewell. He was a very good man. I miss him so.

Touch carried on the wishes of Menrouen. Menrouen had wanted to make sure that issues with transporting wood for housebuilding would be resolved. Touch became our surrogate Menrouen but it was never the same; my friend was gone.

In my deep sorrow miracles happened to fill my heart. First, Sokha came up the stairs; she was a woman living with AIDS, contracted by doing the wrong kinds of things. Sokha was an outcast because of her behavior and she too, was scorned and talked about. She had lost her child, her home, her right to be part of a family. The price she paid for her lifestyle was high. That morning she came into my office holding a young girl by the hand. She walked in with trembling body and tears in her eyes: "This is my daughter whom I lost and have now found again; I thank you for you gave me work when no one else would and I now have respect again. I have reclaimed my child and I am full of hope."

Tharry came and showed me picture after picture of families who have worked their way out of poverty growing vegetables, something they never thought possible and the price for the vegetables was good at that time. These families had started planting before we would give them a well, a rule decided on and implemented by all staff. It was hard to believe in unseen water and yet these families had believed. In less than three months all these families had enough to eat, enough money to change that endless cycle of despair.

It was another year of mixed emotions, of joy and laughter, of unspeakable sorrow and renewed hope; of grace and mercy beyond description. Another typical year in my life.

# 2007

The year began on a positive note after a not so positive incident in December. We had an attempted armed robbery at Tabitha by our hired security people. They came in the middle of the night armed with guns and an AK47. For extra security, Som stayed within the building at night time to make sure that the guards could not enter the building. We also double locked our gate so the security guards within could not open the gate. It was good that we had done so. The armed men demanded to be let in the gate. Som heard them but did not respond. Instead he called the police, but when the calls did not go through as we only had landlines then, he called Soklieng and Heng who in turn called the police and gathered a number of friends to come and save the office. In the meantime, the armed men started shooting in the air which woke up the neighborhood. Several neighbors also tried calling the police but with no success. Within thirty minutes we had several hundred people surrounding the building which made the robbers a little nervous. They packed up their guns and left. We interrogated the guard. We phoned the security company and within hours they were all dismissed. No one was hurt but it was a stark reminder that not everything was as it should be in this land of sorrows.

It was after this threat that we revised our security protocol at the office. Now everyone had to have a Tabitha identification card which included a picture, name, and our official stamp. I had resisted this for so many years as I like to live in trust. I often hear the Biblical phrase that out of bad there is always something good. Our ladies living with AIDS found it very difficult to rent a place to live as people were afraid of them. Landlord after landlord turned them away because they had AIDS. The women couldn't keep their children, they couldn't have a family. Each night they found sleep in a shelter, not a place to call home, not a place to be free but a place to sleep.

When we issued the ID cards, miracles began to happen as all of our women found a place to rent. The landlords would look at the cards and see that these were women had work, had value. These were women who were worthy of being rented to. I shook my head in disbelief and then shuddered with joy. What had been such a terrifying experience had turned into a blessing that I would not have thought of. These women who thought they lost all now rejoiced as their children could come to a place called home.

In 2005, I wrote about two young ladies who had no citizenship in any country. The first time we paid them for their work, they stood in disbelief and wanted to give us some money back as they said it was too much money. Their parents were desperately poor and badly in debt because of medical problems. The young ladies were determined that the debt would be repaid. It took a year and that was done. In this last year, both young ladies had been able to send enough money for their families to rent land and to build a small home. This year, both girls are traveling home in April for the New Year's celebration but they need to cross borders without a passport which was very risky. Their new ID card gives them identity and now they can travel without fear, we want to celebrate life with our families, they tell me.

In the first month of this year, 65 of our families got a home from ten volunteer teams that came. I had met several of these families who last year had no hope. They were in despair because they had no papers and they had no land. Our staff worked hard to change that and land was bought and/or given with legal deeds. As the houses were being built, the family's hopes became reality. We are somebody, a woman told me, we are important.

I was getting increasingly frustrated with the progress of my house as my rented home had to be vacated by the end of the month and my toilets were not yet functioning, the house was not yet painted and the woodwork had just begun. I was assured that all would be well despite the fact that many of the workers had disappeared because of the Chinese New Year which is not an official holiday in Cambodia but because so many Cambodians have Chinese blood in their backgrounds, everyone celebrates anyway.

Frustrated, I went to visit some of the families that we work with. I met a 12-year-old boy with his family. He was laughing and his eyes were wide with wonder. His family's home was made of grass, it was very small; it had no electricity and no toilet, yet he was laughing. His family had just received their savings and for the first time in his young life, his mother bought fish sauce. All his life, his meals consisted of rice and salt, when there was enough money. He had begged his mother so many times to just buy a bit of fish sauce so that he could taste it. Fish sauce was, for the children, a sure mark of wealth, a story I would hear so many times. His mother relented and had bought a whole bottle. I asked him if it tasted as good as he thought. His eyes twinkled as he said, 'oh, I can't open it yet! I want to wait and dream what it tastes like for I have wanted this for so long so I just want to hold it in my hands and look at it for a few days." This 12-year-old boy made my frustration seem insignificant.

We had a team come and build 20 houses in one of our newest projects. On their return, several of the team members were frustrated by the nails they had bent. They told me they were ashamed of what they had accomplished. I shook my head and laughed, we, the perfect people, wanting to give the perfect house, to people who see miracles in the homes they have received.

The families who have received these houses have learned that we are not perfect; they have learned that we are the same as they, for we too, make mistakes. We are human. I saw my house with its crooked walls and its imperfect tiling, and I thought; this was my real home, because it fit the imperfect me with all its imperfections.

In preparation for our move to our yet unfinished home we cleaned out our collected belongings, clothes and toys that Miriam had outgrown. We gave some to the Sisters for the orphans they were raising. The little girls pranced around in their new dresses and the boys built their own imaginary homes from the plastic bricks. Sister Samantha smiled with pleasure and gave Miriam a hug for Miriam's life had its beginning in this home. Miriam begged me to take home a little brother, a boy who looked so much like her. For him, his home had been destroyed by an illness that took his mother. His father visited each week but he too, was very ill. We could not take him, for although his home was no longer there, the love of his father sustained him.

Miriam's begging did not cease and so I told her, no brother but would a dog be okay? Like all children, she promised faithfully to take care of the dog and it was a good alternative to having a brother. We visited Marie, a good friend, who raised purebred golden retrievers as a way of raising funds for her NGO for battered women. On that fateful day, we looked closely at all the puppies, one too energetic, and another one who liked to bite. We finally found our perfect dog, lying quietly asleep amidst all the furor. I should have known better! We named her Lucy. Within a month it became clear that our Lucy in the Sky was epileptic and fit right into our imperfect family.

Miriam's promise to take care of the dog lasted less than a month. Her morning chore was to pick up the dog's waste and put it in the garbage. We had a vacant field beside our home so Miriam's answer to disposing of the waste was to swing the plastic bag around her head and let the bag and its contents fly over the fence into the empty field beyond. We had several heated discussions about this practice but to no avail. Then one morning poor Lucy had diarrhea. Miriam's morning chore was always accompanied by a well-trained gag response. This fateful morning the excessive gagging brought me to the door to see what was going on. I arrived just in time to watch the plastic bag leave her hand and get snagged on the fence post. It burst and spread its contents liberally over my girl. Miriam's total disgust with the incident and my unstoppable laughter put a permanent end to this morning routine.

The move to our new house went unbelievably fast. All the staff and all the Cottage Industry workers came and cleaned and put everything in place. Heng made sure all the electronics worked. Everything was in place within a few hours. The only drawback was that we had no outside doors to prevent anyone from walking in. This made the household staff rather nervous. That first night was a very long night as Tuit, the nanny, heard ghosts everywhere. The next day, the doors were installed and two priests from the church came for dinner in exchange for doing a house blessing. This settled all the jittery nerves and it became our home for many years. What a blessing that was!

One of the questions so many people asked me was why are the people so poor? People always had the answers; too many answers to count; why don't they work, why don't they borrow, why, why, why? It was not just visitors with these questions; new staff also had the answers for the poor. It was and still is something that angers me. It angers me because we decide to answer and pass judgement on others without ever knowing or understanding what the reality of others really is. Instead, we play at being little gods and decide for ourselves what the issues really are. We are the barriers to helping others with our prejudices.

At our annual staff meeting, Tina, who was one of our new staff, had an attitude that left a bit to be desired. When I asked what problems people were having, his statement was rather blunt, "The people are lazy!" My older staff knew better than to use that word around me. I turned on him and asked him how he knew the people were lazy; did he ask them if they were lazy? Was he there with the people all the time to see if they were lazy? I mean what did he really know? The discussion moved rapidly to what is our biggest barrier to our work and just as rapidly came the answer from those who had learned before Tina: we are the biggest barriers to development! Our attitudes and our prejudices affect how we work with people. I made it clear to one and all that using the word lazy to describe people means that we are the ones that are lazy. We are lazy in our thinking; we are lazy in our answers. I expected each and every staff person to do what they said they would do without using the people as an excuse for not doing their work. Anyone who couldn't do this well, Tabitha was not the place for them to be.

The week after our meeting I travelled to Siem Reap to see the progress of the work there. I personally find poverty abhorrent. Poverty diminishes the dignity of people; poverty keeps people enslaved. We went to see Vath's project. It was in a district called Peak Sneng. Three years ago, we had driven down this dusty road looking at poverty that hurt. I was very saddened by it all and had said to Ani, our manager, I wish I had a million dollars; I would build them all a home. This comment Ani had kept in her heart. Now she was anxious to show me what they had accomplished. Do you remember Janne, this is the tree where we had lunch, do you remember, and this is the corner where you told me about the million dollars? Yes, I remembered. As we drove down the road, we talked of the number of families, 370 in all. As we were driving, I began to see houses; nice ones; others in stages of being built. As we talked, Ani and Vath pointed out this one and this one and this one and on and on. At first my mind would not accept what I was seeing; this couldn't be! But it was! We stopped at house after house; each one more beautiful than the last. My disbelief was apparent and I asked each family, how did you do this? Each family shared their story of how savings had changed their lives; how wells had enabled them to grow vegetables and to raise pigs, how each cycle they bought more materials to build their homes. How many families were involved in this? Vath answered 259 families. I turned to all of the staff and asked, why didn't you report this? We did, said Sarouen, this is called Repair House! I was stunned and so thankful. I guess the people here were not lazy after all.

Miriam was attending an international school in Phnom Penh. The school was a parent owned school, set up in 1992 for children of expatriates. The school had become an International Baccalaureate school and was growing very quickly. It was a school that tried to cater to the needs of every child. For parents who had children with learning problems, it became a policy to meet the needs of these children with special needs education.

The school needed to buy land to build a modern school. The board was made up of parents, parents who came and left Cambodia on an average of 2 to 3 year appointments. This made for a very transient and unstable board. Decisions were difficult as parents came from all parts of the world with a primarily Western mind set. The board was unable to make a new school happen so they asked me and Anthony, another long-term resident of Cambodia, to join the board.

I have a very pragmatic mindset. I forced the board to make a decision: will we buy land and build or will we not? It was an important question that would determine what our next steps would be for the school. It was decided that we would buy and build. It was the beginning of a three-year involvement with the school in this capacity.

Anthony and I spent many hours looking at available parcels of land. Phnom Penh was beginning to expand and thrive but was still a small city. The price of land was still affordable, so now was the time to buy. We finally chose 3.5 hectares just on what, at that time, was the outskirts of the city. It was an area consisting mainly of fishponds but scheduled to be a new development estate, a new suburb. To see the proposed site, we took the board members through some very muddy paths at the end of which they were faced with numerous fish ponds. We had to convince the other board members of our vision; of seeing in their minds the future development of the area. The owners of the land were wealthy, high ranking Cambodian families. Between the three families, they had eight children enrolled at the school.

The board agreed and the work of signing a contract began. We agreed to buy 3.5 hectares, fully land filled; with proper environmental concerns answered; including all the infrastructure needed such as electricity, water, sewage, fire lanes, etc. We also insisted on a fair and equitable settlement for the people currently living on the land. Being a parent-owned school, many parents went out to look at the proposed site and argued against the location. They were comfortable with the situation as it was. None of them trusted Cambodia or its people.

There were lawyers, bankers, architects and ambassadors involved in these meetings, Cambodians and foreigners alike. The final contracts were signed and we handed over three million dollars to seal the deal. Very Western, where paper is the honor, not a man's word. As the meeting drew to a close, I stood up and shook the hands of the men who had sold us the land. I looked them in the eye and told them, I trust you and expect you to honor this agreement. Very Eastern, where a man's word and hand shake was his honor. (This is why golf is so important in Eastern cultures, a place where deals are made and hands are shaken, and honor is respected. Paper deals are seldom respected.)

We also needed to hire a new School Director, a long process. We settled on a new Director who would be expected to bring the new school to fruition. It was probably the biggest mistake we made as the new Director had not been involved in any of the negotiations nor had ever served under a parent-owned school board.

The economic crisis was the topic of the day. It was a worldwide crisis and many of my friends were wringing their hands in fear. Some lost their jobs, others were downgraded. Families with children were no longer a priority with large international firms; singles cost less. The cost of housing and school fees affected so very many as their benefits and salaries were cut. We were afraid that the economic crisis would affect us deeply.

In the midst of this, tensions increased between the School Board and the land developers where the new school was to be built. The crisis meant that funding for the development of the new area would be delayed for a number of months, possibly years.

The new School Director was not used to working with a parent-owned school. A number of parents were very disgruntled on the way the land had been purchased. They were very upset that the developers were not beginning to work on the new school. It didn't help any that our elementary campus, situated on a prominent street in the city, was sold and we were given a six-month eviction notice.

Parents, the School Board and the Director were in an uproar. I asked that they give me one day to see if I could rectify the situation. I called a meeting with the owners of the land the elementary school sat on, the Director and myself. I asked if we could delay this purchase until such a time as the new school was built. They were a prominent family and within several hours we had a deal that would allow us to keep the elementary campus until the new school was completed. This cooled the passions for a few months. The Board was busy hiring architects and lawyers for the next phase. Again, being parent-owned and with a new Director, the process was fraught with competing opinions. At that rate, the school would never be built. We finally appointed a select committee to deal with these issues. I thought to myself, how grateful I am that I started Tabitha on my own, not swayed by competing opinions every moment of every day. Nothing would ever get done at that rate.

The building of the school had been postponed because of the economic crisis. The expatriate community in Cambodia was very transient and with the departure of long-time expatriates such as Anthony, new parents exerted more influence on our new School Director. For many of the expats that came to Cambodia, the nationals were not seen in a positive light; in fact, they saw Cambodians as corrupt and lazy. A number of these parents convinced the Director that the purchase of the land had been a big mistake; in fact, the $3 million set aside for the land had not yet been paid but was instead in the hands of Anthony and myself. That there was a signed contract and receipts had no effect on these people. At one of the board meetings, these people came to sort out the issue. Their insistence that I should be removed from the board was met unanimously by the current board with a resounding no but the seeds of dissent had been sown.

The Director and a number of board members decided to sue the developers; to bring them to court. I strongly advised against this move but was out-voted. I reminded all of them that we were guests in this country and treating high level people with disrespect and disregard was not a healthy thing to do. The vote to go down this path was in the majority. I do believe in the democratic system of boards so despite my dismay, I agreed to support the Board in their decision. I did request that I meet with the developers and explain the situation. Everyone agreed.

I explained to the developers the nature of our Board, being parent-owned and transient. I apologized profusely for what was about to happen and asked that they be patient with us in our naiveté. They agreed. In the meantime, the Director and several other members searched for a new location and received a loan from a Korean bank to purchase the newly found land. They did it all the Western way with another $3 million USD put into escrow. Again, this caused a huge problem, as they believed that money in escrow in Cambodia would be lost so the escrow was signed by a judge in Hong Kong.

In the middle of all this negotiation, I became ill with breast cancer and so resigned from the Board. The case against the old developers was started. The furor amongst Cambodians was harsh and I feared for the school. Fortunately, while undergoing treatment in Singapore, one of the developers was also there undergoing treatment. We discussed the issue and I asked again for patience for this process to work itself out. I asked that they not take this personally but as westerners behaving western. I reminded him again to honor the agreement made for the land.

Several months later, the Bank was charged with corruption and misuse of funds. That put an end to their agreement with the school. Sadly, the escrow written by western lawyers and signed by western board members, failed. We couldn't get our money back. The Director came into my office, white in the face. He had the courage to tell me that he was wrong and that he had lost the school and lost the money, he lost everything. He apologized profusely. I did not expect that.

I said to him, we have land, we can build. I would talk with the developers, to which he agreed. About the money in escrow, I knew several very good Cambodia lawyers. Talk with them. They would get our money back. It took almost a year but the money was returned but not without cost. The cost in the broken relationship between the school board, the Director and the developers was great. The custom in Cambodia was that the men handled all legal transactions. With the school, the men never again met with the Director or board members, not for the land breaking ceremony, not for the official school opening, nor for any discussions regarding the issues of the land being developed for the school. Instead, they sent their wives. I reminded the developers of the original agreement we had made and that I expected them to honor those agreements. They did as they promised.

On the day of the inauguration of the school, Prime Minister Hun Sen came to give the official address. He made a point of asking where the developers were. The wives stood up but the PM had made his point that he knew and was not pleased in a very diplomatic way. I understood, but neither the Board nor the Director did. Slowly but surely, the children from the big families in Cambodia moved to other schools. The school had lost an ally; they lost the respect of those families whose respect we needed. The school was an example of foreigners believing that they know everything without understanding anything. It was a harsh lesson.

September was the beginning of our new fiscal and program year. It was also the month we prepared our annual report detailing what we had done in the past year. It was a very good year. We had worked with 33,958 families with 271,664 dependents. 2025 volunteers came from all over the world and built 611 houses, truly unbelievable! We were able to install 997 wells, bringing hope to so very many people.

Our budgets were met in miraculous ways; savings increased phenomenally this year to $1,290,895. From this our 33,364 families made 124,385 purchases changing their lives for the better. The value of these purchases was an astonishing $8,910,861 worth. Families that received wells increased their income to an average of $2.50 per day, a remarkable increase from the less than fifty cents per day.

As I sent this report out to our foundations a question came back: In your annual report it says "total value of items purchased $8,910,861" and "total savings $1,290,895". I don't understand why the numbers are different. Don't people use their savings to buy items? In other words, how are people buying eight million dollars' worth of items if they have only saved 1.2 million?

And I thought now is my opportunity to explain the miracles of our work. Yes, people bought much more than they saved because savings is much more than just saving money. Poverty is something that is at least 90% attitudinal. For our families in Cambodia, it means that they have given up hope; they are despaired when we start working with them. For the past thirty years they have lived a living hell; bombings and genocide; armed clashes; floods and droughts. Every time they took a step forward something would happen and they would lose it all over again. So they quit; they quit on themselves and they quit on their families; they quit on life itself.

The savings process brings back the hope! It is a moral support system that asks each person in our program to believe in themselves, to believe in their families, in their communities and in their country. It is a huge step of faith that these people make; faith that we won't steal their money or abandon them when troubles arise; faith that what they achieve will not be lost yet again; faith that they have the right to choose what their lives should be. And so, they save a small amount each week. Every week, we are there to say well done and every ten weeks they get their money plus an extra ten percent which is our recognition of the courage it took to do this. Every eleventh week we celebrate what they have bought and changed with their purchase and the process is repeated. The people tell us again and again; you have helped us to think again, to dream!

The dreams are much bigger each cycle. Each member of the family begins to think, to dream, of what is possible. For children it is school and a bicycle, and maybe new clothes and for parents it is sources of income and making sure everyone can eat their fill. For all the family, it's the dream of a permanent home that the rains and the winds can't destroy. And the bigger the dream, the more money that is needed. So, our families begin to work together to make these dreams happen; how can each member contribute. They begin to raise animals such as pigs and chickens, they work hard to get a well and with the well they can grow vegetables and they are less sick. They start small shops selling little bits of many things, or they raise money through kids working for their neighbors. They all save with Tabitha. Before, no one worked all that hard; now everyone, even the littlest one and the older siblings can pick grass for the neighbor's cows and get paid.

The dreams now have dates for the future; something not usually done; but it's important that the income from pigs, vegetables and savings all come at the same time, so that the big money is available to buy the more expensive items.

Our hardest times in Tabitha are when we graduate our families, for we are the catalyst to these dreams, we are the ones asking each week, how is it going? We are the ones that celebrate as each step is taken and we are the ones to encourage bigger dreams. No matter if there are floods or the people believe there is no water in their area or if there is a national holiday, we are there to stand beside them and to celebrate as they move from step to step. We become family.

We had visitors who came to see what we do. One of the ladies came back after several days in the village and she said to me "I don't understand the joy, I don't understand these people. A woman living with AIDS took us around her house and showed me every little thing she had done over the past two years. Her eyes were shining with joy! I would have been in despair; yet she, and so many of the families we met, was happy and proud of what they had done." For us in Tabitha the amount of money is miraculous but the most important aspect is the joy. That is the savings program. We are about celebration; about life itself.

October is also the month of Pchum Ban. Pchum Ban is the holiday week when Cambodians remember those who have passed away. It is a season when mood swings tend to be a daily occurrence and depression is just below the surface. Soklieng was one sufferer. Her face was long and drawn each morning. Memories of her lost family were all too real. This past year, so many of Soklieng's friends had passed away in their sleep. People who are in their mid-forties; too young really, to pass on. Often there is no sign of illness, just a quiet passing in the night.

Soklieng said her body hurt. She told me she is too old now; not the same as when we began working together. Her mind doesn't always learn new things very quickly. She was not as physically able as she was before. Soklieng's symptoms were reflected throughout the staff and workers. This month of remembering exacts a high price.

Tuit, Miriam's nanny begged me to take her to Toul Sleng Genocide Museum and to the Killing Fields. She wanted to understand why the older people were so sad; what had made her mother so angry and spiteful. So, I took Miriam and Tuit to both places. Miriam was too young to fully comprehend all that she saw and was told. She kept asking why Pol Pot did this to his people. I answered that all people have a choice in life, to do good to others and in turn, to themselves or to do evil to others and, in turn, to themselves. Neither Toul Sleng nor the Killing Fields had yet been sanitized as they would be in later years.

It was a hard afternoon for the three of us. As we walked through the Killing Fields, Miriam held my hand tightly as she looked at the left-over bones and scraps of clothing left in the ground. We arrived home just before a storm opened up the skies with its drenching downpour. Miriam began to sob and sob. I finally quieted her down and asked her what was wrong. As she hiccupped her answer, my heart broke. "We need plastic, Mum, we need to put plastic on all the leftover bones and clothing at the Killing Fields." Miriam felt the souls of the lost; she felt it every time she took a friend or family member to these very sad memorials.

I went to Singapore for the second of my annual visits. I went to talk at several schools that gave us phenomenal support and the week ended with a Tabitha Silk Fair. It was an amazing week in so many ways. We sold US$94,000 in three days. Children would walk up to me at the schools and want to shake my hand. A number of parents shared the changes in their children who had been housebuilding. As the week progressed, I wanted to share with all our volunteers and schools who helped us of what their impact was on the lives of our families.

I told them that for each of you who have supported the Cottage Industry program, either by selling or by buying our products, tonight, before you lay down on your beds, look in the mirror and when you see yourself then look behind your eyes and see the women and men, your sisters and brothers in Cambodia. Know that tonight they will lay themselves down, physically tired but satisfied. Tonight they will sleep well because their work has been sold; their children are well fed and are in school; tonight it is good because you stood with them; tomorrow is exciting because there is more work.

When you kiss your children goodnight this evening, see your other children here in Cambodia; who are safe because mom or dad has work; whose bellies don't ache with the pain of hunger; who have mom and dad beside them because they earned enough to be able to stay home with them in the evening.

When you see yourself in the mirror tonight, see your brothers here in Cambodia, who are tired but content because today they had enough work to feed their families. Today they planted their crops which have begun to sprout and the pigs they fed and washed and the chickens that scratch beneath their homes; tonight, the men who are your brothers here, can rest in peace.

For each of you who have built a house or paid for a house to be built, tonight when you look around your home, think of the many families here who look around their homes, families who take the time each evening to say a prayer for you, their angels, of the families who are safe from rain and from danger because of you.

For each of you who have given the gift of water through the donation of a well, tonight when you take a shower, feel the joy of thousands of your brothers and sisters here in Cambodia and thousands of your children here and feel their sense of contentment as they wash the dust of their bodies before they lay down to sleep. Feel their thirst slaked with the cup of cold water you gave to them. Feel the stir of hope, of dreams as they have water for their crops and their animals hear the laughter of your children here as they splash each other with the gift of life.

For each of you who stand beside us in so many different ways, see the children here in Cambodia as they have a new set of clothes, or a bicycle to go to school with, or a battery and a small TV to end the day with. See the food on the tables, food in abundance after so many years of hunger. See the parents sit with each other and talk quietly about dreams fulfilled and dreams to come.

It was a good way to end a remarkable week.

This was the first year when we were able to give everyone a cash bonus for Christmas. This was the first year when we were not afraid to say thank you to everyone who worked so hard to make lives for so many so good. The staff had always received an extra bonus at Christmas but never the workers. What a blessing it was to celebrate Christmas and the end of the year in a state of blessings.

# 2008

Several staff were designated to follow in my footsteps should anything happen to me. We instituted much stricter in-house auditing of all our project areas. Srie would go to projects with a copy of the list of families saving in a project. Each family had their own little savings book which recorded their weekly savings, the savings returned and date and the item purchased with that savings. When she arrived in the project, she would randomly choose several families from various villages which she would get to with the staff. There she would question the families, review their passbook, verify this with the project list and then verify it with the monthly report submitted by the staff. She also had anecdotal evidence from the families and took pictures of the dreams purchased. It worked very well for a long time.

Often when I visit our project areas, I am dismayed with the sight of fallow fields. The lack of access to water meant that the one resource which most of our families had, which was land, was unused for nine months out of the year. Their main source of sustenance was their land and the rice that they grew. The three-month growing season was not enough to sustain our families for the whole year. The installation of water sources encouraged the use of this land.

I visited Vutha's area and families who had learned this lesson. We insisted that families must grow vegetables if they received a well and/or raise animals such as pigs or chickens and/or develop fish ponds, all of which provided additional income. These families had grown vegetables in increasing amounts over the past year. From their first planting, they harvested enough vegetables to clear US$250, which doubled their annual income.

Initially, their vegetable plots tended to be very small, just enough for family use but not enough to earn an additional income. The next cycle the plots got bigger, and planting and harvesting were repeated every six weeks. For these families, the income averaged US$250 every six weeks, quadrupling their annual income. How very good that was! They bonded together to enhance their capacity to increase their incomes even more. Their latest purchase was a gas driven rototiller costing $1,310. This group's purchase saved them endless hours of backbreaking labor and enhanced their ability to do even more. It was so very good to see these families move from despair and hopelessness to a state of hope and vitality.

I traveled to communities in Svay Rieng and in Prey Veng with staff from the projects. We went to visit projects that we had first looked at two years ago. In Svay Rieng we had stopped in two villages in Svay Chrum District. Initially, the poverty was appalling. People lived in houses less than two meters square. Everyone at that time was tired and they all had aches and pains. There was no laughter, no joy. It was painful to see this.

The village chiefs in both communities had arranged for families to receive a larger plot of land and we had promised wells for the families. With the wells was the promise from families that they would grow vegetables and/or raise animals. Our staff, Ponluck and Tula, would often talk about how very hard it was to get the people to do so. Poverty does that to people; it makes them tired, physically and emotionally. And, as the staff had told me, the people told them, no one grows vegetables in Svay Rieng, it's unheard of.

I saw a young family with a fish pond; full of fish, a garden that gave them an income of 10,000 riel every day; I saw mango and banana trees planted; I saw land being prepared to build a house. Most importantly, I saw a young family smiling with smiles that wouldn't quit.

Next door I saw a garden full of special herbs for soups which were a staple in the Cambodian diet. I met again an aged couple, standing proud. They had been full of aches and pains the last time we had met. I had given them all my aspirin then. This time, the old man was acting like a child of ten; running and jumping to show me his fish, his garden, his fruit trees. It was hard to get him to stop. We are not sick anymore he chortled.

I saw a man who could not walk last time; a man who lay ill for the last year and a half. He took my hand as we walked through his garden; the vegetables, the fish. I am not sick anymore, look I have new child. Starvation no longer haunted his frame. His lameness was a direct result of lack of vegetables and fruit; he had only been eating a bowl of rice each day.

The village chief took me to his new home, his new garden and pointed at the jackfruit tree. It never bore fruit in all my life, he said, now look, it's a tree bursting with fruit, some so big that they bent the boughs of the tree. His children were clothed; he and his wife had put on weight; their eyes and skin glowed with health. We walked carefully so that I did not step on one of his 60 chickens or his 30 ducks.

And then we went to Mesang District, an area infamous for selling their children to avert starvation; an area infamous for begging on the streets of Phnom Penh. Two years ago, we watched helpless and angry as a child was sold. It was a poverty that was too stark to comprehend and too difficult to understand.

Phat and Choeun, our staff there, worked so hard to change things. It seemed to take so long. Finally, in desperation, Phat had bought seeds and put in a well. Yesterday, I saw a woman I knew well, our second woman who had begged on the streets of Phnom Penh. Before me stood a woman transformed. Her garden bore vegetables, too many to mention. Her excitement about life was contagious; look at this, look at that. If I had a pump, I could do twice as much. You know, she said, people come from miles away to buy my vegetables. Just look at me, I am strong now.

Her neighbor next door showed us their garden. We have 500 bitter melons we can sell right now! Everyday people come to buy. We used to be beggars the man said; I have eight children and this month, four of my children have started school for the first time in their lives.

It was a day of miracles; a day of blessings. We developed a new motto. Tabitha goes green! Our desire was to make all these fallow fields burst with food. Our desire was to see all children live free; never to be sold again! Our desire was to see the middle-aged have hope; never again to beg! Our desire was for the aged to run like gazelles, their aches and pains forgotten. Our desire was to see the lame walk and the ill to become strong! Our desire was to see people work and to receive a just income from their work. So very Biblical!

I took Ing Kantha Phavi, Minister of Women's Affairs out to see another house building team. Phavi is a delightful woman and we walked from house to house and well to well. We both bought vegetables, delicious in their freshness. Then we drove to an area that we were graduating. The changes were amazing. Houses that we built four years ago were now painted and had cement walls filling in the ground level. There were toilets, built sturdy and strong. Everywhere there was food growing, and there were cows and chickens in abundance. Several of the older women came and hugged me. Thank you they said, we have been reborn. Phavi laughed and hugged me as well. Then the women compared skin color, they said mine was so beautiful. I took the hand of an older lady, burnt almost black by the sun. I kissed her hand and said: you have the most beautiful skin! Her eyes grew huge and she looked around and then she kissed my hand and said: we both have beautiful skin. What a lovely day it was.

---

I went to Singapore for our annual Silk Fair. It turned out to be the most successful fair ever. Women came every day for three days. None of them had credit cards, forbidden by their husbands during this economic crisis, so they came with cash instead. Oh my, what a three-day sale it was! We sold $164,000 Singapore dollars! Unbelievable. The women were buying in a frenzy as if this was their last opportunity to shop. It was also a sad time as many of our volunteers and friends in Singapore lost their jobs or were being transferred to less expensive postings. Others lost benefits and life was harder for them.

The success of the Silk Fair brought a sense of relief to our sewers and weavers. So much joy and laughter in this time when inflation was hurting so very many people. We had a constant stream of orders and their income was very good. They could eat and they could share with others who were not so fortunate.

In addition to the economic stress in Cambodia, tensions were running high as another election took place. The government had ordered a mandatory closure of everything for a three-day period. The staff had requested their salaries to be given early so that they could buy extra food. Border tensions between Cambodia and Thailand had increased and no resolution seemed to be in sight. Both camps had military stationed there and everyone was wondering what would happen next. People were worried for it would only take one soldier firing his gun to start off something no one wants and yet everyone talks about.

I met an unusual man on a trip to Prey Veng. Ban started with Tabitha in February of 2003 when he was a motor bike driver and earned $1.25 a day. His house was a small thatched hut and his small piece of land was barren. Over the past 5 years, Ban had saved. He began with two piglets to raise which he sold to buy more pigs. Over the years he was able to get a well and dug a fish pond on his property. He raised 1000 fish and sold them every six months for $1500. Ban bought another piece of land across the road and there he started a piggery. Now he raises 16 pigs every three months and makes $2000 profit after his expenses and buys more piglets. Ban has built a house of tin, he has built a toilet that even we westerners can use, and he has built a cement wall around his house. Ban grows vegetables and sugar cane. He no longer drives his motorbike. His land and his home were where he spent his days with his three children and his wife. I asked Ban how much he sold his sugarcane for. His response touched my heart. Oh, he said, I don't sell the sugarcane rather I give it to my neighbors for free. I want to teach them all how to save and to have a good life like mine. His quiet dignity and his desire to help others improve their lives touched me deeply. I was to meet many more people like Ban in the years ahead.

I had another magical day. I went out to Tanong Village in Takeo to see the impact of our field wells. These wells serviced 28 families; families whom we were told two years ago by the commune chief, don't bother to give them wells because they are very lazy and very stupid people. Just the words needed to challenge our staff.

Last November we started to install the field wells. Our first stop was with four families who were desperately poor. What a joy it was to come. All of the families were there with big smiles, anxious to show me what they had done. They received their field wells in January. Between them they had 50 small pieces of land; the average size was 10 meters square. The well had allowed these families to grow three crops of rice and their fourth crop of rice was growing. Out of every four pieces of land, the fifth piece was for vegetables, bananas, eggplant, morning glory, cabbages, bean and green bell peppers. For the first time, not all the land was for rice. It was their smiles and their health that touched me so. We have enough food to eat, enough food to sell each day; we are no longer hungry. I snuck a look at the chief but he said nothing.

We went to the other families. As far as the eye could see, we saw vegetables and rice growing. These families all owned several pieces of land that averaged 50 meters by 10 meters. They received their wells last November and since then they had grown three crops of rice; enough rice to feed their families and to sell a ton each. All of them had vegetable plots of cabbages, morning glory, beans and chili peppers, but the one I liked most was the field of green peppers which I didn't know they could grow in Cambodia. One of the green peppers was the size of my two hands. I wanted to buy it from the farmer but he wanted to give it to me. I said, no, you worked hard for this; I want to reward you for your hard work. As we were talking in this field so far from any main roads, a Lexus pulled up and a man in a suit got out of the car and approached us. He said he wanted to buy the pepper in my hand. I said that I had already bought it. He asked me for how much. Tongue in cheek I said, $10. Without batting an eye, he said, I will buy it for $20. I held out my hand for the $20 which he gave me. Then he turned on his heel and he left. I gave the farmer the $20 and received the biggest smile I have ever gotten.

Kameak had asked if he could open up in a new province adjacent to his work in Banteay Meanchey, called Pailin, in the area of Phum Malia, the area where the remaining Khmer Rouge were banished to. Kameak had spent several months of preparatory work there and wanted me to come and approve. I went with Soklieng and Srie. The road to Malai was made of dirt clay and the area off the road was still land-mined.

Our arrival in the village was expected and many villagers came out to greet us. So were the chief and a number of Khmer Rouge. It was all a bit unnerving. As I walked with Kameak and the chief, Kameak mentioned the possibility of bringing out a house building team. The poverty was very stark and the houses were very simple. I said that I would discuss it with all the staff but made no promises. I was not too keen on bringing a group of volunteers into land-mine territory.

As we left the village, Srie began to talk. You cannot bring a team here she said. The villagers warned us that if we brought a team, they would be kidnapped and held for ransom. Eventually they would kill all the foreigners, she said. We are lucky that they did not capture you today. It's only because the villagers were there that nothing bad happened. Needless to say, I did not approve this expansion.

———

It was Pchum Ban Festival time in Cambodia. Pchum Ban was equivalent to the Christian holiday of Christmas in significance for the people here. It was the time that Cambodians have to honor and remember their parents and grandparents who have passed away. There are very specific ceremonies that need to be completed in the 15 days prior to the actual Pchum Ban day itself. The belief was that people must honor their departed parents and grandparents by going to seven different pagodas and bringing gifts of food to the monks. On Pchum Ban day itself, everyone must bring a variety of cooked foods plus a variety of dry foods to the pagoda before 11 o'clock in the morning. At that time, all offerings must be completed and the monks sit down to eat.

The belief was that deceased parents sit down with the monks and eat the food as well. Why seven pagodas? Basically, the parents are wandering souls and are looking to see if their children are honoring them. If they cannot find the offerings of their children, the souls of the parents become angry, and the children will suffer from nightmares and problems at home. A secondary problem was, of course, the amount and variety of food a person brought. A small offering of just rice would not satisfy the hunger of the parents nor sustain them throughout the year so the pressure on families is immense.

For families in Tabitha programs, Pchum Ban becomes progressively easier as their incomes increase. When SokLee joined Tabitha four years ago, she lived in a small thatched home with her husband and seven children. During those years, we often talked with this family about getting a field well and putting their land to better use. SokLee had lost all her family during the Khmer Rouge years. She met her husband who was also an orphan, the sole surviving member of his family. Over the 18 years of their marriage, bearing children was one of the few things they did well, but sadly several of their babies died before they were a year old. When I would ask them, why they didn't dare to change their lives, SokLee would talk of being bad. She would reiterate again and again, we are suffering because we are bad. I lost my family, my parents, my land, my right to go to school, my right to earn a living, my right to be a Buddhist because of the Khmer Rouge. My children die or are always sick. I have bad dreams because my parents come to me and ask me why I am so bad. I cannot think anymore. I cannot do anymore.

Their home was small and decrepit as her husband was often away trying to earn money from jobs on the border. Their children would go to bed hungry. Malnutrition was a disease that weakened the body and tired the soul. Encouraging this family, like so many others, takes hours of talking. Peuw, who was our project manager, got increasingly frustrated with this family so last Pchum Ban, he took SokLee and her husband and nine other family heads on a day trip to Tanong. He did it by force, threatening dismissal from our programs unless they came and saw. In Tanong we have several hundred hectares of land under continuous use with vegetables and rice. Both groups met and talked and talked some more. They talked about being bad; they talked about being of no worth, of not being able to think anymore. They talked of the nightmares. Then our Tanong families talked about changes, about dreaming and thinking again, about working their land, about working together to make sure everyone did well. They talked about learning the markets and growing off-season vegetables which resulted in more money for their crops. They talked about growing rice three times a year and never going hungry. The men talked of no longer needing to leave home to earn money for their families; they talked about the health of their children and the schools they are attending. They talked of the homes they have rebuilt and how good it all was. Then they talked about Pchum Ban, how the nightmares had gone and how their parents were at peace.

SokLee and her husband listened and he did the unthinkable. He wanted a field well. It's been ten months since that field well was installed. The change was remarkable! This family grew mushrooms, and cucumbers and they make rice wine. Their income had increased to $20 per day, each day. Unbelievable! But the biggest change was in them. SokLee and her husband laugh a lot, they were eager to have me come, they were eager to feed me good food, to show off their achievements, to brag about their children. They were eager to show me their neighbors and all that is going so well. People ask me why I am so passionate about the work we do. SokLee and her family are the reason.

On my second biannual visit to Singapore this year, I met and talked with the first and fifth grade classes at the Singapore American School. Their response to my presentations was amazing. Mike Ferguson, Amy's husband, was the grade one teacher. In my chat with the children, I had Mike and a female teacher lay down on two-meter mat and then had six students join them. It was a very visual and helpful way to show these young students what poverty really was. It was about learning that poverty means not everyone can sleep safely together at night; some children had to sleep outside. And I asked them how they would feel if they had to sleep outside at night. I asked them how they could brush their teeth without water, or if the rain came, how they could sleep with the rain coming through the roof of their homes. After my chat, Mike and his fellow grade one teachers had the children do a fundraiser for us at Tabitha. Their challenge was to do ten minutes of chores each day at home. The parents were asked to pay their children for those chores. This money was collected and sent to us. That first year, these first grade students raised US$10,000.

Dave Smith was the contact teacher for the fifth grade classes of which there were ten. I showed these students a Power Point presentation of our work and then answered questions. It was a fun hour. Dave and his fellow teachers came up with JUMP-A-THON, an event where the students raised funds for the number of jumps they did. They raised an amazing US$20,000. Both of these grades raised money for Tabitha every year after this. Sadly, Dave passed away unexpectedly several years later but other grade five teachers continued his legacy. I miss you, Dave.

Taking the time to talk with school children was an integral part of my biannual visits to Singapore. A day at UWCSEA always meant talking to the grade two classes who bought our signature geckos and decorated them as art pieces. They sold these geckos every year and raised vast amounts of money for our programs.

Talking with the eighth-grade classes at UWCSEA resulted in an unheard of happening. The question was why they could not come house building? My answer was, I don't know, talk with your teachers and your parents and tell me your answer the next time I come. They did as I asked and they enabled all future eighth-grade students to come and house build. It is, by far, the biggest group of builders each year, except for one other team. The grade eight house builders are now restricted to 80 students and 20 teachers and parents. They have come each year since then with experienced teachers leading the teams.

Our biggest house building group was from a large multinational company. 150 volunteers to build 50 houses. The logistics involved were staggering. They accommodated all of us, staff included, in a five-star hotel. Just moving this team to the village was a challenge; feeding and watering all these people on the building site was a massive effort. We were blessed that no one got hurt, the houses were completed and none of the staff, especially Heng, who supervised it all, quit.

This build was in Siem Reap. The team built for several families of orphans. When the team left, a number of better-off people in the village tried to take the houses away from these youngsters. When Ani heard this she phoned the Provincial Governor and told him the story. The Governor came out immediately and made it clear to all concerned that these houses belonged to the orphans and no one would be allowed to take these houses and land away from these children. This often occurred in all the areas where we worked. The Tabitha managers would immediately phone their respective governors and insist on the houses being returned to the orphans. What a maturity the staff showed in these instances.

It was another year of tremendous blessings. It was a normal year in my life.

# 2009

The year began with a new project area in the province of Kompong Channang. Once again, I was reminded of how I live a life of grace. We saw many families for whom life was a daily struggle. The poverty and meanness of their lives was truly painful to see. In one small community we met three families living in one small house. There were 25 children and seven adults living in a space of four meters by six meters. I thought to myself, how long it would take before I lost my mind if I lived in such a circumstance? They didn't have access to clean water. They walked through the fields to a small swamp where they fetched their water. I thought to myself, how many hours would it take before I developed diarrhea or had sores on my feet that would become infected from standing in swamp water?

We met with a group of ten widows; their husbands had all died from malaria or AIDS. The women lived close together for security surrounded by children of all ages. They were sharing how they earned an income. They gathered tamarind beans from nearby trees and gathered insects from other trees. These were sold at nearby markets. It was hard to find out how much money they earned so I asked, how many nights do they go to bed hungry? One woman replied: we go to bed hungry 18 nights out of one month. I thought to myself, how many days of hunger would it take before I despaired, saddened beyond words that I could not supply the daily needs for my child?

A few days later I visited a project area in Treang, an area where we started two years ago. It was an area that had similarly suffered as those in our new area. This day we celebrated. I met families who had lived in barren surroundings the first time; families who now had many varieties of fruits and vegetables. I saw banana and papaya trees. I saw lemon grass and morning glory which is a staple in Cambodian diets. I saw green onions and peppers. What struck me most is that I saw men at home, working their small plots, men who were honored to have me visit and proud to show what they had done. I tripped over pigs and chickens pecking boldly around my feet. I saw families together, smiling in pleasure at my visit. I thought to myself, would I have the strength and courage of these families, to work long physical hours, tilling soil that is unrelenting in trying to keep its treasures from mortals such as me? Poverty is a hard task master.

House Building was a growing program. With the growth, came more problems. Poor Heng was beginning to spend his nights on the road, leaving home at midnight in order to move the lumber we needed to frame the houses. The sad reality was that most of the trees left in Cambodia were being harvested at an alarming rate. This lumber was being sold across the borders to Vietnam and Thailand. The result was a growing scarcity of lumber within the country. The government had put restrictions on the movement of all wood. This meant that moving lumber from one place to another was subject to road blocks, all demanding payment and occasionally, confiscation of the wood itself.

We needed to solve this issue before it stopped House Building all together. Heng Touch, who had replaced Menrouen as our advocate, authorized us to approach the various Ministries involved. Our goal was to get special dispensation for Tabitha. Fortunately for us, several of the Ministers we needed to approach had visited our projects and had seen house building teams at work. Despite their knowledge and support, it still took many months before we received the coveted Ministry of Forestry and Ministry of Agriculture certificate of exemption. In the meantime, I commiserated with Heng on the burdens that he carried. Personally, I think he enjoyed the danger involved in smuggling wood to our areas of work. Thankfully, they were never caught. On several occasions they were waylaid by cows roaming the roads during the night. Cambodian cows are rather dangerous animals and will attack with very little provocation.

With the growing scarcity of wood, came the increasing cost of the lumber itself. It was very difficult for us to try and keep a steady price for the houses without increasing the costs to our teams but eventually we had to increase the price. This was very important as several project areas no longer had any lumber and we needed to move lumber from one province to another. This made for very long nights for Heng and the contractors. The cost of transporting the lumber became almost unbearable as those we hired to transport the lumber felt the danger and threat involved from being caught as well as having to transport during the middle of the night. Our certificate of dispensation was a very welcome and treasured document; one that we protected faithfully.

In addition, the cost of transporting teams to the villages had doubled. I had asked Soklieng to get me a quote from a number of companies who rented out vans. She came back with five quotes ranging from $130 to $150 a van. There was nothing I could do but pass on the cost to the teams until we negotiated a better price.

## School Building

One of the team leaders of the Margarita's team, Sue Huxley, had developed a virulent form of cancer. We had all become good friends over the years. Despite Sue's suffering, she continued to participate in house building. This year Sue came with the team, but was in great pain. She was unable to participate in the building and returned home to Singapore. I flew over a couple of times to be with her. It was such an honor. She was a phenomenal woman.

Sue had one request that the team and I truly wanted to honor. Sue had a passion for Cambodia's children. In our talks, I shared how we were in the process of finishing our first school. I had met a group called PACE, a group of UWCSEA parents, whose sole goal was to build schools in developing countries. Because of our affiliation with UWCSEA over the years, PACE requested a meeting with me. It was a difficult meeting as their needs and the needs of our communities didn't quite match.

PACE had requested the cost of constructing a six-room school. As we did with all new projects, we did a comprehensive survey in our project areas towards the costs of building a school complete with water sources and toilet blocks. We double checked these prices by costing the list of materials needed for construction and labor if we did the work. Based on these results we submitted the cost of building a six-room school.

PACE was happy but they wanted more. They wanted to be able to come twice a year to the school and teach. They wanted to subsidize the salaries of the teachers and they wanted to bring in specialized equipment such as computers for the students. This was not possible.

Teaching at a school where English was not spoken was problematic. It was very disruptive to the planned curriculum that schools already had. It would mean that school would be disrupted for several weeks each year. Cambodian teachers were no different than Western teachers; a disruption to the curriculum was not feasible.

The subsidizing of teacher's salaries was a problem in Cambodia. A number of foreigners had done this and caused strife amongst the teachers. Teachers were paid by the government. Everyone knew what everyone else was getting. When a foreigner disrupted this, there were ramifications as other schools and teachers demanded the same subsidy from the government. The direct result was the government passing a law forbidding this practice.

Bringing in specialized teaching equipment such as computers was also a huge problem. The issues involved were manifold. This was exacerbated when Bill Gates decided that every child in Africa would climb out of poverty if they had a computer. Suddenly everyone wanted to bring computers for the children and for the schools.

Schools had no electricity and the computers offered were used equipment, equipment that couldn't be serviced. There were no teachers trained in computers so how would they teach? There was no wifi or internet available at this time so what could the students do with the machines? Worst was those computers were not edible so it did not still the hunger of the children. I saw a vast number of schools with a room filled with outdated computers gathering dust. Incidentally, Bill Gates solution to poverty lasted only two years.

Tabitha was completely unwilling to be responsible for the schools after they were constructed. We met with the Ministry of Education and with the provincial governors over this issue. We agreed that we would be happy to construct a school if the government would supply a school director, teachers and textbooks and assume full responsibility for the school after that. The process would be that we would inform the provincial governor through the village, commune and district chiefs who had to approve the need of a school first. The governor would inform the Minister of Education and we would look for a donor. We would be responsible for the construction of the school building following the design approved by the Ministry of Education. The school would be handed over to the government upon completion of the structure.

PACE had agreed to our terms reluctantly and had agreed to fund the first of three schools. It was the beginning of the latest addition to our outreach: the Schools Program. Sue was so excited about this possibility that she requested a school be built in her memory. She died early the following year and her family and friends raised enough to build three schools in her honor.

We had a number of firsts this year; unusual events that touched my heart. Bruce Ford, an Australian friend, ran the first ever marathon in support of Tabitha. Bruce entered an event called Racing the Planet which was a 7-day marathon in the heart of Namibia. The race was very tough and Bruce struggled but he never quit. At the end of that week he ended up in the hospital with a severe infection in his leg. Bruce raised nearly $50,000 Australian for Tabitha; his race so reflected the people he raced for, people who struggle constantly and never quit.

One of the mothers of a second grade student at UWCSEA wrote a children's book called I Hate Peas. She asked her daughter where the money she made from the book should be donated to. Her daughter answered, Tabitha Cambodia. Over the next five years, she wrote five more children's books with all the proceeds donated to Tabitha. The money raised was substantial. This mother-daughter duo helped so very many families work their way out of poverty.

---

I visited a family of six who were desperately poor. They owned two hectares of land but the land was of very poor quality; land that could not grow rice as the water just seeped through the sandy soil. The family received a field well a month ago. When I arrived, the father cried. He cried not because he was tired or because he was defeated, instead, he cried because he had hope; he cried because he could work. I looked at their fields. Their fields were sprouting with new life. His wife Sokha carried her youngest in her arms; her face was shining; her eyes spoke volumes of the joy she felt. The parents and their four young children tilled and planted every inch of their fields. Their house was nothing but a simple canopy to protect them from the sun. All their hard labor was bearing fruit. Harvest would begin in June when they expected to make several hundred dollars from each field. This sounds so little to most of us but for this family, it was riches beyond their imagination.

⁓

This summer, the rains had fallen in a steady, weeping fashion. For some of our families, the rain was a blessing because the rice would grow well this year, if it didn't flood. In other regions, the rain did not fall. As I traveled to our Kampot project, we passed through parts of Takeo province. Here the rain had been sporadic and the rice was not growing. In Kampot, the rain fell in abundance, in fact, parts of the highway were flooded. We looked at the fields through sheets of rain as the families asked for two reservoirs, 25 meters square, which needed to be walled in with cement. If done, the 240 families needing the reservoirs would be able to have year-round crops covering a minimum of 250 hectares. Right now, they grew only one crop of rice a year, which was hard to imagine, as we stood drenched in the rice paddies surrounding us.

For Tabitha staff, rain brought its own challenges for our country roads and tracks that are used to get to our families had turned into a morass of slippery goop. I too had tried to walk in the mess, only I was given a lift on the back of a carabao. I was also transported on a wagon powered by a rototiller which slid into the ditch several times but I survived. I decided that I was getting too old for this!

The most poignant illustration of rain came when a house building team arrived to build in one of our villages in Kandal. Kandal countryside seldom flooded. The team had specifically asked if they were okay to come because of the flooding. I assured them that all would be well; in fact, I would personally accompany them on their house build. It was very important that teams come when they said they would come as the families were very anxious to receive their new homes. In this instance, the vans got mired on the path to the village which was under a meter of water. Heng jumped from the van and called the men from the village to come and push us out but to no avail. The team leader was gracious and just said, oh, we build in water? I gave a sick smile and as I stepped out of the van, eight strong arms lifted me high. Four men of small stature insisted that I not get wet so they carried me to the houses. I was so embarrassed and begged to be put down but they would not hear of it. The team and staff couldn't stop laughing. They were thoroughly soaked but in good spirits. Each time I tried to walk from one house to another, these same four men would grab and lift me high and carry me wherever I wanted to go. It was a truly humbling experience, one that I would suffer numerous times as I got older.

I received a booklet of thoughts about a Tabitha Housebuilding Trip by eighth grade students from UWCSEA. I had just finished orientation with two teams who were building that week and I felt a bit drained. I decided to take this booklet home with me to read with my daughter Miriam. I had not read many of the entries before tears flowed silently down her cheeks. She snuggled closer against me and together we had a magical hour, both of us realizing how very fortunate we are to live the life we live. One excerpt was "At first I couldn't hit the nails, although I was good at hitting my thumb. Every time I hit myself or my back was aching all I needed to do was look down at the little children collecting the nails beneath me. Or I would turn around and look at the men of the village helping put up the walls or even just take a glance at the mothers talking amongst themselves. Right away I would get back to nailing and wouldn't dare complain. Doing something for someone other than myself for once, was enough for me just to get on with it. I took so much from this trip. It was such a privilege to be able to make such a big difference to someone else and that experience will stay with me for the rest of my life. I complain a lot less now. Before I left, I would complain for the tiniest thing but now, I like to believe, I rarely complain. I am so grateful for the life that I have and I am able to fix this world, one house at a time."

This year marked the end of the first UN held Khmer Rouge trial of Duch, the infamous head of Toul Sleng; a torture and death chamber of more than 14,000 Khmer. Duch has said he is guilty and he has said he is sorry, but these words have little meaning for the survivors for he also says "I was just following orders". There is no remorse.

When I started Tabitha Cambodia back in October of 1994, the wounds of this brutal regime were still open and raw. Pol Pot and the Khmer Rouge were still active in many parts of the country. People were struggling to make sense out of their losses; losses which included family, homes, education and their very fabric of society, their faith. We had decided to start Cottage Industry, a program that focused on providing work and income for families who had lost so very much. I decided that we needed to focus on traditional skills inherent in this society. Silk weaving was one such skill.

One of our first weavers was a very old lady, named Tuit. When I first met Tuit, she lived in a thatched hut. She was bent over double for she could no longer straighten her back. Tuit was raising four grandchildren. At 78 she should have had the luxury of resting her weary bones and enjoying her family but her family was mostly gone. Her husband and her four children had been executed by a regime that was only following orders. Her one surviving son had married and had four children. Sadly, the son and his wife died of AIDS. Tuit was raising her four grandchildren, 16 years old and younger at that time.

We talked of the threads of her life. She was raised in a happy home, learning weaving skills that created beauty, getting married and having a good home. Then it all ended with the brutality of the Khmer Rouge. Tuit revived her weaving skills and the silk thread she wove became the income that helped her grandchildren to survive. The silk thread spoke of better times; times when life was normal and good, time when wearing silk spoke of the daily events that people were living. Each silk piece bespoke of the married status of women, of special events being celebrated, of a society that had customs and beliefs.

Several years later, a housebuilding team came and built her home. Tuit was so very touched for in Cambodia it meant so much to have a home to die in. She was so very tired and wanted to move on. I asked her not to die but to live; to live for her grandchildren, to stretch the thread of life a little longer.

Over the next several years, Tuit taught the oldest child to weave and the income of the family was secured. The children graduated from school and all got married with the oldest one still weaving today. She is passing on her skills to her three children. The weaving allowed Tuit to live out her life with dignity and beauty. Tuit passed away three years ago at the age of ninety. She was surrounded by her grandchildren and their children. The thread of life continues, the thread of silk her burial shroud. For a few years, this silk weaver regained some degree of comfort in her troubled life. For a few short years she could be what she was meant to be, a woman of beauty comforted by a thread of silk that bound her family together.

Tuit's story was but one story of so very many; women and men who have gone through unspeakable horror, the silk thread has given them the strength to carry on, the strength to live for a while longer, the strength to regain their meaning in life, the strength to dare believe in life itself.

Our families make a liar out of Pol Pot, a man who believed that Cambodians were simply things, things to be used, abused and thrown away. They make shame out of people like Duch who said he was only following orders in his maniacal desire to kill as many as possible. Our families are survivors whose desire to live far outweighs people like the Khmer Rouge. Tabitha had the very rare privilege of being but a small part of the strength and courage of these people who dared to live. What a great reminder of how precious life is. A very good way to end the year.

# 2010

I started the New Year in Bangkok, celebrating with my daughter Miriam, who was now 11 years old. Like most people, a new year signifies for me new beginnings. Miriam wanted so much to go to the Siam Water Park and so off we went with Melita and her adopted daughter Srie. Silly me, I agreed to go down the biggest waterslide I had ever seen, which had all kinds of loops, with Miriam. At first Miriam hung on to me but with my weight I started to go much faster than either one of us thought was fun. I went so fast I thought I would flip over the side so I did what any sensible person would do; I closed my eyes and promised my God all kinds of things if I survived! I went through water spouts which went up my nose; I slid with abandon from side-to-side thinking would this ride never end? I landed in the pool at the end which in my disturbed mind, I thought was not the end! I actually sat underwater for about 20 seconds which got the attention of the life guard, who came down from his chair and began screaming. My little mind finally said to my little body that it's over, you better stand, which I did, much to everyone's relief! A New Year's resolution will never again be on a water slide!

I travelled with Pon and Srie to our newest area in Krakor District in Pursat province. As we drove through the communities, the poverty was hard to face. A number of families didn't even have four walls to their shelter. We met another 60 families who did not eat every day, their hunger painful to see. A number of families had shelter not big enough for two people, much less the eight or ten people living in those shelters. We saw bigger homes but they housed two or three families. Not so good. We noticed that there were no pigs, chickens, ducks or vegetables; just barren, dusty land. What a challenge. As we talked, the ladies made a New Year's resolution that this too will change.

On the way back to Phnom Penh we stopped in Kompong Channang to see the family that Miriam had given a well to. The husband had decided that he would be the model for his village. In his small garden, he had planted rows of vegetables, nine kinds in total. One was a row of six zucchini plants which were large and healthy. I said I would like to buy a zucchini but he said, no! They had all been sold for a $1.00 each because people wanted the seeds from the zucchini so they could grow their own. He had planted five kinds of fruit trees, such as mangoes, papaya and grapefruit. Across the path, lay his field. There he had planted a row of nine other vegetables because he wanted to see which would grow best. His eyes just sparkled. He had set up an ingenious irrigation system by piping the water into a water jar standing several feet off the ground. He turned a spigot and he could water each plant individually with a hose he had pieced together. He, too, made a New Year's resolution of no hunger for his family this year!

Srie and I traveled to Banteay Meanchey to see the progress in the new areas. The visit was anticipated by Kameak, Long and Touk, our staff there. They had gone through several frustrating years of working with families who had been slow to respond, primarily because the areas were next to the Thai border and troubles kept flaring over the disputed temples. A sense of fear and insecurity kept the families away.

The new areas were further from the troubles and work had begun in September. We have learned that water was the quickest way to move people from poverty on to the road to prosperity. We all knew that we had to convince people that they had to earn income from wells that we installed. The staff took it to heart and began installing wells soon after the program started.

Often the Tabitha staff would tell me about how many times they had to talk to people before they would begin to respond. Banteay Meanchey was no exception. For the first time the staff were excited. The talk had worked. We stopped at Khun's home. He and the neighboring family had received a well. Khun was taller than the normal Khmer so it was rather a pleasure to look up at him while he talked. He proudly showed me a stand of corn he was growing. I was rather pleased as the corn stood taller than me. I admired his work and asked, so when will you harvest? He smiled and shrugged, I don't know, he said, do you know? I was a bit perplexed and looked at the staff. No one looked my way; rather they were studiously looking at the ground.

What do you mean, you don't know, I asked? Oh, said Khun I have never grown corn in my life. Srie found it hard to keep from giggling, no one had ever grown vegetables here, she said. I was a bit dumbfounded. So how did he know what to do? Kameak gave a grin and said, we didn't know either, we just told him to make the ground ready and then throw seeds in the ground and it worked.

Srie mentioned that she had told Khun to cut a few stalks so that each plant had a bit more space to grow. Over my shoulder, other vegetables were growing in abundance; too many in too small a space but they were eating and selling from their small plot. As I was admiring the handiwork, Khun kept asking me when his corn would be ready, but I also didn't know so I guessed that another month would do it. He left it at that.

We visited a number of families, each one growing small fields of vegetables. No one knew the first thing about growing vegetables. All of them were learning things the hard way; through trial and error and it had worked. Lek, with her husband and three sons, had learned how to plant several varieties of vegetables. They were on their third cycle of growing food. Lek found carrying the water to the plants rather burdensome and she had devised a unique way of transferring water by garden hose from her well. She was being innovative out of need and desire.

As we visited various families all learning new skills, I marveled at my staff. They had talked people into trying new ideas without understanding themselves the growing cycles of the various vegetables. They were so proud of their families, so proud of the progress. We talked of the innovation taking place and of other innovations that we could try to make this a bit easier for the families.

The families in our communities were desperately poor; their life style was fraught with hunger and despair. I looked at the huts they lived in; their meager possessions open to all who would see. I looked at bodies, worn with hard labor and so little to show for it. I looked at the staff and marveled at how hard they worked, how much they must have talked, to change just one life. I marveled at how much change occurred simply because all of us talked a lot about how to help without fully understanding the impact of what we said and did. I marveled that my God talked to me about how to help and how I talked with all the staff and how all of us talked with others so that people like Khun and Lek could look at me with shining eyes and ask me, when do you think I will be able to harvest the corn? I think I'd better look up the growth cycles of corn.

Miriam was now old enough to go on field trips to other countries which was a mandatory requirement from ISPP, her school. Miriam was also very athletic and had made the varsity teams in soccer, basketball, volleyball and swimming. All of this required travelling to neighboring countries in South East Asia. Now Miriam needed health insurance. Health Insurance was a commodity that I had lived without since the beginning of setting up Tabitha Cambodia. I found an insurance company that would insure Miriam at a price that I could afford and that would allow her to travel with the school events. The company then mentioned that I should have health insurance as well. They made a proposal that was cost effective and that covered me fully. I was truly in a state of wonder as I had lived so long without health protection. Would wonders never cease?

Within a month of getting insurance, I was diagnosed with breast cancer. That insurance covered all the costs involved with my treatment of the cancer. However, it was also a policy that was not renewable at the end of the year.

For Miriam, my journey through breast cancer was traumatic. This was compounded with the events that occurred as a direct result of my cancer journey, events that changed me, that changed Tabitha Cambodia. It was a journey that was the start of Nokor Tep Women's Hospital, a start that was challenging to all our foundations and donors.

I knew from the first few minutes of diagnoses that I would survive the cancer. I heard God's voice telling me a line from my favorite Psalm 91:16 NIV "with long life will I satisfy you and show you my salvation." I would be fine but I also knew that God had put treatment in place that would eradicate my cancer. I knew with certainty that I needed to build a cancer hospital for the women of Cambodia. In the previous six months I had met so many women in our projects who were living with breast cancer and breast disease turning their breasts into horrific, multi-colored displays. There was no treatment to be had. With my diagnosis, so many people had written and called about my cancer. I was honest and said, all had been taken care of, I would be fine but for the women of Cambodia living with this disease, they would not be fine, they would all perish in a long, slow agonizing process towards death. This inequity was intolerable for me. I could not do anything other than build a hospital for these women.

In the middle of my treatment, the school built in memory of Sue Huxley was completed. Sue's husband David, their children and the Margarita's house building team with Sharon and Lisa and Sue's closest friends came for a special ceremony to open the school. The Huxley family were horrified that I had contracted cancer so soon after Sue's passing. At the celebration of the opening of the school, Chris Huxley, Sue's eleven-year-old son hugged me tightly and asked me not to die. I promised him that I wouldn't.

I informed Dr. Ing Kantha Phavi, the Minister of Women's Affairs, of my cancer diagnosis and my vision to build a cancer hospital. Her response took my breath away; no, you can't build a hospital! We will build it together. Thus, began our journey along with Trac Thai Sieng, Phavi's husband, of building a hospital for women.

Our first task was to come up with a name for the hospital that would convey our values and principals. We chose the name Nokor Tep Women's Hospital. Nokor Tep is the angel of compassion and mercy, one of the central concepts in Buddhism as well as a central concept in the Christian faith. Nokor Tep reflected our faith in a God of mercy and a God of compassion. It was our central and shared value for the building of the hospital.

Building Nokor Tep together taught the three of us a great many life lessons. Our first lesson was that the majority of people we met thought we were very foolish, telling us: you can't build a hospital, it is just not done! I am not a person that listens well to the negativity of others. Of course, we can build a hospital.

The first step was to come up with a vision of what this hospital would look like. Initially, we were thinking of a 60 bed women's cancer hospital. I met with Beat Richner who had built the Kantha Bopha Children's Hospital in Phnom Penh and Siem Reap. He said, Janne don't make my mistake and build too small; within one year you will outgrow your space. With this advice, we changed our plans to a 220-bed hospital with room for expansion.

None of us had time to write up the concept of the hospital so we hired two experts to help us through this process. Yvan Chalm was an architect and did us well. Bruno was the concept writer. I didn't like him from the minute I met him; a cocky self-assured individual who did not believe in our vision. He did believe in earning money so he did a slipshod job for us. We learned right away that people were interested in taking our money while mocking us behind our backs. I will give Bruno credit, he did apologize to us for his behavior a few years later; an apology that gave me no pleasure. He believed that we would never accomplish our vision.

Our next big task was to acquire land. Phavi wanted to show me land in the middle of the industrial area; an area that was ideal for our vision as up to 500,000 women worked in factories with a ten-kilometer radius. The problem was that infrastructure such as roads, water and electricity were not yet built but were part of the city's plan. Up until the last year of construction, getting to the hospital would often be a two-hour bone rattling, car destroying journey.

All of this transpired during my journey with breast cancer. An extraordinary six months.

# 2011

## Tabitha Cambodia

The year started with trouble brewing. On my return home from cancer treatments in mid-December, I was met at the airport by all the staff: staff from the provinces, Cottage Industry workers, and my administrative staff. It was a subdued group of people. Despite my questions of how things were going, no one would answer me. Several days later we had our Christmas party. Srie came and said; promise me, you will visit every project. I asked her what was going on. Her answer made me sad. You had cancer and we all believed that you would die. Please come and visit every project.

I began my promised visit to every project. The staff were delighted to have me come and could not wait to show me what they had accomplished and where they planned to expand to. Srie and Heng came on each visit.

We looked at finished schools, approved new ones to be built and talked with students and teachers about the marvels of education. One young lady, six years old, attached herself to my skirt and hung on no matter what. Her mother had died last month and I seemed to be a good replacement. I felt for the little one.

Then we visited families who had received houses from our volunteer house builders. It was so good to see the improvements being made by each family. We met a family that had filled in the lower level with bricks and were slowly replacing the tin on the upper level with wood. They had taken off the Tabitha sign and were protecting it. They would have a ceremony when the house was rebuilt and then proudly hang the sign on the wall.

Some had bought new staircases; others had extended their homes and many had built or were in process of building a latrine to go with the house. Some planted flowers around the house, others had put up curtains but all reflected the pride and joy they had in their new homes.

We visited the many families who had received wells and who were earning incomes from these wells. We talked with Hout and his wife who had eight children. They were middle aged, their faces worn with the cares of life but they were proud and smiling for all eight children were in school, all of the time. They were earning enough to keep their children in school.

We saw vegetable fields; corn that was taller than me; spring onions that I couldn't have because they only chop off the green parts for selling; bok choy and cabbages, pumpkins and aubergines, chili peppers, there was so much to see. We looked at pigs and saw fish in the ponds; it was all so very good.

The last item on all the site visits was to see the new areas. I sighed with sadness. How could people live so meanly? Houses were so small and so inadequate. There was no water; there was so little food, and almost no clothes. We saw a number of men drinking under a tree. Srie and Da were disgusted. I said, if I lived like this, I too, would drink. Life could be so sad.

Phat, our manager in Prey Veng, asked that I come. Phat is one of our senior managers; he had been with Tabitha almost from the beginning. Phat's area was one of our toughest. In the areas we worked, the poverty was rather stark. Phat wanted me to see Prek Komdieng, an area we have worked in since 1998. It was always frustrating to visit because, despite a lot of effort, very little has changed.

As we drove into the area, Phat had us stop. I was looking at a lot of barren fields with splashes of green, here and there. A number of people were working in the fields and came to meet us. The first man to reach us didn't smile; instead I got a look of utter defiance mixed with pride. Touk looked at me and stated bluntly, I have all my children back from the border. Touk had five children and like so many in the area, when life had gotten too difficult, he would get a loan in exchange for one of his children from a moneylender. His three daughters and two sons had been at the Thai border for two years, the girls sold into the sex trade, the boys sold as carriers for heavy loads and of course, the occasional appointment with a man. What Touk did was not uncommon in this area as many families used this practice. Touk was waiting for me to say something.

I looked at Phat who was so excited. He shared the story. Last year Phat had asked Touk to be a model for the village. Phat would put in a field well and together they would grow rice and vegetables. It was unheard of in this village. Many of the men had gone off to find work, many were too ill to do work primarily because of malnutrition. Touk agreed and in the past year grew four crops of rice and two crops of vegetables. He earned enough money to buy all his children back. They don't need to work anymore, he said. Other men had joined us and the talk began. There were now 12 field wells installed but they needed 20 more! And then what? Come back in March and you will see. We will have rice and vegetables covering 150 hectares. And the children? The children, they replied, will all be home and in school. March is not a long way off so it's quite a challenge.

Touk watched me intently through all this chatter. He had expected me to pass judgment on his past behavior. All I could think was: who am I to judge these people? What do I know of hunger? I see hunger but I eat whenever I want and whatever I want. What do I know of being ill and not having medicine? What do I know of having to choose which child was next to go? I know nothing of this, I just know pain when I see it, and hope when I see it.

I went to see Tharry's projects in Kandal which was near to Phnom Penh and easy to get to. Our first stop was at Preah Put village where we saw 80 hectares of dry season rice growing, all from Tabitha wells. The families grew year-round food for the first time and their lives were changing rapidly. The husbands and the children were all at home. The smiles were wonderful to see.

We went to the new area of Duang. What a different story. I met 18 of 50 families who have been deeply affected by AIDS and malaria. Because of this, the families had sold off their farmland and all had less than five square meters to call home. There were lots of children. It seemed that this was the one thing in life they could do. None of the children went to school. They could not for they needed to scavenge whatever they could in order to eat each day. Each small shack had two families living in it, three square meters is not a lot for 15 or more people. These families had heard of us and asked us to come and work there. We estimated that there were a thousand desperately poor families in this area, half of them ill. Some still had land and so the pressure was on to put in wells. One young husband was growing mushrooms in a space 10 meters square. His income for the next six months will be $600 a month but then the rains will start and the mushrooms can't be grown. So, he planted another small field with cucumbers and another with trakun, a type of spinach. He gave us the energy to hope and to do as much as we could for all the families.

I was asked a question by a volunteer, are you sure there are eight people in an average family that Tabitha serves? It was a fair question and one that I thought deserved a fair answer. In Pursat, I met with 30 families who were about to receive houses from our house building volunteers. I asked how many children there were in the families. Giggles started and the answers: one lady has 12 for she had four sets of twins. Another mother said I have 10 children and on it went. In village after village the answers were similar.

We visited a school in process of being built. The director and teachers were so excited to see us. More than 900 children would attend school said the director, as I looked at an 80-pupil grade one class. How could they learn with so many children in one class? Then I asked the big question, on average, how many children in a family? Once again, the laughter broke out. Nine, said the director.

In Battambang, I visited with over 50 families. There was no road into their community rather we walked through uneven fields, looking at plots and plots of vegetables and fruit trees. These people had been waiting a long time for my visit. It was a good community, with young married couples and middle-aged families. The size of families was consistent, those just married had two to four children, those between 30-45 years were more varied. On average, 30% of families had 10 or more children, 30% had eight to nine children, 25% had six to eight children, 15% had less than six children. In all our areas, 70% of the families were raising an additional child or two that were not their own, usually from relatives who had died and left orphans or from relatives who needed to be away from home to work.

We had a wonderful time just chatting. A young married man of 27 said that every year he had to leave his home to find work. With the field well, he no longer had to leave, in fact he said, I don't have to buy food, I can pay my expenses and I have money left in my pocket. He was so delighted. The parents of seven children reiterated how good this all was. The only thing we buy now is a bit of meat or fish. Everyone said that they felt much better physically. I, of course, ended up heading home with cabbages that weighed two kilos, spring onions and long beans, all very delicious.

We had started to talk about the women's hospital so I came back to the number of children and the reasons for this. I asked the women how they felt physically. All of them had a similar complaint: they had an infection that resulted in a vaginal discharge which smelt bad, left them with sore bellies and caused them to be hot inside. Some had gone for medicine but it was too expensive and didn't clear up the infection. I asked about family planning; medicine to stop having babies. The women were unanimous in their answers: we tried the medicine they said, but it didn't work. We bled heavily, our bellies really hurt and we were hot inside. In my mind, I thought perhaps the infections were the cause of some of the aftereffects but I didn't really know. Whatever the reason, none of the women were interested in this medicine any longer.

In all these project areas it became clear that 90% of all rural women over the age of 16 have some form of infection that causes vaginal discharge and pain. Sometimes this would clear up when the husbands were away for work but would return when the husbands came home.

I had learned to present some sensitive questions in the form of a joke, so I said to the ladies, perhaps the next time your husband wants sex, you should just close your legs? Pandemonium broke out as the women said no way, but now the men spoke up for the first time. No, they said, we want lots and lots of children. When we are old, our children will take care of us. Our brightest children we will put into school, the rest will help us with the farming. I was straying close to a sensitive area. For the women, sex with their husband would hopefully ensure that the husband would not leave for another woman. For the men, children were seen as a form of social security in their old age. It was the one clear incident of the people thinking and planning for the future. Family planning would have to be taught taking this social aspect into account.

Over the years we started handling more and more cash, and it started to be a concern, both from a staff security standpoint as well as one of temptation for theft. I mentioned this to Phavi and her husband Sieng. Sieng put it all into perspective. He told me that it was no longer wise for Tabitha to handle all our funds in cash, rather it was better to use the banking system which had become well established. There were now banks in every sizable town throughout the country.

Carrying cash was not a wise thing. I listened to his advice with a sense of dread. Change was not something staff handled well. Sieng also suggested that I shouldn't be travelling to areas where people knew we worked with a lot of cash without security. I capitulated and Miriam and I had personal body guards until the news spread that Tabitha no longer dealt in cash.

At our next staff meeting I explained how things were going to change. We were going to use the banking system for everything, from paying salaries, to paying for materials for schools and wells, for paying subcontractors, everything. The next few weeks were difficult as it became clear that half of the staff and workers were totally illiterate. We had a number of people who could not even sign their name. The bank personnel were very patient and they taught people how to write their names. By the end, there were just three staff who could only sign with an x and a special symbol. It was a true eye-opener.

I asked Heng to become my right-hand person; the one who would take over should anything happen to me. Heng needed a few days to think it over. He agreed. Heng was and is a very humble man. He is quite strict but accompanied with a fine sense of humor. We hired Manang as our new accountant. She had worked as an auditor with the firm that did our audits. For a number of years, this worked very well but Manang was a Filipino and did not respect Cambodians very much. This brought its own tensions at the office. The lack of literacy amongst some of the staff was something Manang could not understand nor tolerate very well. She made the mistake of assuming that the lack of literacy was a sign of backwardness. They were illiterate but not stupid, a mistake many people make.

This was the year of water. We received grants for water sources from a number of groups: EMC, The Wheeler Foundation, The Leonard family and from FAWCO, The Federation of American Women's Clubs Overseas. It was unbelievable. For the first time we were able to meet the needs of a large number of families with life-giving water. But these grants resulted in more than just water. Yolanda Henry had made the FAWCO grant happen. A member of one of the FAWCO clubs decided to nominate me for a special award, the Veuve Clicquot Initiative for Economic Development Award. Unbeknownst to me, Claudette De Groote had made it her mission to see that I received this award. I would receive it in February of the following year.

The impact of water on our families was immense. It changed lives in a way that little else could. We were able to install 2,015 sources of water, with over 3000 hectares of land put under year-round cultivation, earning more than 6,500 families an average of US$500 per month, or US$6,000 per year, up from a low of US$300 income per year.

I met with the staff and talked about what had been accomplished this program year. We talked about the number of school-aged children in our program; in the communities where we worked and how many were able to attend school this year. We had a dream to build seven schools and we ended up building fourteen schools. We talked about the impact it had on the children in our program. In our new areas, an average of one child per family was able to go to school while in areas where we were in mid–program, the average was three out of five children. In the areas where we built our schools, four out of five children attended school. This year we enabled 120,878 children to attend school for the first time.

Our dream this past year was to have 55 teams come and build 950 houses. We had 97 teams come with 2,425 volunteers to help build 1,182 houses for our families. It was so very good. The volunteers became friends and supporters, people who had a deeper understanding of poverty and its impact on people.

Our goal was to work with and reach out to 42,145 families with 340,228 dependents. We ended the year with 43,546 families with 348,368 dependents and we worked with another 358 families in Cottage Industry.

Their initial savings wasn't much, usually 25 cents a week but those little bits of money grew into big money. Our families saved US$2,037,313.90 this year but the miracle was the purchase and life changes brought about. Our families purchased US$10,919,450.00 worth of goods and services. Savings works, for families pull together all their resources to make a positive change in their lives. As Tabitha staff we are cheerleaders, encouraging and celebrating each achievement. The families say to us, you helped us to think again. The attitude has changed. It was so very good.

## Nokor Tep Women's Hospital

Along with all the activity with Tabitha, work for Nokor Tep Hospital continued. We continued to develop our vision and our architectural plans for the hospital. Together we wrote a synopsis of the vision and plans for the hospital.

Our vision of Nokor Tep was comprehensive. At this time, less than 7% of the rural population had access to medical care. It was also very clear that 90% of the women in Cambodia suffered from long term infections of various kinds. The hospital would be the venue to treat women in desperate need of gynecological medical care. The hospital was the core of the outreach to these women.

An Education and Preventive Unit would be an integral part of the hospital. In this unit, materials would be developed to educate women about their various issues, preventative measures they can take, and when to seek medical intervention.

Our outreach would be to all parts of Cambodia through the use of mobile units. Nokor Tep staff would be trained to screen women in their communities; provide education and provide treatments for ailments. Severe medical cases would be brought to the hospital for treatment.

The hospital would have a research unit where research would be carried out on the various illnesses affecting women in Cambodia, the causes, effects and treatments. The hospital will be the core unit where training in all aspects will take place. In short, the Nokor Tep Women's Hospital would be the heart of our vision.

The vision was huge and taken as a whole, seemed impossible to achieve. Rather than us becoming overwhelmed with the vision, we broke down the vision into achievable parts which we believed would result in the whole.

Our first step would be the actual building of the facility itself. The design and architectural concept had been completed and detailed drawings were being made, permits were being applied for and the land for the hospital had been secured.

Our vision was to begin building the facility in the year 2012. The cost was estimated to be US$5.8 million for the building. None of our vision could be made concrete without the building being completed so serious fund raising needed to begin. We created a Wall of Caring; a wall that would recognize all donations of US$100 and above.

The building of the hospital, our vision for the people of Cambodia, was not readily accepted nor applauded by either nationals or foreigners. Culturally, Cambodian women were seen as second-class citizens. Their role in life was to serve their husbands and children without complaint. They were not to be heard and, in many cases, not to be seen either. Men were the rulers of the nation. Boys were the preferred children, raised to be kings in their personal lives. It was an affront to many men that we would place women as our greatest need rather than men. There was resistance to our vision at many levels. If we had made men the central focus of our vision, that resistance would not have been an issue.

For foreigners, the building of a hospital was a vision that was not plausible. People like myself and my co-founders did not understand that this was impossible. There were attempts made by several outsiders to stop this vision. Painful as that was, it was not the naysayers who we were serving, rather it was the people of Cambodia.

I met so many women with their sad stories about their health issues. I met Sokha for whom life was extremely hard. She had 10 children with the oldest being a girl of 16. Several years ago, Sokha became ill. At first, she lived with the discomfort for she would faint without warning and she was often breathless. She began to go to local elders for help and they encouraged her to take herbal teas, which she did, but things got worse. In desperation she and her husband sold a

305

hectare of land and with that money they began the rounds of doctors in nearby towns. Each visit cost money and each doctor would guess at the illness. There were no tests done and each doctor gave her medicine, but nothing changed. They sold their last hectare of land and with this money she went to Phnom Penh. The money dwindled fast as clinics couldn't help her. In desperation she finally found a hospital that carried out some tests. She suffered from high blood pressure and heart palpitations. Their medicine worked.

Then her husband became ill. Every day he passed blood in his urine, but there was no land left to sell, no money left to eat with, no way to find help. In desperation they sent their two eldest daughters to Phnom Penh and find work in a factory. One was fourteen, the other sixteen. With their income, there was food on the table.

But the girls were frightened to be on their own so far away from home, so they hooked up with a man who offered them a room to sleep in if they would but sleep with him. He offered safety in a sea of confusion, hundreds of workers, long days and short nights, surrounded by men who took advantage of the young girls, girls who were frightened and away from home, girls who had no knowledge of what life was all about. Inevitably, the youngest became pregnant. She continued to work because the family needed to eat. As we talked and Sokha finished her tale, she looked at me. I didn't know, she said, I didn't know where to find help with my illness, I was afraid to die. We sold all that we had and now my husband is sick. I didn't know about the factories, I didn't know what goes on there. I just didn't know. Sohka's story is one on a long list of so many.

It would have been easy to give in to the naysayers without knowing the women of Cambodia. Nokor Tep Hospital was a field of dreams

306

for so many women like Sohka. Our design incorporated an atrium which would provide a stream of light and air that that would infuse the building, a stream of hope for women like Sohka, to welcome them and bathe them with the light of hope, of love. Our design was one of brightness and natural beauty for those women who were living with disease. They will be welcomed with natural beauty surrounding them, welcomed with sights and smells of the homes they will leave to come to our field of dreams.

The year ended in peace. All our programs were impacting the lives of thousands of people. Our latest vision of the hospital had started.

# 2012

## Tabitha Cambodia

The year 2012 had started with so many dreams. We had over 47,000 families in our program, which meant that at least 376,000 people were working out their dreams with Tabitha.

In recognition of our work, I had been chosen to receive an award for which I was humbled and grateful. I would receive the Veuve Clicquot Initiative for Economic Development Award, an award that Clydette De Groote nominated me for. The award would be presented in a gala dinner in Paris, France.

To celebrate this miracle, I went on a site visit and met with several families. Kan Thai shared his story with me. He had five children, two boys and three girls. He was a farmer who could only plant crops during the rainy season, which was not enough to supply all the needs of his family. He received a field well from Tabitha. He loved Savings because it helped him to focus on achieving specific dreams of moving out of poverty. With the well, Kan Thai could plant vegetables and rice all year long. He was so excited as he said to me, "Now I still continue saving money more. I bought water pump, water jar, stair, build kitchen and I can raise pigs and chickens also. I am so very happy"

I went to a school that was being built in Kampong Channang. What made my heart so full was the sight of children who were the future students, actively participating in the building of the school. It was a bit of a problem for the contractors as the students often got in the way of the actual construction work but the children were so anxious to have the school completed. In anticipation, they had already bought school uniforms and wanted to help where they could each day. They were young and full of hope and dreams!

Graduation is an integral part of our work in Tabitha. Graduation is probably the most difficult part of our work. The staff become like family to our families. We are cheerleaders in the steps people make to come out of poverty. It is not easy to say farewell to people the staff have invested so much time and energy in. The families don't want us to leave. We are their emotional and spiritual support in life. They look to us for encouragement and ideas, for being told, well done! The truth was that we had too many families which really did not need us any longer. The families had become self-sufficient, they had become middle class.

We began to talk of which families should graduate and which families should continue. It was not an easy process. Sokeang and her husband and six children joined our program five years ago. Life was very difficult but Sokeang quickly joined our Savings Program, much to the disgust of her husband. She took his abuse for the ten weeks it took to get through the first cycle and then bought her first sack of rice. His attitude changed dramatically. Over the next few years, they received a well and started to raise pigs, chickens and ducks. They grew rice year-round. They built a latrine and saved to buy materials for a new home. It took time and courage and strength but they continued. I asked them how it all felt. Her husband looked at me, you gave us water, cool, clean, abundant water and we could do everything. You gave us a way to protect our money; to do things step by step. Now look at us for we are happy! We work hard but we are happy. We cannot say thank you enough. Graduation is a good thing!

We had families who didn't have enough land to grow rice year-round. For them the challenges were harder. As staff, we talked about families who didn't have enough land, what else could they do? We talked about raising different kinds of animals such as field rats. Vutha decided to raise crickets which are considered a delicacy for Cambodians. Vutha and his wife had five children and the pressures of life were great. It was hard to start such a business but it had become a life changing one. Since they started raising crickets a year ago, they had been able to buy and raise pigs, start a small shop and buy rice security. What was even better was that this family was helping several other families to begin a cricket business as well. Over the next few years, graduation became a necessary goal for all our projects.

I was asked so many times this year why do you do Savings? I once again explained that poverty was partly an attitudinal and psychological state. In Cambodia, the past forty years of war, genocide and its aftermath have left people feeling disenfranchised from life itself. The lack of security, the loss of family members, and the loss of their original homes over so many years has resulted in a severe poverty that is both physical and psychological.

In addition to their recent past, several cultural and societal issues resulted in poverty. Cambodians saw their children as an assured method of social security. They believed that their children must take care of their parents in their old age, therefore they have many children.

A second issue arising from this was that when a male child got married, the child would receive a portion of the family land. As their children reached a marriageable age, the land a family owned shrunk to a point where the land could no longer support a family unless the land could be harvested throughout the year. Currently, one crop a year is the norm.

A third issue which caused poverty was illness within the family. Whenever a family member became very ill, the family began to sell off what they owned in order to find and pay for medical treatment. Usually a family sold their animals, then their land and in severe cases they would sell their children.

In order to break the attitudinal and psychological barriers to development, we focused on Savings. The rationale was that Savings was a non-threatening way to make choices, a very necessary component for a people who had a very low self-esteem; who needed to have security with little threat and who must make their own choices without fear from us or others. Savings created a pathway for our families to takes steps to a better future.

With a change of attitude through Savings, a source of dependable water had the greatest impact on our families. What we meant by direct was that the water sources were installed for specific families because these families must be able to earn an income from the water but families in the community who do not have their own water source, do have free access to the water for family use; uses like taking baths, washing clothes, water for cooking and cleaning.

The impact on our families was immense for their disposable income changed dramatically from less than 50 cents a day to an average of US$6000 per year ($16 per day). How was this done? For families who had land suitable for growing rice: the change was from growing rice just once a year to growing rice year-round.

I visited our Takeo project where I was stunned by the intelligence of our families. The families had an average of two hectares of land but the land was broken into various smaller plots of differing sizes. What the families were doing was growing rice at different stages. When I arrived a number of plots were being harvested, in other plots the rice was half grown and in others they were just beginning to plant rice. The effect was amazing as our families were constantly harvesting and earning incomes every month from the rice they were growing. One lady, Theira, was so excited and her eyes full of joy as she showed me her various plots being harvested that day, other plots that were half grown and plots they were replanting. But it is the men who made it so very clear the impact this had on their lives. A consistent comment from the men, who stood proud and defiant before me was "I bought my children back." I could not begin to imagine under what circumstances so many of the men had chosen to sell their children but I do know the circumstances that were bringing the children home.

For our families who had land that was not suitable for growing rice, growing vegetables of all kinds brought about change. In our Kandal project I visited 60 hectares of newly grown vegetables. What a joy it was to see; better yet, how delicious the vegetables were to eat. The variety of vegetables was amazing: corn, tomatoes and lettuce of all kinds. Vegetables like Spanish onions, large green peppers and ginger that really surprised me. I never knew that Cambodia could grow such a wide variety of foods.

For families whose land was not large enough to grow vegetables and rice for sale, the raising of animals took a priority. Families were able to start raising pigs, chickens, ducks, fish and frogs. The ingenuity of our families always amazed me. Raising crickets and tarantulas as an additional source of income gave me the shivers.

People always asked me why do you do House Building? Well, there were many reasons. One of the main reasons is that House Building was a great leveler. Our poorest families had a very low self-esteem. They believed they were bad, they believed that they were not very smart. They believed that foreigners had all the answers. House Building changed that illusion. Through House Building, Cambodians needed to share their expertise with the volunteers that came. They taught foreigners how to hammer and saw, they taught foreigners Cambodian ways, they taught volunteers about their culture.

Foreigners liked to have a meaningful volunteer experience. They would like to feel like they have left something behind. They would like to feel as if they have interacted with the people of Cambodia. House Building fills that need.

Through House Building, volunteers were dependent on the Cambodians for instructions on how a house was finished. Volunteers played with the children and learned some Cambodian words, volunteers left with a deeper appreciation of the strength of the human spirit under harsh living conditions.

This past year we had plans to build fourteen schools in our communities that had no schools or the schools were no longer usable. The request for schools comes after our families have met their basic needs. When the daily struggle just to eat a meal a day was past, then the parents begin to focus on other needs. Schooling for their children becomes a priority. It was at this stage of their journey that they contacted us to see if we could build a school. The school was a community project as chiefs, villagers and Tabitha staff worked hard to make it happen.

—

Cambodia's King Sihanouk had passed away. It was a time of mourning for the people of Cambodia. For older people, like my staff Chao Da, it was a time of trauma. The passing of the King marked the end of an era of turmoil, uncertainty, tremendous suffering and pain. For Chao Da and so many others who remembered the time of goodness before the turmoil, the King was always there. Through all the years of uncertainty, the one sure thing was the presence of the King. For Chao Da and so many others like him, trauma marked his days as his fears returned. He was afraid that Cambodia would pass away just as the King had passed. He was afraid that the turmoil would all return.

For Sieng there was a deep sense of loss, a feeling of emptiness but there was also hope. The King Father prepared Cambodia for his passing for he had abdicated the throne and had placed his son King Sihamoni on the throne. It was the end of an era, one marked with deep sadness and emptiness but also a new era marked by hope and renewal. My heart hurt to see their pain but I was encouraged by their hope.

It was a time of joy for 480 children for their new school was completed and opened. What excitement as the donors, Corinne and Mike came to see it! What an excitement for the students to show their work, written ever so neatly in their notebooks. What an excitement to see a 16-year-old sitting in grade three, proud to be learning despite sitting with children much younger than him. What an excitement to see the grade five students relearning the alphabet for the past few years going to school had been sporadic as their old school building had rotted away. Rain kept everyone away but now all the students came all the time and the serious business of learning to read and write, the serious business of learning numbers, of learning about the world outside their village had begun in earnest. For me personally, visiting completed schools and meeting the children and their teachers brought me a deep sense of peace, of contentment, of hope for the future of Cambodia.

I was amazed at the boldness of the Tabitha staff. We would like to show our donors just one more place, they said, just one more school for it is not far away. As we travelled I was amazed at the transformation taking place in these communities where we worked. Three long years of savings, wells, house building teams, and now a school. The fields were bursting with rice but the wonder of the houses changing stunned me. Small patched, thatched houses were being slowly replaced by sturdy cement houses. Tabitha houses that were built by volunteers' teams were being transformed into larger homes with cement lower floors and extensions in the back. I rejoiced as a new era had come for so many. An era of hope and pride, an era where hard work was resulting in the dreams that people all over the world have; a safe home, secure sources of income and of a future filled with possibilities rather than simply waiting for a time to die. It was so very good.

Mara, our manager in Kampot boldly showed Corrine and Mike the next school that was needed. It currently consisted of two rooms of battered cement, filled with too many children. Then we had to see the building next door which was made of cement and wood but with no floors and no complete walls. The rooms were dangerous and when it rained, no one came to school. The threat of a child being hurt by falling debris was just too great. We just need six rooms, that is all we need, pleaded Mara! Corrine and Mike looked and saw, they heard and felt, and then they made their promise, yes, we can help. I was humbled yet again by all of our donors but as we talked, I thought of all the other schools that were needed, I thought of all the other children that were waiting to learn.

As usual, my life was full of emotions, full of dreams met, and dreams in process. It was full of people whom I call friends; some who are in great need and others who have a great capacity to give. I stand in wonder to see how my God had filled my life with fullness, the fullness of his creation, His people who are all of us as we stand together. As the needs of Cambodians are so many, I was reminded that all things are possible to those who believe. (Luke 1:37 NIV)

The year ended with a special day. It was special because my daughter Miriam and three of her friends came along on a site visit. It's not often that these young ladies could come as their lives at fourteen were rather busy with school and home activities. We went to Kampong Speu to see a school in the process of being built. As we passed through the village where these children live, we were reminded of how blessed we were. We passed one old school which was a small wooden building which held two classes, the rest of the classes were open air and on the corner of a dusty and very hot intersection. The girls were very quiet.

We passed by homes which were made of thatch and straw with not much in or around them. We arrived at the site of the new school. We walked into the old wooden structure, with holes in the roof and sagging support posts in danger of collapse which made all of us a bit nervous to stay inside. We were surrounded by children of all shapes and sizes. Over 1,100 students in those few rooms! My girls were nervous and a bit overwhelmed. While I talked with the parents and teachers, the girls started a volleyball game with some of the boys. At first it was very quiet but as the game progressed the cheering started. Each successful serve and volley was greeted with loud cheers from the rest of the students. For a few moments differences were forgotten, for a few moments it didn't matter if they were rich or poor, educated or not. For a few moments they were just kids.

Our second stop was at a school completed a year and a half ago. The differences in the villages were startling even though the roads to both areas were bumpy tracks with stunning scenery and poverty the norm. In the second village the school was finished and children were not afraid to be inside. The rooms were cool in the heat which was a pleasant and welcome respite.

Then we visited the homes of the children and the differences between the villages became marked. Three years ago, this village had also been barren and desperate but now it was full of food and dreams coming true. At each family home, the girls started to count the many ways the families were earning money. Every family had pigs and chickens and each family had just harvested rice; unheard of before! What a difference a well makes. All of the families were growing crops: bananas, papayas, lemon grass, pumpkins and peanuts, chilies and sesame seeds with at least 12 different small plots of vegetables per family.

For myself, it was a wonderful way to end this year of phenomenal blessings and miracles. This special day, my Miriam and her friends stood with our families for a few short hours. They shared the lives of the village children, rejoiced in play, counted and tasted the food grown, chased the chickens and laughed with the kids. It was so very good!

## Nokor Tep Women's Hospital

We needed to do a local fundraiser for the hospital, and came up with the concept of a Walkathon to be held in Phnom Penh. Nokor Tep was actually an extension of the work of Tabitha but because of the cost of Nokor Tep, I had decided to separate the two entities so that the hospital costs would not affect Tabitha development funds. The staff were so thankful for the hospital as they shared stories of women in their projects who needed our help so badly.

I cried as they shared their stories. I didn't cry when I was diagnosed with breast cancer; I didn't cry throughout the treatments; crying doesn't help. Pheow was my manger in Takeo. He was in his mid-forties, was married and had four children of his own. Pheow, like so many of my staff, gave so much of himself to the families he worked with.

Pheow was very supportive and desperate to have Nokor Tep Women's hospital up and running. One of the women in Pheow's district was Chan Saran. She was 63 years old and had given birth to four children. Her husband was still living. Four and half years ago, she suffered from a prolapsed uterus. She went to a doctor who told her to get an operation but she had no money and so she never went. For the past four and a half years, Chan Saran had walked in pain. When the pain was too great, she would take local herbal medicines to help. Chan said to Pheow, please take a picture of it. Cambodian women are very shy about their bodies; even more so about private parts. It was in her desperation that she begged Pheow to take a picture of her prolapsed uterus. That was what made me cry. How much suffering can one person have in her life? For Chan Saran it had been filled with war and genocide, unbearable poverty and now she was ending her life in great pain, so great that she was willing to forego her dignity in the hopes of a hospital in waiting.

Apo, my manager in Kompong Thom shared a story. Poun Roeung was 39 years old and had given birth to six children. Poun's breast began hurting five years ago. She went to seek medical help. It cost a lot of money and the medicine she got didn't work. She and her family were very poor. She could no longer work because her breast and her arm hurt when she moved. This made her husband very angry. When he came home from the fields he expected his rice ready but when it wasn't he beat her severely. He refused to allow her to go and look for help.

As I explained the concept of a walkathon to raise funds to build the hospital, there were tears in the eyes of many of my staff. This is about us they said in awe, we will build this together! For many the idea of raising funds was new for they come out of deep poverty themselves. Yet the idea of a hospital for women, for their wives and daughters, sisters and aunts were truly awe inspiring. They all asked for sponsor sheets and held those papers as if they were made of gold.

Two days before I left for Paris to receive my award, I flew to Singapore to meet with a corporation who had given over 500 wells in the past year. As I shared the impact of their grace for so many of our families, Steve, the Regional CEO, asked that I talk about Nokor Tep Hospital. Eleanor, Sharon and Lisa were with me, women who selflessly have given their time to run Tabitha Singapore and now had set up Nokor Tep Foundation Singapore. They too, had set up a walkathon for March 8, International Women's Day, to raise funds for the hospital.

As I shared this with the leaders of this corporation, they decided on the spot that they too would walk. How could this be that a multinational corporation whose leaders and staff would take a half day off in the middle of a work week to walk so that the hospital for women in Cambodia can be built? I had never heard of such a thing; my heart was full. To make the miracle even greater, Bruce Ford and Sam Gobran had decided to arrange for a 1000-kilometer bike ride through Cambodia. This was a sponsored bike-a-thon with all proceeds going to the building of Nokor Tep.

I came back to Phnom Penh for a few hours, to pack and pick up Miriam for our trip to Paris. In those few short hours that I was home I talked with several of our sewers, women who lived in areas where poverty was still rife. They shared their stories. They had gone house to house, shack to shack, where they had told their neighbors and friends of this miracle in the making; this vision of a hospital for women, a vision that needed all of them to achieve. They were met with tears and with offerings of 500 and 1000 riels, ten to twenty cents, and at the end of the day they had collected $35. Everyone had understood the vision and that their need was great. I was awestruck by this generosity given by those who had so very little.

When we arrived in Paris we were met by Clydette and Charles De Groote, people whom I had never met, people who had recommended me for the award. Over the next four days we were surrounded by their grace. One evening they had a few people come into their home to meet me. I shared the work of Tabitha and the vision of Nokor Tep Hospital. Miriam was with me and shyly asked for sponsors for her walk and they all graciously responded. Within thirty minutes she had collected $900. Then Michael came to me and asked me to send him information about the hospital. I am a member of a small foundation, he said, and we will donate $25,000. Karen came to me, I am a hiker she said, I will have a Hikeathon on the same day that you have your walkathon on March 24th. How could this be, for in the space of several hours, people whom I had just come to know, had given so generously for women they did not know? My heart was full.

The next morning, Clydette and Charles came with news! A private Foundation would match every dollar we raised for the hospital by double that amount up to US$500,000. I couldn't quite grasp what they were saying: this foundation wanted to encourage all of us to unite in raising funds for the Nokor Tep Women's Hospital by a double match of all funds raised. My heart stood still for that meant that Miriam's sponsorship of $900 suddenly became $2700.

Nokor Tep Women's Hospital was suddenly becoming reality for as soon as we had our first million dollars we would begin to build! My heart was so very full! When we came home and shared this news, Tuit, Miriam's nanny, had been out every day talking with all her friends in the markets. She had raised $300 while we were gone. This means that my money is now $900, she asked? And then the tears came and we held each other for a long time. Our vision of comfort and healing for women who had no voice and who had no choice was happening.

I was a woman who was filled with awe and a deep sense of humbleness. I was a woman who was so thankful to my God for His unceasing mercy, who filled my life with such grace. I wanted to start building Nokor Tep Women's Hospital as soon as possible for I wanted to stop the silent suffering of so many. It was a selfish desire that wracked my bones.

The next day we had a house building team arrive from the Netherlands. For the second year in a row they presented us with the gift of an extra hundred houses and 50 wells. They listened as I shared about Nokor Tep Women's Hospital and the walkathon. On the spot they decided to sponsor every worker at Tabitha for $10 each. As our women lined up to have their sponsor sheets signed by this gracious gesture, there were tears in their eyes, tears of thankfulness and awe and then applause. I was shaken by the deep emotion of these, our women and men, who have suffered so much.

We had our first 10-kilometer walkathon for the Nokor Tep Hospital here in Phnom Penh. 600 people walked that morning; many more gave support when they couldn't walk. How do I begin to tell you of the miracles that were happening? How do I explain to all of you the so many special moments? The offer of double matching funds started a snowball of support. So many came forward with support. I think what tickled my funny bone most was the support that Miriam got from so many people instead of sponsoring me! My initial response was, "What am I, chopped liver?" which got Miriam laughing! It also made her compassionate for so many Cambodians gave out of their poverty with tears trickling down their cheeks. They raised more than $30,000 with their 10 cents and 25 cents donations. Our entry fee was US$15 to participate so Miriam asked if it would be okay if she shared some of her support so that some of them could walk.

More than 300 Cambodians walked that day. It was a magical time for them for they had never done such a thing. They walked through a small village and then through farmland with the smell of rice being harvested and trees laden with mangoes, with aubergines deep with life. Three hundred foreigners walked with them giving the walkers words of encouragement, words of laughter and near the end, words of tiredness from many. For others it was, is this it? We did it? You sure did. Villagers came out of their homes all dressed in their finery to wave at these strangers walking through their life.

And then our walkathon committee, not a large one but people with big hearts and strong arms had gathered 70 young Cambodian volunteers, young people who helped man water stations every two kilometers; young people who had never seen such a thing but wanted to do it again.

At the end of the walk we all gathered together under a field of mango trees, we ate noodles together and cheered together. Many received prizes for their efforts while others received hugs and congratulations. We will do it again, when is the next one, so many asked. Our response was the end of next January. The three of us co-founders; Phavi, Sieng and I, each spoke. When Phavi spoke, the silence was complete. She spoke of how this hospital would affect every woman in Cambodia and every man; husbands would have a way to care for their wives and their daughters.

The weeks before the Walkathon, the enormity of the need for Nokor Tep Women's hospital became so very clear. Sohka, a woman in one of our villages was dying. The cancer that wracked her bones was slowly eating away at her body. When one of our staff spoke to her of the walkathon and the hospital, she got up out of her bed and over the next two days she visited every house in her village and talked of this vision. A neighboring woman who was dying from a blood disease joined her. These two women whose lives were ebbing away shared of how their vision of their neighbors not having to go through what they were going through touched every heart. In two days they collected $223 with Sohka herself donating $10. She said to me, this is all I have but I will give more as soon as I have it. My tears were hard to hold for this woman of dignity and strength, this woman of courage and vision, this woman whose days on this earth were limited. We raised a little over US$140,000 through the walkathon. An event which would be repeated for the next five years.

We had exceptional news for the hospital. The Prime Minister, Samdech Techo Hun Sen, signed off on our hospital. His message to all was very clear. We need this hospital very badly. I don't want to hear of anyone obstructing the building of the hospital. That put a complete stop to all the negativity we had been receiving within Cambodia. How good that was for now people wanted to encourage us instead of mocking us. What a relief!

Phavi, Sieng and I had made a promise that once we had one million dollars in the bank, we would select a contractor and the building of the hospital would begin. We selected a company, a company well experienced in building hospitals with organizations that were well funded. They had no experience working with an NGO that was not well funded. The company asked for $800,000 to start the project. I was not happy with this at all. Instead, I proposed $500,000, and show us what you can do. Writing a check for that amount made me physically ill. So much money at one time. Whoa! The company's response was to add on another $500,000 to our budget for the hospital. That bothered me no end.

We asked the company to delay starting the project until we had a ceremony asking for God's blessings on the land. The morning of this auspicious occasion I arrived to be met by a rather upset and disturbed company project manager and a overturned bulldozer. What happened, I asked. The gentleman was very upset. We had asked him to wait until the ceremony was over before beginning the work. In his wisdom, he decided that he should begin to dig the foundation. With the first scoop of dirt, a mighty wind had sprung up and blew the bulldozer over. The wind was just on our land, nowhere else. You need to learn to listen, I said. The hospital was a project out of faith, faith in our respective God. Our ceremony was one that addressed our God through animistic and Buddhist traditions as well as the Christian traditions. Very few people understood how important that was. The company learned a valuable lesson that morning.

In Cambodia there was a set of rules for women's behaviors called *"chhap srey"*. These rules dictate how a woman should behave. A woman should be silent; should not talk of her problems to others, should serve her husband first in all things; should not make noise inside the home. A woman must be a shadow, a fleeting figure in a man's world.

Women like Von Savvy. She was a young mother just 22 years old. She was pregnant with her second child. Like so many other women, Von Savvy was working in her fields planting rice when she felt faint and fell. It was clear that all was not well. Von Savvy was transferred to a hospital where she gave birth to her son, three months too early. She could no longer breathe on her own. Her neighbors, her family, the village chief, our staff, everyone gave money to make it possible. But it was not enough. Her husband sold all that they owned, all they had bought through savings. At first the small things like TV, battery, table, chairs, bed and then their land and finally their house. All was gone, there was nothing left. Von Savvy's mother-in-law was angry for she blamed the baby. The baby had brought misfortune therefore the baby had to go. I was saddened for there was not much that I could do.

All of our workers lived with *chhap srey* rules. Many of our women suffered from physical as well as emotional abuse from their husbands. The rules dictated that they should accept the abuse. For the men, there were also rules. One of the most important was that a man had to provide for his family. Many of the men lived in poverty and worked in jobs that were precarious, that could end at any time. All were severely underpaid despite working 10 to 12 hours a day. Men with these issues were not seen as men for they could not fulfill their roles as providers. This led to abuse. Our women took the abuse on themselves but when the man began to abuse the children, the women became angry and would divorce the man. This was done under the auspices of the local chiefs; men who had the responsibility of enforce the law within the villages they ruled. I respected these men for they were unusual. They knew the women had paid for their small plots of land and their small homes. They knew the women provided the food and clothing for the children. The chiefs would grant the divorce with a settlement from the woman to the man of US$25. The man was then banned from the village and the women were protected from his abuse. It was another reason why I loved Cambodians.

# 2013

## Tabitha Cambodia

The year started out well with a new Tabitha Cambodia website, a website that gave a much better overview of what we do, where we do it and our progress for the current program year.

I went to Kep in Kampot on a site visit. This trip amazed me and reminded me about the ingenuity of the families in our program. Oy Tien and her husband lived in Kep. They had three children and two hectares of land. Four years ago, life for the family was extremely difficult. The land lay barren and they lived in a bamboo shack. They got a field pond from us and their life changed. They began to grow crops all year round: three crops of rice and three crops of corn. The rice yield doubled from two tons per harvest to four tons per harvest, enough to eat and enough to sell. They began to raise fish for family consumption, raised chickens and ducks and then raised pigs. From their incomes they started a small shop which had grown and now included several tables and chairs for people to sit and to eat.

Their income increased to a point where their eldest son could go to high school, a dream they never believed would happen. He learned about biogas and so they started a composting project that released enough gas and energy for all their cooking needs and for all the lights in their home. Their house changed dramatically. First, they built a two-story 12 x 5 meter cement home and then recently they added a new addition in the back for toilets and water.

But the biggest change was in their outlook on life. Oy Tien was so proud of what they had accomplished. They were content in their labors, content in being able to provide for all their children, content in their willingness to share their life with others in the village. They were a constant source of encouragement to others whose dreams were similar. It was time for graduation. Graduation was about celebrating life itself and marking yet another stage in the lives of our families for they will continue to grow and flourish. Tabitha will begin the process again with other families who are just beginning the journey.

Graduation of families like Oy Tien and her family, gave me an opportunity to reflect on who I was, what I was doing and why I was doing it. Fierce opposition to the building of Nokor Tep Hospital by some foreigners increased my need to define who I was. My passion for the people of Cambodia started many years ago when the bombing and genocide were taking place in this country. I knew then, as I know today, that this is the country I must serve. I am a woman of extraordinary passion that makes me different from many others. My passion is rooted in the pain I see in others, pain that I know I can impact and not turn away from.

Like all people, I am terribly ignorant of all the types of pain people suffer. I have discovered over the past 35 years that helping to ease pain is something which is learned not from books but from life itself. Over the years I have learned the pitfalls of community development. I have also learned that there are better ways to do it, not because some book told me or some professor taught it but because I could see and feel whether or not what I did actually alleviated the pain.

I learned through all these years that the cost to myself in some ways was enormous but in so many other ways, was nothing. As long as I persevered and was faithful doing what I knew was right, not for me, but for the people I served; then there was no other option. The learning had not always been easy. Starting Tabitha, I had only one other person who believed in me, not in what I was going to do, but in me. My brother John said to me, sis, I will help you but understand me, no matter how many will stand with you, you are alone. It is your vision, your faith that will make this happen. We can only stand with you.

Tabitha is my vision and drive, and every aspect of Tabitha came about through personal knowledge of the pain and suffering of others. Savings is the only way to help those who live in fear. It focuses on their choices with no threats. Cottage Industry I knew was the only way for women who had their dignity stolen from them through sexual violence and abuse. Being handed an orphanage full of children filled with pain gave me no choice but to find them a home. My gorgeous daughter who was a defiled child, a throw away child, I had no other choice but to call her my own. House Building, I learned from people who had no home and from people who needed to serve. Water programs came from the death of one of my staff who on his death bed said, they need water Janne, give them water. Schools came from people who needed to serve, and from children surrounding me because there was no school, or space, or money. Nokor Tep Women's Hospital came because I suffered and it was my own suffering that made me so aware of the suffering of women here.

In all these instances there was one clear marker for me, I could do something about the pain! Once I knew that, I never had any other choice but to do so. Doing less would have taken away who I am; it would have made me empty. I am who I am. The visions I have, and the work I must do. I can do nothing except to do it.

I know that for many people, my visions at times seem to be far-fetched, yet I must be who I am. I know I can make a difference in the lives of millions of women through the women's hospital. It is not an easy task, nor a quick one, but it is one I must do. I have no other choice.

And yes, people will stand with me in this vision, people we know and people we have yet to come to know. Each person will add and be a part of that vision. For some, in ways they, nor I, could ever have imagined. And that is good, for that is what life is all about.

My inner strength and conviction comes from my God who has been and always will be with me. In that sense my brother was wrong. I have never been alone. I am grateful to each and every person who joined me on my journey and shared my vision for the people of Cambodia.

Phat came to the office one day and excitedly told Heng how the Prime Minister of Cambodia was going to give him an award. The Prime Minister wanted me there. Heng and Srie and I were a bit dumbfounded as we knew the award was not for Phat but for me. How do we tell Phat this? I didn't have the words, nor did Heng or Srie. I assured Phat that I would be there and we prayed that someone else would tell him. I was a coward!

I was given an award by the Prime Minister of Cambodia: Samdech Hun Sen. It was also my 65th birthday and I received an award that was created in the year I was born. The Royal Order of Sahametrei is a chivalric order conferred by the Government of the Kingdom of Cambodia. The Royal Order of Sahametrei was instituted on 9 September 1948. It is a prestigious award for distinguished services by foreigners rendered to the people of Cambodia.

It was a special day because I didn't expect this high an honor. It was special because the award was given in the back of beyond, in a small rural village where we had built a school, did savings and put in wells. The protocol people had been phoning a number of times that morning, where was I? I was on a road with potholes large enough to swallow the car. It was very special because the honor was given amongst the people we have come to serve, 6,000 villagers; people we worked with were there to share the honor with me. It was an honor because it was given with pleasure and received with a deep sense of humbleness and thanksgiving.

The months of October and November are always very busy months for us at Tabitha. A large number of house building teams as well as visitors come and spend time with us. I often wonder what the impact of these visits had on our visitors for the impact on our families that I know! I would like to share some of these moments.

In October we had a team of teachers from the Australian International School in Singapore come to build houses. One of these teachers shared a reflection on his experience for he was not overjoyed with the possibility of house building. He came reluctantly, fully convinced that he could not contribute to the process. He believed that he had nothing to offer and Cambodia had nothing to offer him. He told me: We travelled into a little village about two hours outside of Phnom Penh. We were given a little demonstration on how to hammer nails into floor boards and sheets of tin into wall frames. It looked simple enough. Oh, how wrong I was. I started hammering the nails. And no word of a lie, every single nail that I tried to hammer into the same floorboard bent … and this took place for almost an hour! I like to think that I am a patient person. I like to think that I cover my anger and frustration from others, but I was seconds away from throwing my hammer into the jungle and giving up completely. Everyone was so capable. Everyone could do it so why couldn't I? At this point, a young gentleman from the village climbed up the ladder of the hut we were working on and literally grabbed me by the arm and took me away. Without thinking, all I took with me was my hammer. I was taken to the next hut where another team had begun working. Through the rain I could see a man wearing a grey, floppy, full brimmed hat walking towards me. He looked to be in his mid-60s. This man stroked my arm, ever so gently, and stood beside me. And without speaking a word of English, he started hammering a nail through a bottle green colored sheet of tin and then gestured for me to do the same. I said I couldn't, shaking my hand 'no, no, no. I am better at floor, hammering nail into floor. Again, he touched my arm, pulled me closer and hammered another nail into the wall, although this time, he only hammered it half way in. Step by step, nail by nail, we walked the perimeter of the house, hammering away, laughing at the nails I kept bending, me apologizing profusely, him just beaming his magnificent smile as if to say it is okay.

For someone to recognize that I was struggling, even without speaking a word of English, to show me how to do something, to stand by me and offer his patience and encouragement was just, oh, I just can't describe it, it was just so special.

But you know what, after my little moment with my friend in Cambodia I've realized something. I've realized that I am capable. I can do things that seem impossible. I need to admit that I'm hopeless at some things. I need to reach out to those who are good at doing things and let them teach me.

I've also realized that this wall I put up really doesn't exist. It's in my mind. It's crystal clear now. From this day forward, I'm going to 'do' things in order to understand. I'm going to stop listening and watching and sitting back. I'm actually going to do something about it. And if I can't do it, I'm going to ask someone who can to help. And on the flip side, when I am teaching, I'm going to allow my students to 'do' the things that they think they can't. I'm not going to just talk to them and show them, I'm going to let them do it. And I'm going to be by their side all the way.

One of the greatest privileges in my life and our work in Tabitha was hearing the words of our volunteers and visitors. It was good to hear about the changes in their lives. It was an affirmation of the vision I had from the onset of Tabitha that if I just put people from all backgrounds together, to simply give people an opportunity to serve, then we could change Cambodia and we could change ourselves. We could bring peace to a country torn apart with sorrow. This year was a year of affirmation of Tabitha and of myself.

## Nokor Tep Women's Hospital

The year had started with much excitement for the Nokor Tep Women's Hospital. Unbelievable how good the foundation earth works looked! It actually brought a sense of deep awe to me, and I couldn't resist going and seeing this miracle in the making. I took some of our Tabitha staff to come and see the progress. There was so much laughter and so much awe; it was a wonderful hour together.

We were preparing for our second annual Walkathon for Nokor Tep. As the staff and I were standing looking at the land, several of the staff came forward and said, it's so beautiful and this is in Cambodia! They said it with wonder and several had tears in their eyes. I want to walk but I also want to donate from myself, can I give $100, asked Srie. They were so shy with their gifts, so humble, which made this a moment to treasure.

Then the awe left them and they turned to me, well Janne will you walk this year? Or will you just welcome us at the end? I knew their thoughts; a challenge is a challenge! I laughed and replied, only if I have a personal sponsorship for US$100,000 will I walk. I figured that was a pretty safe statement to keep me out of trouble, but then you never know.

We held the second annual Walkathon. It was a morning when your nationality or skin color didn't matter, your age or your wealth; everyone was the same for a few hours. The weather was beautiful, the countryside showed its abundance and beauty in crops and our walkers showed their compassion in walking the walk for so many of our Cambodian women.

In the process of registering walkers, a long-time friend came up to me. Caroline works with many of the labor unions, working on women's issues and the conditions of the work force. She said to me, I didn't quite believe what you told me last year about women's health in Cambodia so we did our own survey. We confirmed what you were saying but we learned even more. Did you know that 40% of the women surveyed have a prolapsed uterus? My mouth dropped for I was stunned. The average age of these young ladies was 19. How could that be? How much suffering is there?

Did you know? Magic words because it was exactly this statement that covered my own ignorance, did I know? No, I didn't, for ignorance was bliss! What I didn't know about others could not affect me but I was beginning to understand that although I may be ignorant and blissful of the pain of others, it did not mean that others didn't suffer. It was all about the silent suffering. I could not imagine what pain, what thoughts these young ladies must have about their own bodies, what guilt and what shame was attached with something so personal.

Work with the contractor was turning into a nightmare. After they had completed the land works, their productivity ground to a halt. What did not stop were their incessant requests for more money. I was adamant in my refusal to grant any more funds until they had reconciled the spending of the first $500,000. Then the lies started. We have ordered 1,340 20-meter cement foundation posts from Thailand. From Thailand, I gasped, why would you do that when we make them in Cambodia? Show me the receipt! This they could not do so they badgered Sieng for a few weeks who in turn sent them back to me. It became so onerous that I would no longer meet with them. The task of turning them away fell on Manang's shoulders.

This continued for several months until they finally delivered and installed 340 locally sourced foundation pilings and then work stopped again. It was exactly a year ago that we had given our first payment to our contractor. We were full of hope and of excitement, it was all beginning. But sadly, we chose wrong for we chose a contractor that, despite all their hype, loved money but hated to perform. They were always asking for more money and more money and increasing the budget for the building by leaps and bounds. They were unwilling to do anything and so they held us hostage, give us more they said, but you have done nothing I replied and then they would do a little more. Give us more they said but you haven't done enough I said and then they would do a little more until we came to an impasse. They were holding us hostage and our dreams of turning tears into laughter, of turning pain into health were held in abeyance. For a while, 12 long months, we allowed to let them hold us hostage, we allowed them to bring our spirits down.

In total frustration I talked with Sieng and told him that I could not do this anymore. Sieng was so relieved for he too could not deal with it anymore. So, we terminated the contract but not before I had full reconciliation of the funds given to them.

Now we made a bold decision. We decided that we would take control of construction. We would do so by using local contractors and local people to build the hospital while maintaining international standards. It was the best decision we made.

Over the next several months my daily trip out to the site was fraught with anxiety! How many pilings had been done? Will the rains hold back? Will the machines all be working? The trip to the hospital site was ridiculously perilous. There were no paved roads although the roads were planned by the city and would be eventually completed. The potholes and the traffic were a nightmare.

And then came the morning when the land cried out. I was standing on the lip of our foundation watching the pilings going in. What a noise that was. And then I heard the land groan, a groan so deep and painful, that it shook my soul. I phoned Sieng and told him he needed to come because the ground had cried out. He asked me in astonishment, you heard it? Yes, I heard it. We were from two different faiths yet we served the one God. Sieng came immediately with the proper offerings and prayers for his Buddhist faith. I prayed in my Christian faith. It became our daily task. The ground never cried out again. It affirmed that our hospital was a walk with our God, each of us expressing that faith in different ways.

We hired a project manager, Mr. Para, who was a lovely man with the skills and temperament to be able to do the work. Our vision was to be a teaching hospital so we contracted to become a teaching ground for the Institute of Cambodian Technology, ICT, and their skills in survey work and architectural design. We became a classroom for professors and their students, the best of both worlds.

What a pleasure this all became. How much I enjoyed working with Cambodians who were full of life and hope, who wanted to build and learn and contribute their many talents for the women of Cambodia. There were many challenges that lay ahead but how good it was to be with people for whom challenges were just that, something to be resolved and to move forward with.

⌒

Cathy and Matt arrived with another house building team for Tabitha. Cathy and her husband Matt were strong supporters and had been coming for the past four years. Cathy was diagnosed with breast cancer a couple of weeks previously. She was already a colon cancer survivor and now she had breast cancer. It was a daunting diagnosis. We were talking about what lay ahead for her and we were comparing notes. Both of us were survivors but more than that, we both had a positive look on life and all its up and downs.

As we were comparing notes we talked about the options that we had. Why did I have a lumpectomy and she was having a double mastectomy. Then the jokes began. On my last visit to the doctors, I had six mammograms done which were not pleasant. I started developing an aversion to my own breasts. I said I believed that my breasts had gained at least two inches in droopiness. Cathy laughed and said; see I will have new perky ones. We laughed because we could laugh, we laughed because we had options and we were in control of how we would fight and survive these obstacles.

Another friend, Glen Stretton, was here and he had brought his son Harley, a young man who is rapidly becoming famous as a musician, going by the name Flume. Glen had come for a number of years on house building and made our first video clip about Nokor Tep. He asked Harley to come and see what was going on and to put on a concert for Nokor Tep Women's Hospital. Glen was also prepared to do a second video clip. In that process we interviewed several women in our projects, one of whom was quite ill. Glen asked me, how do you feel when you leave a village with a woman so ill? At that moment, I was so sad for this woman for she had no options. She had no jokes to tell, she had no future to look forward to. That was the stark difference between rich and poor.

Finally, all the pilings had been completed just before the rainy season started. What was even more amazing was that the cost was much less than what had been estimated. Suddenly, we were back on budget. Halleluiah!

Our next phase required innovation. The rains had fallen with abandon and many of our Tabitha project areas were under several meters of water. Sieng was an innovator, a man of vision. How could we do the heavy labor with technical expertise? Sieng's response was to design and build special machines. These machines were to enable us to do the capping. Capping was a process where all of the 1,340 piles needed to be buried up to a meter's depth below the soil. Each pile needed to be broken and rejoined in sets of three or six or nine piles which would be joined together with a six meter wide and deep cement cap. These would become the 220 main support columns for the hospital. The things I was learning about construction, things such as load bearing, about measurements and surveyors, it all left me breathless! Yet it all left me with a deep sense of contentment as yet again I was learning about things I never knew. It was all quite good fun especially when I suggested that we drill a small hole in each piling, put in a touch of dynamite and blow the tops off. This suggestion was met with wide eyed disbelief by our young engineers. No sense of humor.

Sieng decided that since we were teaching new skills to so many people, we should hire farmers from our Tabitha projects, farmers who had lost their rice crops to the recent flooding. It was a great idea. He decided that these men and women would first break the piles manually with chisel and hammers. Oh, how hard these people worked. Then he brought in the innovation: jack hammers! If we had brought in the jack hammers first, these men and women would not have accepted the innovation for it was something they were not used to. With the methodology of using what they had learned to do and the harshness of the work, the people were very willing to learn the new technology. It sure made the work faster but much noisier.

As the building progressed, there were expectations amongst the women we worked with. For some, the expectation was not for themselves, for their lives were coming to an end. Im Sot was ill with pains that wracked her body, with memories that disturbed her sleep yet she faithfully collected and donated a few dollars each year as her faith in Nokor Tep stood firm. Im knew that her time was short for in her mid-sixties her body was no longer strong. She believed that her daughters and granddaughters would receive the care that was not there for her.

Then there was Sok Che and her neighbors, women who struggled each day to put food on the table, women who talked in secret about the way their bodies are betraying them. They were ashamed of the smells that emanated from their bodies, afraid of pain that haunted them and prevented them from being the wives their husbands expected. Despite the situation, they had faith, faith that once Nokor Tep was built, we would welcome them with open arms.

Then there were the young people, young men and women who had faith in their own futures, in the goodness of life that lay ahead. These young people had faith that the hospital would be there when they begin to suffer. In their faith they clamor to join us in our fundraising events here. Young university students so terribly upset that they did not know beforehand of the Walkathon this past year and who will join us in the walk next year.

How good it was that faith still existed, that belief in the goodness of humankind was evident even when it seemed that there could be no good at all. I was so thankful that faith and expectation were a part of all of us. It was a good way to end the year.

# 2014

## Tabitha Cambodia

The year started out with a new epidemic spreading throughout Cambodia. This epidemic was not a disease but financial ruin. It marked the acceleration of micro-finance. In 2006 Grameen Bank had been awarded the Nobel Peace prize for their micro-loan program to the poor. This opened the floodgates to unscrupulous people and institutions that took advantage of this lucrative business.

Micro-finance was based on giving loans to the poor and lower middle class. These loans were legal and always included collateral. Collateral usually involved land, house and chattel, often children. Micro-finance boasted about charging low interest rates but what they failed to elaborate was that these interest rates were monthly, averaging 36% annually. In short, interest was based on usury.

For the poorest, loans were seen as an easy source of ready cash. The poorest are often functionally illiterate; they do not understand the legality and impact of having a loan, nor the impact of collateral. In Cambodia, the poorest were drawn to the easy money without worrying unduly about the repayments and collateral involved.

Cambodia was developing at a very fast pace. The tourism industry and the garment industry were a huge employer of the poorest. Going to work in the city for teen-age children in a family was very popular, with the understanding that these children would send home money to the families. Construction was growing in leaps and bounds, so it all seemed so good for our families. But the salaries of the workers were low and it was not secure in any of these areas of employment. Garment factories would hire workers on a three-month trial period before the worker received benefits and secure work. As the end of the three months grew closer, the workers were dismissed. It was so very sad.

And so, the poorest took out loans with abandon, never understanding the ramifications of not being able to repay a loan. Our managers began complaining of villages being emptied of families. Whole villages were decimated because of unpaid loans. The families believed that if they were not at home, the micro-finance companies could not collect on collateral. How wrong they were!

The problems increased to a point where the only people in a village were the micro-finance staff desperately trying to collect on loans. We had to close down a number of our project areas as there was no one left in the villages we served other than a couple of elders and a few children.

We also needed to take away the ten per cent interest that we paid on savings. We were contributing to this mess because of the interest. Just like people worldwide took advantage of the Grameen Bank as a way to make money off the poor, rather than help the poor, so was the word interest becoming an evil word, a word that meant people would lose their homes and land. The interest that we paid through savings was being correlated with the percent of interest charged on loans. The average interest on loans was 3 per cent per month or 36 per cent per annum. People were confusing the interest we paid with interest charged on loans. Several of our staff were attacked by angry villagers who had taken loans but could not repay. The people believed it was the interest that caused the problem. It now became too dangerous for our staff to pay interest on savings.

To overcome this, I insisted with all the projects that graduation and repaying all our savings was of outmost importance. I insisted that each project staff then re-enroll families that wanted to do savings only. The impact of micro-finance brought a sense of urgency to making sure Tabitha programs were beyond reproach. It was a very difficult time. US$36 billion had been loaned out to a population of 16.5 million people. This was totally unsustainable! Villages were emptied, the suicide rate of the young workers quadrupled, the internally displaced people living within Cambodia quadrupled as families desperately wanted to start their lives all over in a different part of Cambodia. Land grabbing was at an all-time high.

Despite the mayhem caused by micro-finance our work continued. We had received a great number of donations for water sources in the past two years. I made the mistake of supplying water before the donations actually reached Cambodia. We had a promise of US$100,000 for water sources this year so I let the projects install these water sources without waiting for the funds to arrive. This started to put us into financial jeopardy for the contractors needed to be paid, yet the funds had not arrived. This promised donation took two years to arrive. Manang, our accountant, was beside herself as the funds used to pay for the wells were meant for other programs. We decided at that point to never again install water sources without receiving the donation first. We were walking a financial tightrope during those two years, an experience never to be repeated. A lesson well learned!

House Building had an enormous impact on so many people. Over the years so many volunteers had shared with us their own personal impact. I often got the question, but what about Cambodian house builders? Miriam attended the International School of Phnom Penh (ISPP). Every year the tenth and eleventh grade students went house building with Tabitha. One of the privileges was that I shared my thoughts with all the students, but most importantly with the Cambodian students. This year I was very privileged to hear several reflections of their house building experience, their own personal journey which was a journey very different from all of us. For these young people, the recent history of Cambodia was very personal. It was a privilege to hear their thoughts.

One young Cambodian shared the following with me: The first learning outcome I would like to address is undertaking new challenges. The phrase "new challenges" before meant little to me; it meant taking on new things and just experimenting with possibilities, example sports and languages. However, the orientation at the Tabitha main headquarters led me to a realization that the term new challenges is far broader than I had thought it was and can also be used to describe a change in lifestyle. The one most important thing that was demanded from us house builders was respect. Respect. True, as the founder of the organization had said, our generation is a rather spoilt generation. We do not fully understand the word respect, and nor can we fully understand what hardships in life really meant. The fact that the one thing she had stressed on was just respect really surprised me, and my first reaction was that even without having to stress on it, respect is needed wherever we go and for whatever we do and that it was obvious. I did not realize, though, the gravity of the term, until the one-hour long orientation was over, and until I started to grasp the reason behind her words. Thus, I concluded that being respectful is the most important 'new challenge' in this activity. Compared to this, the nailing of floorboards - my previous 'new challenge' - seems rather insignificant.

Lastly, in this reflection, I would like to thank you and Tabitha House Building for giving me this opportunity. I was not only taught about the implications of this house building job, but I was reminded of important life values. Most especially, when during orientation it was said "our faces are going to be the last thing [they] think of the day [they] die", I was reminded about how we forget what really matters. These people will judge us by the good we do, not by who we were, or where we are from. In our easy lives, we tend to complain, and when not given enough attention, we automatically assume "nobody cares", forgetting the people who DO care. I was reminded once again of how we take things for granted, how we are never really thankful for what we receive. Unlike these people who have only seen "evil" and once given something good, never really forget the feeling of gratitude. The sad thing is that for now, I am reminded, but I know as a fact that in a couple days' time - maybe a week - I will forget once again."

Another young man shared the following: Before the trip to Toul Sleng and Choeung Ek, the orientation with you at the Tabitha House Building headquarters brought me to a realization. Even though I have heard many stories time and again from different people about their experiences during the Khmer Rouge Regime, not one of them have ever mentioned anything about being traumatized. Your talk made me realize that many of the people who survived the war would have had post-traumatic stress disorder and this made me more cautious and mindful when speaking to survivors about their experiences. Additionally, even though I have lived in Cambodia my whole life and understand that most of the Cambodian people who were victims of the war are incredibly grateful and caring due to what they have gone through, I seem to have forgotten these things until your emotional reminder. I feel that even though I know quite a lot about my country and what my relatives and many people around me have gone through, it can be so easily forgotten because the people have moved on, or at least tried to move on, and build their lives from what little they had left. Your much-needed reminder has stuck with me and taught me to respect my elders because of how they have come out victorious even after all they have gone through. It is easy to hear a story from a victim and feel empathy for them, but it is also easy to forget their struggles when they can hide it so well. Your talk not only allowed me to gain inspiration from the victims and how well they have coped after the war, but you also taught me to never forget people's struggles because even though they might be happy now, bringing back the memories of their trauma could hurt them; therefore, it is incredibly important to be more cautious and understanding of their past.

Another young Cambodian shared: Out of all the activities I think that house building had the biggest impact on me because it really connected to me on a personal level due to the issue of the Khmer Rouge. Especially on the day of the field trips when you gave the speech I gained so much knowledge and you educated me a lot that day. When visiting the graves and the jail I felt a very emotional connection because my own father had lost his siblings to the Khmer Rouge I felt very angered and at the same time sad because of all the suffering these people had to do for one dictator. After the field trips I learnt so much that I will hope to let the future generation understand also. When going on the actual house build I learnt a lot of things such as how to hammer properly and where to hammer the nails. I just felt a joy I never felt before seeing the smiles on the people's faces when completing the houses. I cannot put how unbelievable the experience was."

How thankful I was to my God for this life He had granted to me. How thankful I was for these young people who taught me so much. I prayed that none of our house builders ever forget the lessons that house building had taught us.

⁓

As we were finishing our twentieth year as Tabitha Cambodia, our development staff spent a week together, evaluating the work of two projects, Prey Veng and Svay Rieng. The rules were different this year for I insisted that none of the staff from these projects were allowed to be with the other staff as they interviewed several hundred families from each project. At the end of the week we had a debriefing session, a session that was unusual in its impact on everyone. We interviewed a cross section of families in the Savings Program: some who had graduated from our programs several years ago, some who had just graduated, some who were mid-way in the program and lastly, new families just beginning.

The debriefing was very emotional as staff talked of families who had graduated and are graduating of being in tears. Why the tears, I asked. These were tears of thankfulness. Families talked of their despair before they were involved with Tabitha, with the common description of how they felt as "We were miserable, we could not think anymore, we had given up. With the savings program came encouragement with the message you can do anything and always being there to celebrate each step of progress which was exactly what we needed", the families said.

As the discussion progressed, several of the managers were in tears. Why are you crying I asked the staff? Apo said it best: "I was nothing before Tabitha but now I am everything. I am proud of who I am for I have a wonderful husband and family; I have a home. All the things I never thought I would have. This is what we give to our families, the same ability to take pride in themselves, to be confident in taking new steps, in making the choices. It takes courage to make these choices but we do it."

The managers of Prey Veng and Svay Rieng, Phat and Ponluck respectively, glowed with pride and a sense of achievement. It was so very good.

Two weeks later, Ponluck passed away. He had been diagnosed with an infection in his leg. We brought him to Vietnam where we found out that his infected leg was not the real problem. Ponluck was riddled with cancer. He died knowing the impact that he had on thousands of fellow Cambodians. On the day he died, he took his staff to the bank to deposit savings from our families. He instructed his staff to continue to do the work with integrity and with passion. When he was finished, he fainted on the bank floor, and went into a coma. We all miss him terribly because we were family, because we took pride in each other's achievement, because we loved him.

We had a number of families who had lost all that they owned through illness. The most striking community was in Saang, Kandal Project. What do we do with families who have lost it all was our hardest question to answer? In this village, 753 families were reduced to living three families to a small shack of two meters square. They owned no land and had no means of bringing in an income.

It was a daunting and painful visit. What do we do? We decided that families needed their own homes so a house building team came and provided houses for a number of these families after the commune chief gave each family a small plot of land for these homes, six meters by six meters. This was good but their incomes had not changed and the pain was still there.

We had a staff meeting, what could we do? It was very easy to walk away from the problem; pretend that it did not exist. I suggested that we start thinking outside our normal boundaries. What could families do? Some families could raise pigs and chickens but most families had no space for even this! How about raising insects, which were a delicacy in Cambodia, I suggested. Our staff were not so sure about this.

We had visitors come who wanted to see the work. Tharry was her usual charming self yet she was also very nervous. I want to show you something she whispered in my ear. As we drove back to this community, I was a bit confused and so I asked Tharry, is this what you want to show me? We walked through fields of rice and vegetables as so many neighboring families flourished because of field wells. We walked by a patch of pumpkins and again I was confused. Growing pumpkins during rice season? Tharry stood proudly and said yes but did not elaborate.

Finally, we came to this village. Tharry brought me to the first home and there it was. Underneath the Tabitha house were four cement pens and each pen had crickets; lots of crickets! I was amazed for there was a nursery and several pens of almost fully-grown crickets. I was stunned and asked how many crickets? The answer was about 300 kilos worth of crickets. They are sold every five weeks and the income averaged US$200. This was indeed a very welcome change to the famine status of so many of our hurting families. I couldn't help but laugh. Several other families were growing pumpkins for that was the favorite food of the crickets. We had noticed a number of egg cartons on our site visit that day and so I asked what are they used for? Raising crickets!

Life could be very hard for our families, sometimes we are not sure which way to turn. Sometimes innovation and lots of talk can turn the futures of those who hurt so much, towards a life of hope. Who would think crickets could have such an impact? I was so grateful to my God for all He had created, I was so thankful for staff who took a risk and walked outside the boundaries. Mind you, I am not a lover of God's little creatures so I made sure we had no crickets in the car or on our clothes before we left.

I was once again reminded of what poverty was on a site visit to Prey Veng. "Absolute poverty or destitution refers to the deprivation of basic human needs, which commonly includes food, water, sanitation, clothing, shelter, health care and education" according to Wiki web site. The visit was disheartening at first for there were 1,500 hundred families of which 90% were living in absolute poverty. It was a hard thing to see people living in absolute poverty. So much of Cambodia was stunningly beautiful, especially at this time of the year when the rains have come and food was growing in abundance. The colors of the greens and blues were a treat to the eye and brought balm to my soul but the poverty was not a treat to the eye and it burned my soul.

Tabitha had been working in this village for two years. The stories of the families were heartbreaking for I could not imagine living my whole life in a small thatched hut with each day a struggle to survive. I talked with a grandpa who was 85 years of age and had 10 grandchildren living in his home. There were no middle-aged people around; they had all passed away leaving behind the elderly and the young.

Our conversation centered on his life and the impact of the field well on their lives, the ability to grow food year-round was beginning to change the life of the villagers. 30 field wells so far but they need several hundred more. A house building team had come and built a few houses. Water jars and new tin roofs on thatch huts were visible, a bicycle, a pig, slowly things were changing.

As we talked, his thirteen-year-old granddaughter stood scowling behind us. Why are you so unhappy I asked? I want to go to school, she said with defiance. The tension amongst us grew as the other children nodded in agreement; none of them had ever gone to school. Over 500 children - another challenge to overcome.

Across the road I met Nan with her children. Her 19-year-old daughter was having trouble breast feeding her baby. The story of the 19-year-old was so very typical of the poorest. She was married too young to a husband too young who was unable to care for his wife and child so he left. Nan was now raising her granddaughter, her own daughter with no education and no real skills to change much. Their field well is bringing in some much-needed food and money.

I was so thankful for all that I had for I didn't live in absolute poverty. I knew that I had to be patient and that two years from now, so much more will have changed in the lives of these people but it hurt me to know that so many have lived this way for too long.

A visitor asked me, tongue in cheek, how do you bring peace to a country like Cambodia, where life can be so hard? I thought about it and decided to ask some of our families. I had the opportunity to ask a few of our children, what present would they like, what gift would make their families have some form of peace, what would give them some relief from the daily grind of life.

I asked a nine-year-old if she could have any present what she would want. I want a bicycle so I can go to school, my mum could make her business bigger, and my dad would take us for a ride and start his business. A bicycle would be so good. Then my family would be happy and we would have some peace.

I asked a 12-year-old what he would like. I would like a team of cows so that they could carry my loads; take the family to town; help me to plow the fields; my dad would be happy because the cows would have babies to sell. Sometimes though, cows butt people but I would like them anyway.

Peace on earth comes with making the day-to-day pressures of life a bit easier, the burdens of life, lighter to carry. Peace was about savings and dreams, about water and housing, it was about schools and income, it was about labor that produces good income. It was about dignity and respect; it was about enjoying life's pleasures and being undaunted by life's hurts.

## Nokor Tep Women's Hospital

There were two major obstacles to maintaining the progress made by our Tabitha families and that was illness and micro-finance. Illnesses like Ponluck's, illness that were terribly misdiagnosed and caused death. Our vision was to begin addressing the next major cause of severe poverty in Cambodia. Earlier I wrote about a village of 1500 families where 763 families have sold all that they have achieved because of illness. We had begun to address this issue through the building of Nokor Tep Women's Hospital, a hospital that would begin to address the needs of the most vulnerable in society, the women of Cambodia by focusing on effective, efficient treatment. It was a part of Tabitha Cambodia yet separate so that we were able to continue to bring people out of poverty, while developing strategies to keep people out of poverty. The hospital was a huge venture and so we kept this program separate financially so that all our programs would thrive.

For Nokor Tep Women's Hospital this year was full of promise as construction continued. I learned so much about construction and its ins and outs. I now know what capping was: reduction of our 1,340 piles down to 197 caps, each containing at least 2 piles and several containing as many as 10 piles. What a lot of work and concrete but how good it was to see.

We always had visitors come and see the progress of the hospital and a number of these visitors mentioned the lack of safety equipment for our laborers. So, in our infinite but not so much wisdom, we outfitted the workers with steel tipped boots, helmets and gloves. And the accidents began to happen. Cambodians very seldom wear shoes, in fact they wear flip flops instead. Their toes grip the ground and steel like fingers. With boots, this was no longer possible and they began to fall off the pilings. The helmets prevented them from seeing. The workers began to revolt. We let them go back to their old ways and we closed our ears once again to the wisdom of foreigners.

A good friend who worked for the UN mentioned that 25% of his Cambodian staff had cancer. Several had been sent to Singapore for treatment. For one woman it was too late. As we talked, we mused about the women who work for NGOs and companies who have compassion. For these lucky women, hard as it was to go through this alone and in a strange country, at least they had treatment and a sense of hope. For the vast majority of Cambodian women there was no hope, for many there was not even diagnosis instead, just a growing awareness of pain; a growing awareness that all was not well; a growing sense that life itself was ebbing away. For these women this journey was one of despair, of fear; a journey of silence because there was nowhere to go and no one to talk to.

In all developing countries, the simple choices of health care of any kind are choices limited by availability. Cambodia was no different. This past week, we talked with several families devastated by illness.

Srie Thon had a stroke at the age of 33, two years before. She had four children all under the age of 13. The stroke left her unable to do anything which drove her husband away from the family, leaving them alone to fend for themselves. When he left, there was no longer any money to feed them and so slowly they began to sell all they owned, the land, the animals. Now just a patch of land where their shack stands was all that they owned. The oldest boy became the man of the house. He left to find work as a construction worker in Phnom Penh, leaving the three youngest to work for neighboring farmers in the rice fields or cutting grass or finding frogs and geckos to eat. Thon's tears slid down her face as she said "I am invisible, I am no longer a human. I should be taking care and raising my children but I cannot". Tears flowed down the faces of our staff for there was so little to say, so little to do.

It was another typical year full of blessings and hardships. A time of growing and renewal and a time of reflection.

# 2015

## Tabitha Cambodia

Happy New Year. Happy, it was one of those overused words that I actually dislike but I went on a site visit where I saw true happiness! It was senior citizen's day at Tabitha. Being a senior in Cambodia means anyone who survived past the age of 60. I travelled to Saeb Village in Kampong Channang to visit with two families who had received a field well from us three years ago. The road to these field wells turned rapidly into a dusty track.

I first met Norng Sim, 63 years old, a woman worn by the years of hardship and suffering. The only members left of her original family were herself and her 83-year-old mother. She raised six nieces and nephews whom she adopted as her own because her siblings had passed away. She was so excited to show me everything she had done with her well. She had grown rice, watermelons, morning glory, long beans, gourds and more on her one hectare plot of land. She was very excited to show me all the changes that savings and income from the field well had brought her: a rotor tiller and wagon, a bicycle, a new house and all its furnishings, and her youngest adopted son's telephone shop. All her adopted children were now successfully employed and they all lived under one roof.

But her true happiness, the thing that pleased her most and made her body shiver with joy, she told me was, "I now eat three times day, can you imagine this, three times a day And anything I want to eat!" What hunger this woman must have endured in her 63 years of life that food, in its variety and plentifulness, was her happiness!

Two hundred meters down the dusty track I met the diminutive Hout Hun, who was all of 4ft 8in, and her husband and children working their two acres of land. She was 64 years old and had eight children and grandchildren living in her house plus one son with six grandchildren living next door. Once again, I was shown with great pride the food that the field allowed them to grow all year round: rice, watermelons, beans, and morning glory. She too, showed me with pride her rototiller and wagon. No more cows for her! Her two daughters and their children were helping her grow this food.

Her house was not yet rebuilt for a new road was being planned by the government and she did not know how much land that road would take from her home. But, she winked at me, it's okay for you see my pocket is full of gold! Once I know how much space I will have left, then I can build my house!

But her true happiness, the one thing that made her giggle like a school girl was the fact that now she could buy anything she wanted. She was not talking about the big things in life but rather the simple day to day things that make life worthwhile. She giggled as she told me, "Before I could only look at things, I could never buy and it was always so hard. Now I can buy what I want!" What hunger this woman lived in her 64 years that buying a fish for lunch brought her so much happiness.

We sat and chatted under the shade of Norng Sim's house whose 83-year-old mother joined in the banter. It was the repeated word of happiness that touched my soul for both women were so delighted to work in their fields each day. Hout Hun said with passion, "I just love harvesting the watermelons and taking them to market, all by myself, and selling them. Oh," she said "it is my favorite day of all." Sim chimed in and said that was true for her as well, to be able to have my own money, to do so many things but the best is yet, I can eat three times a day.

Neither woman complained about aches or pains. Neither woman wanted to stop work and sit under a tree, life was too good for that; for working hard and bearing the fruit of their labors was true happiness. May I have that happiness all the days of my life!

---

I was so very angry at our manager in Kompong Speu. I was angry because of his passion for the people he worked with. I was angry because he broke the rules and installed 48 ponds without talking to us first; without asking if the funds for these ponds had arrived. I was angry because I saw the results of his work and in my heart, I understood why he did this but angry that he would put Tabitha back in a position where we were not able to pay for the work done by the contractor.

I was angry because yet again the passion of our staff for the people they work with, overrode their responsibility to us as an organization, putting pressure on me that I did not want, yet I loved the results. His excuse for doing this was something I truly understood. The roads to his villages were at best passable and at their worst, bone jarring hours to cover but 20 kilometers. The contractor would not bring his machine out on these horrible roads without ample reason to dig ponds. Obviously doing 48 ponds was enough incentive. It was the dry season as well so the machine would not get stuck in muddy fields. All legitimate reasons.

The village had 420 families and over the past 5 years, 173 families had received water. The poverty in the community was palpable. Houses made of grass, no food, no water, no sources of income. With water came changes too remarkable to ignore. Families began to raise chickens, which multiplied with abandon, which were sold to buys pigs, and then chickens and pigs were sold to buys cows, which multiplied and were sold to become rototillers, motorbikes, new houses and simple basics like food and clothing. Faces that were once so downcast were now shining with joy.

And then there were the have-nots watching those with water and their desire to change their lives became my manager's burden. He was not so dumb! He made sure I saw the fruits borne by these ponds that were dug over the years before I met the families with new water sources. The men were so proud of their labors for all had begun the process of turning chickens into pigs and turning chickens and pigs into cows. All had fields prepared for mango trees and watermelon. These were men who were normally not home but away trying desperately to earn enough to feed their families; home because now their land, their labor will change the lives of their families. My manager knew I would be overwhelmed with the looks of pure pride, men standing with dignity, so proud to show me what they are achieving.

I was angry because I hadn't done everything in my power to make sure that we could install 3,000 sources of water this year, angry that in some way, I had led him into a very legitimate temptation to break the rules. I was angry that I could not meet all the needs of the current families in our program with water now. I was angry that poverty was a reality for so very many of our people.

We had a special visitor come to spend a week with us. Andre had worked for 40 years with an organization called FAO, the Food and Agriculture Organization of the United Nations, and had visited and evaluated development and agriculture projects throughout the world. Andre spoke in almost every country in the world and addressed the UN on various development issues.

With this kind of resume, I was not sure what to expect. What a delight it was to meet a humble and gentle soul, one who had seen much and done much. Personally, it was a delight to speak with someone who understood what we were doing without having to give a lengthy explanation. Andre was fascinated by our Savings Program, a program that impacted the way the poor look at themselves and look at how to achieve simple but positive goals. He interviewed a number of families from various project areas, what was life like before Tabitha and savings and what was life like now.

One example was Tev Seahvey who had been in the savings program for ten years. As she told Andre, before she started working with

Tabitha, she was truly miserable for life was very difficult with just one meal a day and one rice crop a year. When we arrived at her home, we were greeted by 12 cows sleeping peacefully, four sows which were in different phases of pregnancy, plus ducks and chickens. On the outside of her home was a small pond with a thousand fish which they kept exclusively for home use, trees with edible leaves, plants of okra, long beans and more.

Seven people lived in the home. Her daughter was expecting her second child. This child would be born in a maternity clinic which was an amazing achievement. Andre asked about the impact of the well she had received. Her rice crop yield had changed from just 10 sacks of rice for the one harvest per year to 30 sacks per harvest, three times a year or 90 sacks in total. The next question concerned the cost of pesticides and fertilizers. The answers came with quiet pride. 90% of the fertilizer came from animal manure and leaves from certain trees. She had to buy 10% of the fertilizer because growing crops year-round meant the livestock didn't produce enough manure.

The pesticides used were homemade and she recited her recipe which included leaves from certain trees, lemongrass as well as chili peppers. Andre asked her where she had learned this recipe. Tev had been able to pay school fees and her son had learned this at school.

The house was full of belongings, clothes, cooking utensils, farming equipment, all bought and paid for through the Savings Program over the years. There was a rather unique water filtering system for clean, cold water. There were bicycles and motorbikes; there were happy faces and healthy bodies. What struck me most was quiet pride; she spoke calmly and looked us in the eye for she was not afraid to answer all our questions. What a difference from when I first met her when her head was down and her voice nothing but a soft whisper.

Andre spent several days with staff in different projects, hearing the stories and asking the questions. On the last day we went out together to one last village. Andre summarized what he thought were our strengths. The most important aspect with Savings was the time we allowed our families to develop a process of increasing wealth and contentment without threat. He demonized micro-finance and its impact on the poor in countries such as Ethiopia and India. I told him about the impact it was having in Cambodia. Micro-finance was not a one-time quick fix to poverty but rather it was tearing down the fabric of society in many villages.

Andre loved the way we encouraged our families to think in increasingly broader ways of generating income and using that income in a planned and careful way to improve their living conditions. He commented that people having to put in their own funds within all our areas of project work was so very good for it meant that the people owned the development rather than development being imposed on them.

Andre had visited more than 40 countries in his work over the years, including Cambodia. He believed that Tabitha's development work was one of the three best development projects he had ever seen. Andre thought I should bring this to the United Nations.

I demurred telling him that the same thing that happened to Grameen Bank and micro-finance would happen with savings. People would only hear what they wanted to hear. Many would go all over the world to the poorest and take money from the poorest, not to help them, but to enrich themselves. It was a risk that I was not willing to take. I did not want to be responsible for others taking parts of our ideas and changing this for their own benefit.

2015 was a year of miracles, a year of blessings. With the restructuring and renewal of our programs, we had the privilege of talking with so very many families who had journeyed from absolute poverty to middle class Cambodians, people who had become friends. As one woman said, even though I no longer need Tabitha because I am strong now, I feel like I owe Tabitha for my very life. I was so miserable and suicidal and then Tabitha came and showed me a better way. How very humbling this was!

## Nokor Tep Women's Hospital

Construction of the hospital was coming along. The basement and the walls and floors to the ground floor were completed and work had started on the first floor. Elevator shafts were poured and support pilings to the next floor had been completed. Stairs from one floor to the next had begun which was a tremendous relief to me as I no longer had to climb makeshift ladders to the next floor.

It all cost money and we were very busy with fund raisers such as the Walk-a-thon, Ride-a-thon and others. Our Tabitha foundations around the world held special events to raise funds, except Australia. We decided that we also needed to raise funds in Cambodia. My co-founders Phavi and Sieng were devout Buddhists. In this tradition they held a ceremony called Bon Phkaa Samaki. This ceremony was one where people were invited to come together and work together to complete a task which for us, was to help complete the building of Nokor Tep Women's Hospital.

People of all classes of life came and participated, it was a time of peace and of contentment. It was also a time of tears as we walked through the building under construction. I explained what each space would do, leaving many women in tears, tears of wonder, of excitement and of hope.

I shared the success of the ceremony with our staff and workers at Tabitha. Tears flowed freely and hugs in abundance as the women spoke of the hope and faith of a place where they could come in the future, a place of safety for all women in Cambodia to share their hidden pain and shame, a place of comfort and shelter, a place of peace.

Good friends of mine, Cathy and Peter Emmerson decided that they would set up a foundation for Nokor Tep Hospital in Australia. This would allow many in Australia to send tax deductible donations for the hospital. I was overjoyed and so very thankful. Cathy and Peter decided that I should come to Australia to meet with a number of groups and share the vision and our work. The most touching meeting was with the Cambodian community in Melbourne. They welcomed us with open hearts and joined us in our vision. Over the next several years, they raised several hundred thousand dollars for construction. The advent of Nokor Tep Australia was to bring in many supporters, each of whom added a special aspect to the growing hospital.

It was a typical year for me, one filled with too many blessings to count.

# 2016

I had a project manager for whom my heart bled the most. She was five when the Khmer Rouge took over Cambodia, too young to understand the enormity of what was happening. The Khmer Rouge executed her father and three brothers in front of her; they took her away from her mother and put her into a children's camp.

She was too small to work in the fields so the Khmer Rouge put her in charge of 60 babies, all under the age of one. When the Khmer Rouge would visit the crèche and a baby was crying, they would take the infant and smash the baby against the wall. She felt personally responsible for these deaths. Too young and too sad.

After the Khmer Rouge years, she was reunited with her mother. Her mother had remarried as protection against the Vietnamese army, who tended to rape single women. Her step-father didn't want her so she lived on the stairs leading into their apartment. Her mother soon got pregnant and gave birth to another daughter. The husband was not happy and he began to beat her mother. She was ten when this all happened.

One day the step-father had beat her mother badly and came storming down the stairs looking for her. He had a knife in his hand when he reached out to grab her, he tripped. The knife embedded itself in his body and he died. She believed that she was responsible. It was out of this pain that she became one of our most compassionate managers and my example to teach the impact of the Khmer Rouge to our volunteers.

A number of people asked me over the years why I did not become bitter and disillusioned with all this sorrow. Why did I still trust everyone? The answer was simple. I could not live with distrust and seeing only the bad in people. My greatest fault was that I believed in the goodness of people. It was what I looked for and encouraged in as many people as I could. 98% of the time, I got the best out of people and they brought out the best in me. The two percent that let me down made me sad for a short time but then were forgotten.

Removing the ten percent from Savings and the graduation of families who no longer needed us was good. It reduced the number of our families dramatically to a little over 17,000 families. The accolades from families who graduated affirmed that we were doing the right things. I began a process of auditing the projects and programs myself. It was a good way to reaffirm that what we were doing was right.

Cambodia had been hit hard by drought and phenomenal heat. The average mid-day temperature throughout the country was between 42°C and 44C. It left us all feeling extremely hot and very tired. It was not a pleasure to be outside. But the hot temperatures were spawning erratic and very dangerous thunderstorms with storms with high winds and lightning but very little rain. The result was devastating as homes were blown apart and families no longer had shelter.

We had a number of house building teams come in this weather when the heat was overwhelming and the lack of electricity and water on site left the volunteers gasping but they did not quit. They continued to build and at the end of the day some families had a home.

All of our house builders left me in a state of wonder. It was not easy to come to a strange country, a country where the weather was never predictable. A country that had different customs and culture. Our volunteers came with a desire to serve, they worked hard in difficult circumstances and they did it with grace and humility. The volunteers left having gained more than they gave.

## Nokor Tep Women's Hospital

It was an exciting start to 2016 because my sister Nancy and her husband Wolf came on their annual visit. They had seen the progress of the hospital from a field of rice, to the biggest pond in Cambodia to today. What did they see in this time with us? They saw the construction of two large septic tanks; the construction of another ten percent of the third floor and then the pouring of that section; they saw the beginnings of the next section to be poured; they saw our new road in front of the hospital to the main road, they saw a new toilet block being built and they saw the preparation of the road around the hospital.

It was wonderful to see the road being built not only in front of the hospital but the adjoining, treacherous roads that we travelled since the onset of the hospital. It meant a lot more traffic but it also meant that the bone jarring travel was coming to an end. Now I had to learn to put up with the traffic jams that came with the new roads as well as the expansion of housing.

Phavi, Sieng and I entered into discussions with a possible partnership of a medical group already established in Cambodia to run the hospital. We learned a lot from them in terms of the challenges involved in running a charity hospital where everyone would receive free medical care. We had been friends since their small hospital had opened a number of years earlier and I had advised them that free does not work very well, nor is it sustainable over the long run. Charging patients from the onset was the way to start. The hard part was deciding how much to charge patients, especially the poor.

This group had never had strong government support and was anxious for us to open those doors for them. They were properly registered with all the appropriate government ministries but had not developed the relationships required with that registration nor had they earned the respect of the government. I suspect it was because the foreign leadership of the hospital was always changing with short term assignments.

They saw Nokor Tep as their opportunity to earn the funds they needed to run their hospital, a factor that we saw as less than optimum. We also felt that their lack of relationships within Cambodia and within the medical community had become a problem for them, one that would reflect poorly on Nokor Tep. Phavi, Sieng and I decided that it would be best if we ran the hospital ourselves with doors open to receiving foreign expertise on a voluntary basis. It would be better for us to have many partners rather than a few.

We had a group of women from the French community come and see and learn about the hospital. The questions of why came up, why do this at all? It was such a big vision with so much effort involved. My answers were not flip. I asked the ladies, if you and I have breast cancer, how many of us would get help immediately? Not only would we get help, we would almost expect it as a right? Everyone raised their hand.

But if I was an ordinary Cambodian woman and I had breast cancer, I would have no options, nowhere to go, no one to hear my cry. I shared how when I discovered I had breast cancer that the answers to my illness came very quickly and so I got help. I received the best care and had been cancer free for almost six years. At the same time as I had cancer, we had several Cambodian women in our program also ill with breast cancer, one of whose tumor had ulcerated. There were no options for these women and they died a very painful and agonizing death.

Then I asked the question: why could I expect and receive treatment when Cambodian women couldn't? Was I of more value than these women; were any of us of more value than a Cambodian woman? By what standards do we judge the value of people? We were worthy of treatment simply because of an accident of birth, born in nations that had evolved to providing such treatment. Should we not do the same for these women in Cambodia? I concluded that if I had been an ordinary Cambodian woman with breast cancer, I would be dead today. They could not answer my questions.

I had the privilege of bringing all our women from Cottage Industry out to see the progress of the hospital. These women have had harsh lives, were sold into the sex trade, half of them were living with AIDS.

Tabitha had allowed them to become women of integrity and beauty. As usual, I was talking and showing the spaces within the hospital, what we would do, etcetera. At first there was a lot of chatter but then the group had turned quiet. I turned to see what was going on. The women had tears streaming down their faces, this is for us, they said! How very good that anyone would build something so very beautiful for us!

The Queen Mother of Cambodia, Her Majesty Queen Mother Norodom Monineath Sihanouk invited Phavi, myself and several other support people from Nokor Tep to come and visit her at the palace. The Queen presented us with a cash donation towards the building of the hospital. Her Majesty was delighted about the progress of the building and talked of the great need of the women for our services. She spoke of the battles Cambodian women faced in order to receive treatment when they were ill. It was a special hour, an hour where we talked and stood together in our efforts to bring health care to the women.

The First Lady of Cambodia, Samdech Kittipritthbindit Bun Rany HUNSEN, President of Cambodian Red Cross, also presented us with a donation towards the construction of the hospital. It was a special moment as we discussed the hospital; how it will work, how it will touch so many lives. We were very honored.

The second level floor structure was now complete. Work on the support beams for the roof was progressing rapidly with over 170 square meters of concrete poured in one day. How wonderful it was to see one cement truck after other come and pour their precious cargo. In addition, the brick walls on the basement level had been started and were progressing very well.

The Margarita's house building team came and built 30 houses. They had a lovely build but they also became acutely aware of the need for Nokor Tep Women's Hospital on that build. One house that they built was for Yea Chien and her family. Yea was 55 years old and had been ill for two years. She had a lump in her belly, a lump that has swollen to the size of a basketball. Yea took herbal medicine for she could not afford anything else for they were so poor. The team was saddened and helpless in her plight. My soul ached for her but my hands were empty. In Cambodia a house of your own was so important to die in so she was comforted. For me the question was simply, why must she suffer so?

Soon we had 70% of the roof poured. How good that was! The rainy season had started and we wanted to complete the roof before the big rains arrived. Then we needed to finish the interior structure which we could do when the rains fall. We wanted to complete stairs, finish elevator shafts, brick and mortar the walls, and finish the floors. So much needed to be done but it will be beautiful!

We needed electricity to run the hospital. In order to run all our equipment including the operating theaters and radiation units we needed to increase our capacity to 800 KVP. A very generous Cambodian donated the cost of wire and electricity poles plus installation costs to the hospital, but we needed to buy an expensive transformer to make it all work.

We had finished pouring our fifth floor which I thought was to be our roof but Sieng thought we should have a sixth floor and authorized pouring the foundation for that floor without consulting me. I was beside myself with disbelief and horror. Phavi, Sieng and I had discussions about this, some very difficult discussions. The talks revolved about the future. If we had five floors we would have the space for growth over the next 10 years but if the fifth floor became a roof, then we probably needed to add to the building in 4 years' time, at great expense and to the detriment of our patients. We agreed to build a roof over the fifth floor but our decision was dependent on donations coming in, enough donations not just for the roof but finishing the inside of the building. It was a bold vision, a vision we would hold on to for two more months to see if the funds would come in, otherwise the fifth floor would be our roof.

Our fundraisers around the globe were going into their fifth year when our financial needs had grown considerably with our need to both finish the interior as well as the structure of the building. Two miracles happened. The first was from a couple of housebuilders. Veronica and Leo had come house building for a number of years. In addition, they had built a school. They took me for lunch and asked what kind of funds we needed for the hospital construction. They told me they would be able to donate A\$400,000. Veronica and Leo were the most unobtrusive people I had ever met. My reaction took them by surprise. Who are you people? They shared their story. I was left in an emotional turmoil; people such as this couple, donating such an amount with no expectations, no name on the wall. Just use the money wisely and let us see the work, was all they ever asked of me.

Then, Margret and Russel came with news that brought me to my knees. Russel was the CEO of a major company and this year he was receiving an extra bonus for he had brought this company from the brink of bankruptcy to a well-run, profitable multinational. The bonus was US\$720,000 and they wanted to donate the total amount towards the construction of the hospital.

The last miracle came from Harley Streten, aka Flume, who donated $100,000.

I was overwhelmed by these gifts. Gifts that were given from the heart and for a sharing of our vision. Our God had a strong hand in all of this. We could do no more than fall on our knees in thanksgiving and praise. What a blessed way to end the year.

# 2017

## Tabitha Cambodia

Heng was promoted to Assistant Director of Tabitha Cambodia. It was time to train him in the many ins and outs of Tabitha. We started our new year with a trip up country to visit new families and ongoing families. What a lovely day it was. Heng, Srie and I traveled to Takeo to visit a new community of families. It was a day of enjoyment as Heng reveled in walking through the villages for it was a day of comforting and a day of new hope; it was a day of celebration.

We met with 67-year-old Mao and her neighbors. Mao was saving for pots and pans, at the advanced age of 67 because she had never owned pots and pans. This day she received her savings and she was excited for the big moment of buying pots and pans.

We met with 43-year-old Chantha who wove mats of reeds. Three years ago, her daughters aged 14, 11 and 9 had developed a fever and three days later all three were dead. She started savings, what courage that took as she started to dare to dream of a better life. I was struck how very sad life can be but mostly was struck by the strength of the human spirit. I was not sure whether I could come back from losing my children in a space of three days.

As we were walking to the next set of families, Heng stopped us to show the job he performed during the Pol Pot years; the plants he needed to cut for fertilizer and the cow patties he needed to collect. He was only 11 when his father, two brothers and two sisters were killed by the Khmer Rouge. He himself had been beaten half to death for taking a few grains of rice growing by the wayside. This time there was no sadness just a bemused rendition of the jobs he had to do and the life he lived.

We met 34-year-old Neng with her three children. She had already bought water jars and pots and pans. She was raising chickens but they had to be kept in the hut she lived in for Chinese New Year was coming and chickens were very valuable. People were stealing chickens in their village so they needed to be hidden.

We met 52-year-old Po who was very sad for on the coldest day in December her 84-year-old mother complained of chest pains and died. Po was feeling very guilty that she was not by her mother's side when it happened because she had been busy in the fields harvesting her rice crop. I told her it wasn't her fault for at 84 heart attacks were not uncommon. She had taken care of her mother for years and obviously love had been part of their relationship. I told her there could be no greater gift than love and service to her mother.

We visited 49-year-old Li who with her son and husband were making sugar from sugar palm trees. Every day they made and sold ten kilos of sugar. We were laughing and talking and ordered 30 kilos amongst the three of us. Li turned with her wizened face and said, not now but in April when the air was dry. Now impurities from rain drops fell into the sap and the sugar was not as good. I paid for my ten kilos in advance and the giggles turned into laughter as Srei and Heng told her not to show her husband the money. At five feet tall, Po retorted, I tell him one time only and I will hit him then he does not bother me anymore.

We ended the day with visiting several families who were in the program for five years. Ton was so proud to show us his home as he held a broken sign from a Tabitha house build from three years ago. Those materials were now used as walls for a much bigger house and small restaurant. So much laughter and so much joy this day we had together, so much sadness and despair turning into hope and dreams of a better life. Heng's sense of humor was one of his strengths. We got along so well because our one-liners got both of us laughing and laughter was a major part of our visits.

We went on a site visit to meet new families in Kompong Speu. What a lovely day it turned out to be. The weather was perfect, the rice harvest was in and the families were delighted to show us their passbooks and their purchases. I taught Heng how to check passbooks against project reports, making sure everything balanced.

Some families said they had bought chickens but I could see no chickens. Other families had bought pigs but I could see no pigs. Where are your animals, I asked? And the chatter began. At 7 o'clock in the morning, we turn our animals loose and the pigs go into the fields to forage. The pigs roam far and wide while the chickens roam the surrounding fields. I was a bit dumbfounded. How do you know your own pigs and chickens, I asked? The laughter increased at my ignorance. Oh, the families chortled, they come home when they are hungry, usually when the sun goes down. One wizened grandmother looked me in the eye and said, my pig sometimes stays out overnight, I think maybe he has a girlfriend.

Clearly, I was someone who was short of an education for I asked: how do you find the eggs from your chickens? They laughed as they told me that when the chickens come home, they are all hot and bothered, clucking and clearing a spot and then they lay their egg. Bewilderment at my inability to grasp these natural events was a concern for each and every one.

It was all too strange for me because insecurity throughout the country was known to be high, stealing and drug abuse caused much grief. So, I asked, don't people steal your pigs and chickens, are you not worried? Oh no, they responded, for the past year we have a security brigade in the village made up of residents who live in the village and their task is to make sure that everyone behaves properly. Now we don't worry any longer about thefts of chickens or pigs. We still worry about our cows though; they are still watched and brought into the house every evening. The Prime Minster had set a *prakas* (law) to develop these village security groups and it had changed the village. Unbelievable for how good it was to see their sense of well-being and safety, something which had been lacking for so many years. People who took drugs or were unruly drunks were now reported and arrested. I loved it. Cambodia was developing in so many ways.

The decision was made to send the children out far and wide to find some pigs for me to see. While the children were running and looking, Heng, Srie and the chief stood talking under a tree. Heng bent over and pointed to a plant and said, this is what the people smoked during the Khmer Rouge years. The conversation became animated as Srie and the Chief showed me how the leaf was plucked and dried under a sleeping mat, then how it was rolled. The old people still smoke these, said Srie, because they taste better than the new cigarettes.

We left the village and travelled to visit with farmers who had received ponds. There was a sense of joy and excitement as the ponds were clear and provided good water. It changed their lives as they showed me their corn and watermelon patches. The woman of one household pointed proudly at her clean clothes. Life was so much better despite the fact her home was still of humble proportions. Hope and dreams were in the air.

It was a very emotional and difficult time for me as Miriam graduated from high school and left to go to university in Canada. Miriam's graduation ceremony left me in constant tears which in turn had my friends in tears. All the important people in her life were there to celebrate with us, including Tabitha staff with spouses and children, our close friends whose children were also graduating, our religious community with Father Charlie, Sister Regina, Sister Lilian and the Mother Theresa nuns, the Mormons, the Alliance Church with Pastor Anne, all celebrating watching Miriam grow up.

I marveled at all of this. How could it be that this scrap of humanity who was 1.1 kilo at birth, HIV positive, lactose intolerant, with a dim future, turn out to be such a lovely young lady, ready to prepare herself to, as Miriam would say, I need to give back, mama!

I remembered moments when at the age of four, she was very disillusioned with life because you could not take a goldfish out for a walk! What use are they, she demanded as we buried yet another one. I remembered the day she snapped a pencil in grade one in a moment of frustration and then cried for hours because she had disappointed a teacher. The day in sixth grade when she was selected to be part of a varsity soccer team even though she had never played soccer before. The day in grade nine when she played Othello in a school play and brought the house down with her performance. The day in grade twelve when she finally got an A- in chemistry, this from this girl who struggled with math.

I remembered her first laugh, her first step, her first boyfriend, her first drink, her First Communion, so many things, and now it was time for another first, the time to spread her wings and to leave the nest and start a new phase of her life's journey.

I missed Miriam's zest for life with her insatiable appetite to learn new things, her sparkling eyes when she shared another moment of discovery, her tears in moments of disillusionment, her hugs and her pokes as she reminded me of my privilege of being her mama!

Yet I will see Miriam when she is gone, I will see her in the faces of children in our projects who just got a new school, in a teenager so determined to learn that he would sit with the first grade class to begin the process. I will hear her laughter in the laughter of children playing in the school yard, in children showing me their work in their school books. I will feel her presence when the children hold my hand and give me a spontaneous hug in the joy of the moment. I will see her wonder as children gently touch my skin, so white, or pull the hairs on my arms. I will see her beautiful presence as children give me a shy smile or a high five. I will rejoice as children here begin to spread their wings in the knowledge they will gain in their new school.

Despite all that, I felt heart broken and empty as she boarded the plane to take her to her new country. I did not believe that I could bear the pain. Miriam's leaving and so many of my best friends leaving with her at the same time, left me tired, a tiredness of giving of myself to Cambodia, of denying myself the pleasure of family. So, I made the decision that once the hospital was completed, I would split my time between Cambodia and Canada. I would change my role to being an advisor, an evaluator of all our programs, a visionary of new ways and new programs, of speaking for all the programs and raising funds.

The announcement of my decision was met with disbelief. Heng wanted more time with me; Phavi and Sieng and I struggled with how this would work. The staff were unhappy but reassured that I would be back to check on them for as long as God allowed me the strength to do so. For many of my friends all over the world, it was good, good to see me look after my own needs for a change. For others, the question remained, who will take care of Tabitha and Nokor Tep, once you leave. I told them, I remembered when Mother Theresa died and so many people lamented that it would be the end of the Missionaries of Charity. I said then, as I do now, Missionaries of Charity was her vision but the vision would outlast the visionary. Others would take over. They would not be Mother Theresa; they would be their own selves with their own way of expression and of management. It is the vision, not the visionary that is the central core. That is as it should be.

## Nokor Tep Women's Hospital

We were ready to start outfitting the inside of the hospital. Sieng was content with doing the outside of the hospital but was a bit lost with the inside. Moni joined our team to look after logistics. In the last few months of last year and the beginning of this year, Moni and I spent an evening a week with two medical experts from SOS International, an expat medical clinic. Mel and Nan had a tremendous amount of experience between them. Together we went to the hospital and did a walk-through of what our vision was of the working spaces. We took copies of the architectural drawings and we began the process of filling in the spaces. This was essential before we could start raising bricks.

With the assignment of spaces, I had done a first draft of equipment required in each room. The list kept growing longer. We had talked with Philips Health Care about sourcing equipment. They made a comprehensive list for us but alas, the money they wanted for equipment was far beyond our ability to meet, $17 million! They reminded us of the needs for special treatment of walls, the depths and thickness of materials specifically required for machines such as a CAT scan, mammogram, etcetera. This helped us a lot.

Moni and Sieng did a lot of research on the radiation requirements for thickness and design. So much information! We needed to sort out ventilation and electrical needs. We needed to have IT plans and spaces. The list seemed endless. But we persevered and the inside walls began to go up. As the walls were going up, we had endless discussions about safety, security, how high the walls should go, how to ventilate the hospital so that the building could be aired naturally and that microorganisms would not be an issue in the ventilation system of the hospital.

And then there was the aesthetics of the building. I wanted it to be a welcoming place for patients, choosing colors and designs that would make them feel welcome. Sieng's extraordinary skills in innovation and design were amazing. If I had an idea that was out of the ordinary, he would think about it and in time, come up with an innovative solution.

The toilets and showers were to meet both western and eastern needs. We wanted to be eco-friendly so the exchange of water and saving of water became innovative. We wanted to be as energy efficient and low cost as possible so the electrical plant had to be designed in a way to handle both. Sieng was so innovative in these aspects. I didn't understand it all but I trusted him. This required special transformers from overseas.

We wanted the flooring to be as bacteria resistant as possible. We decided to only to simply polish the concrete that we had poured. Aesthetically it was not as pretty as tiles would have been but as we found out later, we were a forerunner, as hospitals in developed countries were beginning to do exactly that.

We had so many visitors come through. One visitor was Anita Bourke, a cancer specialist from Australia. Anita had donated a school through Tabitha and had come to see the school. I took her out to see the hospital. As we were walking and talking, she shared that she was a doctor. I stopped and said: we need your help. Without blinking an eye, she agreed.

We shared our equipment list with Anita and Cathy from Nokor Tep Australia. These two ladies worked endlessly to meet these equipment needs. Crossroads from Hong Kong volunteered equipment. Over the next year and a half, our hospital received enough equipment from these three sources to open up the hospital at a total cost of less than $10,000.

We shared our need for smaller equipment that could be hand-carried in. A number of house building teams from Singapore came laden with bags of smaller items. It was a miracle.

We had a remarkable first at the hospital. Seventeen young volunteers came and helped paint a part of the hospital. It was challenging for the students had to learn how to paint like professionals. This was all in preparation for a group of 400 Cambodian young people coming for a day in November to help paint the hospital. What was so very poignant about all of this was that Sieng was deeply touched by these young people.

Fundraising continued with many events happening around the world on behalf of the hospital. The Walkathon, the Ride-a-thon, Nail Paintings, and so many more events made it all happen. We had a special Gala in Cambodia put on by our lawyers and close friends. What an evening that was! Six Ministers from the government were present but what made the evening truly special was that these Ministers formed their own band and played songs from my youth. That evening they were just men who gave of themselves to give us all a special night. The money raised that night was ten times more than all of us expected.

We received so many presents this year from so very many people, Nancy with her painting class; Charlotte with her concerts; Jemane with her half marathon; Russell and Margret with their faithfulness repeated again this year; Leo and Veronica with their gift and the list continues, too many to mention but not one forgotten.

We had so many visitors come and hear and see. One woman asked me, why Janne, why? Why all this work and worry and heartache and hope? For me it was all so simple for my Cambodian sisters are hurting, hurting so badly that it was painful to meet with them coming empty handed and bereft. In one village of 260 families, we had 15 women in various stages of losing their lives to diseases for which I was helpless to change, yet I myself had so many options. Sokleang is a very sad story of losing her battle with breast cancer. I listen to Sarouen as she talks of her horrific pain from uterine cancer. Fifteen women in one village. Fifteen women I walked away from, fifteen women who believed that somehow, someway they must be inherently bad for this to happen to them. It does not matter what village we go to; the story is the same. I could do nothing less than build Nokor Tep and fill it with compassion and mercy for those who have none.

I look back over this year and I stand in wonderment, in disbelief of what stands before me. The hospital was coming into being. So many people involved in so many ways. I heard so many stories of pain and suffering. One day, this will change to stories of hope and comfort. It is a story of Amazing Grace. Who am I that I should be a part of something so wonderful?

# 2018-2019

## Nokor Tep Women's Hospital

**W**hat an extra ordinary year and a quarter this was. The challenge was to complete the hospital to a point where we could finally open our doors to the women of Cambodia. This was no easy task. There was an endless list of things that needed to be completed.

Painting each floor its own unique color while the outside of the building needed to be white was time consuming. The building was huge. Sieng had found a way to keep the paint from fading with time and was also washable.

Sanding the concrete floor took forever. What a noise and what dust there was. Finishing the atriums was a challenge as we wanted a retractable roof in the big atrium to provide additional air could flow through the building. We needed endless railings for stairways and steel doors. More noise and more frustration as everything took time.

Finding enough bricks to complete the last walls was a huge challenge as the port town of Sihanoukville had been sold to Chinese consortiums. Over one hundred casinos were in the process of being built, and they needed bricks and every construction worker they could find. This left us scrambling for both workers and for materials.

And then there were the endless windows we needed. The window casements had to be improved. Glass was in short supply along with the doors we needed for every room and toilet in the building. We had a contract that would see all the doors installed over six months, which turned into eight months.

The plumbing had to be completed: toilets, both Asian and Western styles, sinks and dispensers and the list kept growing. And the plumbing lines, oh my what a task that was!

And then there was the electrical plant to be built and furnished. The size of the equipment and the innovations that Sieng designed so that we could have both grid and solar power were mindboggling. The 800KVH generator and plant, the electrical wiring compounded with the IT wiring that we needed. And the squabbles that came with so many craftsmen and trades working at the same time. Unbelievable.

Outfitting the hospital with furniture and medical equipment seemed to be another endless task with so little funds available. We had started to receive donations in kind from Australia and Hong Kong. Enough computers for all our needs along with an enormous amount of medical furniture and hospital linen all of which needed to be checked and cleaned. We received ultrasounds, colposcopes, and hospital refrigeration units, which needed to be checked and made useable. We received boxes of pharmaceuticals, endless boxes of syringes and dressings, face masks and thermometers. All had to be checked and stored in the appropriate place which was not easy as all areas were under construction. We were so very grateful for these donations but it all added to the workload.

We hired our first employees filling in our top line needs. The laboratory became a beehive as it needed to be completed to the latest standards while signing contracts with companies to rent the analyzers through promising to buy their reagents.

The pharmacy took shape as staff were hired and shelving units installed. Air-conditioning units became a priority so that drugs that needed a constant temperature could be safely stored. Security cameras, doors and systems needed to be installed and security protocols needed to be written and abided by.

We needed a fully integrated hospital IT system designed and installed. Endless hours were spent on designing this, time required to determine every need and every interdependent action. A system that would allow medical staff access to patient information and tests, and pharmaceuticals. It needed prices and inventory and action taken as well as follow up. It had to include a full accounting department and an inventory of every item in the hospital. Not an easy task!

In all this busyness we had visitors come and see the progress. Their comments lifted our souls, comments like how spacious it was, how beautiful the colors were, how good the atrium looks, how beautiful the floors were, what a wonderful place for women to come to. This buoyed our tired souls.

It was a time when we three founders were tired and stretched to our limits. There were days when each one of us in turn, would throw up our hands in frustration of the mayhem around us and want to quit. But we didn't, we persevered! The three of us were in danger of losing our sense of humor. Then we knew it was time to take a meal together and forget the hospital and just be ourselves for a few hours.

We talked with our lawyers about expanding our board. Siphana looked me in the eye and asked me the hard question; would Nokor Tep Hospital have been built if you had had a bigger board? In my heart, I knew the answer, no, because it would have become about board members rather than the building of the hospital. It was a difficult discussion and still is. He assured me that every board member will have their own agenda, often in conflict with the agenda of the founders. It was the nature of having a board.

The few months before the opening were hectic with a thousand things to be accomplished and staff needing to be trained. My saving grace was that my sister Nancy and her husband Wolf came for several months as well as Dave Johnson, a very good friend. I asked that Tabitha staff come and help us as well. Together we moved endless beds and equipment. We sorted all the linens, uniforms for staff, blankets and soaps. Thousands of pieces that needed to be laundered at a cost of several thousands of dollars, reduced to $400. We cleaned floors and walls and windows, toilets and sinks, machinery and equipment. The installation of electrical, IT, the plumbing, the installment of our front doors and front steps all going on at the same time. The setting up of consultation rooms, offices, patient wards, we had not a moment to spare. Slowly it started to come together.

We had issues with the opening dates as our government representative could not come on the planned day because of unforeseen circumstances, yet we had invited so many people for that day. So now we had two openings two days apart. We decided that the opening had to be a soft opening as we wanted to open the hospital in phases. This was good as we needed the time to set up training and scheduling for each department.

The week of the soft opening in March was a wonderful week. Friends arrived from all over the world, many in tears to see what we had done together. My family was there with Nancy and Wolf and with Miriam and my niece Paighton. We celebrated in the Buddhist and the Christian traditions; God was the center of all we had accomplished. We proudly showed everyone what was completed and what needed to be completed. We were so thankful for every person present.

In between the two days of celebration, we had a special visitor. We had just left the hospital at the end of a long day, when a woman came and stood in the front of the hospital. Several Cambodian staff greeted her and asked her name. She said: that is my name as she pointed to the sign on the building. I am Ms. Nokor Tep. You have taken my name, live up to my name, the angel of compassion. And then she disappeared. The three of us had goose bumps when we were told what happened.

The official government opening went very well. The Deputy Prime Minister, Hor Nam Hong was gracious in his praise as he wished us well. He stood for several moments in front of our wall of caring, listing several thousand names of donors who had given from their hearts for this vision of ours. He was amazed at the fact that donations had come from so many parts of the world. It was so very good.

We ended our celebration with a special meal together as founders. Each one of us was in a state of wonder. What had started as a response to my cancer, became a united vision; what had started with just a few dollars, had been completed almost within budget; what had started as a dream had now evolved into being. What made it amazing was that the three of us had become deep friends, we had become family. What made us stand in awe was that our respective faiths in a God of Mercy and Grace had made this miracle happen. What we started will serve the lives of endless numbers of people, long after we are gone.

## Tabitha Cambodia

The year 2018/2019 was the completion of 25 years of service through Tabitha Cambodia. Micro-finance continued to be a bane to Cambodia. At the end of 25 years, 38 billion USD had been loaned out but not collected. Villages were still being emptied but there was also a change in the attitude of people. Everyone knew of someone who had fled in hopes of not losing their home; everyone knew of suicides and people losing possessions. Everyone knew of families where the adults remained hidden away in the fields, day after day, so the money lenders could not find them. The Prime Minister had enacted a law that banned a vast number of micro-finance groups. Seven remained but they were large ones. He banned the use of usury and no institution could charge more than 18% per annum on any loan. It was all too sad as so very many lives had been affected adversely by micro-finance. It was little comfort that I had been proven right.

Our 25 years had been and continues to be an amazing journey. It began when Cambodia was still in transition from a country devastated by war, genocide, isolation by the international community, insecurity through war lords and transition to peace. Life when we started was worthless, taking life and causing mayhem amongst the population was the norm. Twenty-five years later Cambodia had achieved a modicum of peace. Life was more valued now. Discussions now focused on where the country wanted to be in the future, questions that were not easily discussed or answered. The concept of globalization threatened the fabric of Cambodia. There was too much temptation involved in selling the assets of Cambodia for instant wealth but not for long-term sustainability.

Twenty-five years ago, 99% of the people lived in great fear, insecurity was rife. 90% of the people lived in makeshift homes. Finding a livelihood that brought food each day was a challenge. Travelling from place to place in the country was full of danger with warlords, competing factions, landmines and roads that defied the description of being a road. The infrastructure was minimal at best and lack of all basic essentials was a struggle. Twenty-five years later security has improved considerably, the infrastructure continues to improve at a rapid rate, and people tend to eat every day and are able to work if they wish to do so. Twenty-five years ago, the population was 7.2 million. Twenty-five years later it is 16 million and growing. There has been so much change, life is so much better.

Tabitha Cambodia was privileged to be a part of this transition to peace. When we started, travelling within the city was fraught with danger. Working with families who were fearful and traumatized taught us so much about the strength of the human spirit, taught us all about respect and dignity for each person, taught us the value of each life, inestimable value despite coming out of an era where life was worthless and people were reduced to things where their only value was to be used, abused and thrown away.

In this 25-year process, Tabitha Cambodia was privileged to work in 17 provinces transforming whole villages with our work. We changed the lives of more than 579,546 families, or a staggering 4,610,127 individuals, moving from absolute poverty to middle class citizens. We were humbled by the need to show respect and dignity to the people we worked with by instituting a savings program that focused on the dreams and visions of each family. We were entrusted with their funds, entrusted with their dreams. Their dreams of basics, food, clothing, shelter, income generation were met. The people saved over 22 million USD which they transformed into millions of dollars' worth of change in their lives.

We were cheerleaders in that process. My site visits always involved having to see and admire each small step forward as families showed me their accomplished dreams. One of my fondest site visits took place in Siem Reap, in a small village tucked away at the end of a trail. I met with 50 women all carrying six plates and six real drinking glasses. The villagers had brought out sleeping mats for all of us to sit on. Every woman passed me her six plates and six glasses. I had to admire each piece. As usual, I would run out of adjectives to describe the wonder of each item by the tenth woman. The laughter started as I struggled with enthusiasm for yet another plate and another glass. It broke down the constraints that were there on my arrival. We began to talk about our families, our joys and sorrows, our hopes and dreams. Each lady had a chance to touch the hair on my arms, to check on my blue eyes and to pinch the fat on my tummy. Then the miracle happened. We became as one, we were just one huge family talking and sharing and just being. Our differences were forgotten, our sorrows were diminished, and we just enjoyed being together. As the sun began to set, it was time for me to go. There were genuine emotions as we hugged each other good bye. The site visits were for me the highpoint to all I had envisioned.

Not every site visit was as beautiful as that visit was. My most awkward visit was to a village where 30 families had bought pigs. The search for words after the fifth pig was hard enough but it was the visit of one of the largest boars I had ever seen that did me in. I was mesmerized by the size of this animal that had come to service a number of the pigs. I was so totally enthralled with this vision that I failed to heed warnings of staff and villagers alike to move out of the way. Clearly, I was an obstacle that the boar was not pleased with. He harrumphed loudly and then started to charge. I was nimble enough and with it enough to recognize that I was the target of his wrath. I moved faster than I have in a number of years much to the laughter of all around me. It was the one gift that I brought to thousands of Cambodians, the gift of laughter.

For Tabitha development staff, site visits were a time for each one to have me to themselves for a few short hours. We shared our work, our families, our hopes and dreams. Times when each of us cared deeply about each other in concrete and wondrous ways. One of my best moments, amongst the very many, was the day, Phat took me aside in a field, just him and I, and he took me by the arm and told me, you don't have to worry about Prey Veng anymore. Phat, who never spoke a word of English, spoke English for the first time. Then he hugged me and said, thank you for Tabitha.

In this 25-year process we enabled more than 26,000 families to receive a new starter home, moving from two square meters of living space to 20 square meters of living space. We were humbled by thousands of volunteers who came from all over the world to help pay for materials and to help finish these homes. These starter homes became the means for our families to continue the process and end up with firm stable homes, expanded, refined and meeting the needs of the families. We cheered as another 470,000 families rebuilt their shacks into beautiful homes through the savings and income generation projects they did through savings.

Throughout the years of housebuilding, I had many memorable moments. I understood what these homes meant to our families. Culturally, Cambodians needed to die in their own home, a sturdy home, for then their soul would travel to heaven directly after death. If people died in any other space other than their home, their soul would be lost and would struggle to find their way heavenward. When I first heard this, I began to understand the enormity of the pain of losing your life during the Khmer Rouge years, where more than 2.5 million Cambodians died in horrific ways and never in their own homes. There were endless stories from Cambodians and foreigners who had seen ghosts in their homes and in the streets. This lessened after the first ten years but was still common when someone died far from home or was someone who had done wrong during their earthly life. These people would float around in space for a period of seven years and were totally dependent on the offerings made by their family for their release from earthly bounds. This made the Pchum Ban holiday so very relevant when, for thirty days, families were required to make offerings at the wat for their deceased relatives.

Our house builders did not appreciate how important these houses were for our families. But the families knew. One team had built a number of houses in a village. At the end, a number of older people spoke and thanked this team. The main spokeswoman was a woman in her mid-forties, raising her own children and six orphans. She said to the team, you will forget us as you go back to your busy lives. That is as it should be. But, she said, on the day that I die, it is your face I will see. House building brought peace in a way that few other things could.

We were humbled by the women who had come to us from the sex trade to become women of beauty and dignity through the making of silk products. We enabled more than 400 silk weavers to rebuild their lives; we watched as the silver smiths rebuilt their home villages. We stood with our women living with AIDS as they rebuilt their lives, retrieved their children and raised them well. We did this through selling more than $US10 million worth of products.

Cottage Industry touched me deeply. Sina, outcast by her family, came as a not very good sewer and developed into our sales manager. Apo, my manager in Siem Reap was sold by her family into the sex trade. Her sister was sold with her and died at the age of 19 because of the abuse. Apo, who believed that she was unworthy of ever being happy has turned into one of the dearest people, a strong woman, married and living happily, forever insisting that I name her children. Six of our Cottage Industry women named their daughters after my mother, various forms of Rose. They knew that name because my daughter was Miriam Rose. These strong, courageous women were the crux of every holiday for we always ate together, sang and danced together, hugged each other whenever we could. Threads of silk bonded us together.

We watched as vast areas in our programs were changed from dry barren swathes of land, to food bearing and animal husbandry oases of prosperity through the installation of water sources. Over

22,000 sources of water impacted the lives of thousands of families throughout Cambodia.

Site visits that involved checking the water sources were wonderful. I was often very hot and sweaty and being able to splash cold, clean water on my face was a gift. It was the endless ingenuity that water brought our families that I enjoyed. I marveled at the ingenuity of piping water into their homes from a field well or watching as children splashed and played in the cooling water. I marveled at the systems that families worked out as they shared a well, making sure that every field got its share of water to grow life-giving food. I marveled at the variety of vegetables and fruit trees that could be grown in Cambodia, from Spanish onions to green peppers, from the rice staple to morning glory; raising crickets and spiders to raising fish and fresh water lobsters. It all tasted so good.

Twenty-five years ago, when we started, schools were just beginning to open. Education systems had been destroyed by the Khmer Rouge and forbidden by the Russians and Vietnamese after the genocide. People such as Heng attended underground schools, threatened by imprisonment if caught. We were humbled by the desire of old and young to learn about how grass grows or why does the sun come up every morning. We were privileged to have built 103 schools, impacting hundreds of thousands of children in our projects. These schools will continue to serve as the future becomes the present which in turn has a future. It is wondrous to imagine all the children that have been, are being and will be impacted by these schools.

I was very touched by teenagers sitting in grade one with the little ones, desperate to learn how to read and write. There was no shame being a teenager in with the little ones. I was deeply touched by the parents eagerly awaiting the return of the children from school, anxiously waiting to be taught what the children had been taught. I admired the school directors and teachers who hungered for decent space but when there was none still taught the children in the open air under a tree. I was in awe of donors whose desire it was to see the children educated, like the six-year-old who still could not attend the school despite us building 12 rooms. Just too many children and not enough space; the donors would not say no to yet more rooms.

Over the past 25 years we have been struck by the gains made by families reduced through illness; illnesses which could be diagnosed and treated in the Western world. Our response had been to start a process of impacting this scourge through the building of a women's hospital, Nokor Tep Women's Hospital. We are privileged to have been a part of the opening of the doors of this hospital in our 25th year. We are humbled by the vision of the hundreds and thousands of women who will be touched by its healing powers over the next 25 years.

My most cherished and important moment was the day my daughter Miriam Rose was placed in my arms. She has become a beautiful young woman, mature in so many ways from living in a country of sorrows, from living in a truly international setting, of learning how to make friends and losing good friends as they moved on. My girl participated in all our activities from house building to having a well put in for her birthdays; from meeting and getting to know so many visitors, many of whom we now call friends. She is now learning how to live the Canadian dream, a process that is so different to what she was used to. She has come to terms with being my daughter, of being a Canadian, of being Miriam Rose Ritskes.

I am humbled by our Tabitha Foundations in six countries, run by volunteers whose only reward was the knowledge that their efforts changed the lives of millions. I was humbled by all of you who have stood by us all these years through your donations, your housebuilding, and your care for the people of Cambodia.

I am humbled by the Grace that God has shown me, Tabitha and Nokor Tep, His unfailing mercy in all these years, His steadfastness when I was not so steadfast, His care when I was weak, His joy when with each family we touched. His hand was an integral part of the process. How very good that was!

# ACKNOWLEDGEMENTS

There are a great number of people, literally, in the thousands, whom I would like to thank personally but that would be a book all its own. There would be no book without each one of you who volunteered, donated, prayed for us and stood beside us. You are my miracle.

But there are a few whom I would like to mention:

I would like to thank Yolanda Henry at Tabitha Foundation Canada, who continually encouraged me to write my memoir. I would like to thank Canadian board members Angela and Craig Snell, Holly Scott, and Elaine O'Conner, along with David and Audrey Meadows, Jim and Elaine Pollock and Corrine Gurry for taking the time to read as I wrote and who gave me encouragement and advice.

I would like to thank my brother John Ritskes, for his faith in me from the onset. John with family and friends set up Tabitha Foundation Canada to support my work. I would like to thank Andy and Mary Payne, Amy and Mike Ferguson, Marg McCormick, Nerida Nettlebeck, June Cunningham, and John and Janette Fawcett who supported me through in early years.

I would like to thank United World College (UWCSEA) in Singapore: Susan Edwards, Kate Lewis, Chris Wise, Anthony Skilicorn, the administration, every student, teacher and mother's team member for your awesome support.

I would like to thank Singapore American School (SAS) for its constant support all these years from first graders, fifth graders, to our Walk for Water students, and both teacher and student house building teams; what a difference you made in so many lives.

I would like to thank The Australian International School (AIS) who supported us with student teams, Mother Day sales, The Margarita House Building team; you are my family from down under.

I would like to thank the Canadian International School in Singapore (CIS) for your teacher and student teams, it meant so much.

I would like to thank our foundations, Tabitha USA with Mary Broach as the founder, Erika Kies Hoffman, Gary and Jeneyne Williams for your unfailing support. I like to thank Dave Richter for his faithfulness as a board member but also for his faithfulness in bringing teams each year.

Tabitha UK led by Jeff and Jenny Spaeth, Rosie Dean, Chris Fensome, who have remained so faithful. I thank Eleanor Craig, a stalwart board member who stood with us in Singapore and with the start of Nokor Tep Hospital against naysayers to the project.

Tabitha Australia led by Mike and Corinne Gurry, Bob Page, an extraordinary group who stood with us in times of trouble. My special thanks to Sharon Doubikin, who has become a dear friend and encourager for many years as a board member in Singapore and now in Australia.

I would like to thank Tabitha Singapore for the very many hours of service through Cottage Industry sales, speaking engagements, galas of all kinds, you volunteers were amazing. Tabitha Singapore was the group that encouraged service not only in Singapore but in other countries when volunteers moved away. A very special thank you to Lisa Michel, Valerie Kholmayer, Sharon Dubikin, and AnLee Cox for your superlative care during my cancer travels.

I want to thank Tabitha Hong Kong, Frank Yazzi and Ariel Hung for your patience and perseverance in obtaining tax deductible status in HK. That meant so much to me.

I want to thank Stichting Toetssteen in the Netherlands, Cor and Lies Hogeveen, Giulio and Nicolette Tomaello, Laura Shep and Marcel Straver, for your outstanding support in so very many ways: housebuilding, water sources and the hospital. Your Gardens of Eden are still flourishing.

I want to thank the Christian Reformed Community in North America, especially the Kemptville Christian Reformed Church and the Brockville Christian Reformed Church for standing with me from day one until the present. Your prayers and financial support made it all happen.

I want to thank the Roman Catholic Community in Cambodia, especially the Maryknoll Group, SR Regina Pellico, Father Jim Noonan, FR. Charlie Dittmeir and so many others, the Missionaries of Charity and the Bishop. We have done so very much together. You stood beside me every step of the way.

I want to thank the Latter Day Saints Community for its support, especially my sister in arms Margret Ellwanger and her husband Russell. Thanks for all the house building teams, the Cottage Industry support and the generous donations to the building of the hospital. For all of the missionaries in Cambodia especially the VerHarrens, the Dowds and the Thurstons for you became my friends, you laughed and cried with me. How good that was.

I want to thank Clydette and Charles DeGroote who started the hospital off so strongly with their support. For Leo and Veronica Howman and their hospital support but also for the schools and the housebuilding, which touched me to my core. I want to thank Dr. Erin Ellison and Dr. Anita Bourke for their constant support of the hospital. It meant so very much.

I want to thank my housebuilding teams, people who came from all over the world. A special thank you to my oldest builder, Kevin Byers and his wife Barb. You are my hero Kev.

I want to thank the Wagners, the Rickards, S.H.A.R.E. Foundation, Bill Szego, Casey Willemse, and so many more of you for the schools and water sources. You have given new life to so many people.

I want to thank Cathy and Peter Emmerson, Brendan and Hazel Allen for their work with Nokor Tep Australia, for the containers of goods and for encouraging the Khmer community to sponsor the hospital. It was so very good.

I want to thank each and every staff member and worker, from Tabitha Cambodia. This is our story, what you and I accomplished together.

I want to thank Phavi, Sieng and Moni, for an extraordinary journey together. The building of the hospital was a miracle. You were part of my miracle.

I want to say a special thank you to my large, extended family. Your constant prayers and support meant so very much. Thank you, Nancy and Wolf, especially, for your willingness to suffer through both good and hard times. You were my strength.

Thank you, my daughter, Miriam Rose for being my girl, for encouraging me, making me strong and forever bringing joy into my life.

Most of all, I thank my God for always being with me, for keeping me strong in times of sorrow, for comforting me in times of hurt, of enabling me when I thought I could not go on, for standing with me in times of joy and laughter. I thank my God because without my God, none of this would have happened. It cannot get any better.